Praise for

ZERO
HARM

This book represents a turning point in patient safety. It describes principles that, if internalized and executed, will unleash the power and talent of entire health systems in pursuit of transformative safety and experience.

—A. MARC HARRISON, MD, President and CEO,
Intermountain Healthcare

A definitive blueprint for how to solve the safety issues in healthcare, *Zero Harm* should be required reading for frontline caregivers, leadership, and board members. Replete with real-world examples of health systems' safety journeys and the expertise of leading healthcare experts, the book shows the way to accomplish the goal of zero harm.

—ROD HOCHMAN, MD, President and CEO,
Providence St. Joseph Health

Eliminating preventable harm to our patients and employees should become the strategic goal of every healthcare organization. *Zero Harm* is a terrific book that presents a clear road map for healthcare leaders on how to get there, especially for CEOs whose obligation is to personally lead the work.

—JIM SKOGSBERGH, President and CEO,
Advocate Aurora Health

HPI and Press Ganey bring a fresh and important reminder—despite the current deluge of change issues affecting healthcare—no issue is more important than safety. As a safety zealot, I found the book to be both inspiring and deeply moving. This is the ultimate playbook to accomplish zero harm. It will serve patients for generations to come.

—MICHAEL R. ANDERSON, MD, President and Professor
of Pediatrics, UCSF Benioff Children's Hospitals

Zero Harm is the gold standard for healthcare teams and organizations aspiring to provide the best care and outcomes for their patients. Authored by a Hall of Fame lineup of quality and safety leaders, this book provides practical guidance and tested strategies for making the transformational changes necessary to achieve the Holy Grail of zero harm. As the CEO of a major children's hospital, I have seen firsthand the impact and success that these principles have brought to our patients and caregivers. Whether you are in the C-Suite, on the front lines, or in the board room, *Zero Harm* should be required reading.

—KURT NEWMAN, MD, President and CEO,
Children's National Health System

The stories we tell are the most potent force for change for they define how we act in the world. This impressive book reframes two stories that have been holding improvement back: harm is preventable rather than inevitable, and zero harm is realized by viewing safety as an integrated management system integrating governance, leadership, culture, processes, and accountability. This nuanced book offers wisdom for how organizations can accelerate their journey toward zero harm.

—PETER PRONOVOST, MD, former Senior Vice President of Safety, Quality, and Service and Director of Armstrong Institute, Johns Hopkins, and author of *Safe Patients, Smart Hospitals*

Achieving zero harm is a journey into uncertain territory that goes on forever. Any such journey requires expert guides along the way. There are no better ones than the authors of this book.

—STEPHEN E. MUETHING, MD, Chief Quality Officer and Co-Director, James M. Anderson Center for Health Systems Excellence, and Professor of Pediatrics, Michael & Suzette Fisher Family Chair for Safety, Cincinnati Children's Hospital

We have an ethical and moral duty to improve dramatically and to spread best practices quickly. Though improvements in safety have been progressing for some years, the progress to zero harm as a system is way too slow. We need to build the will for change and to offer leaders and clinicians the ideas that are proven to provide safer and more patient-centered care. We need tools to implement quickly and reliably across all of our systems. Our promise should be that we deliver the safest, best care, every day, everywhere. This book gives you the ideas to inspire change and the tools to execute this necessary transformation.

—MAUREEN BISOGNANO, former CEO, Institute for Healthcare Improvement

Zero Harm provides practical, reader-friendly guidance to any healthcare professional interested in the critical link between safety, experience, and quality care. The book highlights the value of developing fundamental skills such as communication, leadership, teamwork, and strategies to support a culture of excellence.

—LAURA COOLEY, PhD, Senior Director of Education and Outreach, Academy of Communication in Healthcare, and coeditor of *Communication Rx*

ZER●
HARM

HOW TO ACHIEVE PATIENT AND WORKFORCE SAFETY IN HEALTHCARE

Edited by

Craig Clapper, PE
James Merlino, MD
Carole Stockmeier

of Press Ganey

New York   Chicago   San Francisco   Athens   London   Madrid
Mexico City   Milan   New Delhi   Singapore   Sydney   Toronto

1 2 3 4 5 6 7 8 9   LCR   23 22 21 20 19 18

ISBN   978-1-260-44092-8
MHID   1-260-44092-3

e-ISBN   978-1-260-44093-5
e-MHID   1-260-44093-1

Library of Congress Cataloging-in-Publication Data

Names: Clapper, Craig, author. | Merlino, James, author. | Stockmeier, Carole, author.
Title: Zero harm : how to achieve patient and workforce safety in healthcare / Craig Clapper, James Merlino, and Carole Stockmeier.
Description: New York : McGraw-Hill, [2019]
Identifiers: LCCN 2018037653| ISBN 9781260440928 | ISBN 1260440923
Subjects: LCSH: Medical errors--Prevention. | Patients--Safety measures. | Medical care--Safety measures.
Classification: LCC R729.8 .C53 2019 | DDC 610.28/9--dc23 LC record available at https://lccn.loc.gov/2018037653

McGraw-Hill Education books are available at special quantity discounts to use as premiums and sales promotions or for use in corporate training programs. To contact a representative, please visit the Contact Us pages at www.mhprofessional.com.

To those who have been harmed—
may your experience inspire others to embrace
Zero Harm *and make all of us better*

Contents

Foreword

Thomas H. Lee, MD, MSc

DURING MY CHILDHOOD, my Chinese immigrant parents exposed me in countless ways to elements of Chinese philosophy. The central questions of this philosophy—What does it mean to be good? What can I do to become better?—were baked into the way my parents lived their lives and raised my brothers and me. More recently, I've come to realize that these are the very same questions we in healthcare ask all the time—or should ask.

Zero Harm is a powerful inquiry into what "good" is in healthcare and how we and our organizations can achieve it. The book recognizes that the answers are complex, interesting, and challenging—that they involve far more than simply following a set of rules. Rules, protocols, and processes are, of course, vitally important in healthcare. Before performing a physical examination on a patient, the rule says you should always wash your hands. Before inserting a central line, you should check a patient's coagulation status. But on so many occasions, rules don't suffice. What rule should a clinician follow in deciding when to begin discussing end-of-life care preferences with a patient? What rules dictate to clinicians how to build trust and respect among other caregivers with whom they collaborate? It is in such vast gray zones that highly reliable healthcare organizations demonstrate that they possess more than just policies and procedures: they have philosophies and cultures.

As the chapters in this book demonstrate, organizational philosophies and cultures bear on all aspects of performance, including safety, patient experience, technical excellence, and efficiency. Individuals and teams can't improve in these areas simply by following new and better rules. Rather, they need a basic set of values, norms, and behaviors in place that they can judiciously apply in the moment to address specific situations. When asked what it meant to be good, Confucius famously gave different answers in different contexts. In his view, people couldn't define goodness by mindlessly applying rules. Rather, goodness followed from learning behaviors and developing instincts that equip us to do the best we can in any situation, however unpredictable it might prove to be.

Throughout my career in the United States, I've been amazed at how many of my colleagues have seemed to practice in accord with Confucius's teachings. They don't like it when organizations define excellence in rule-bound ways, and they are even ambivalent about guidelines. Certainly, they have a point. I don't know any quality measures that define the proper course of action in every situation. I can always cite a reason why a "rule" might harm some patient I have seen in the past or might see in the future. Such concerns cause all of us to shift restlessly in our seats when we receive quality data suggesting room for improvement, and they provide us with an easy way to resist the imperative to improve.

At the same time, of course, we must improve. We all know that patients are injured as a result of our efforts to help them, and that they endure unnecessary suffering and fear. These challenges only increase as medical progress accelerates. More people have to work together to provide state-of-the-science care, and those people often maintain increasingly narrower perspectives. Opportunities for errors, intentional or not, proliferate.

What would Confucius do? I actually think he would embrace the safety science approaches embedded in this book. The book's authors cover a variety of topics, but they share a common understanding of culture as the primary vehicle of improvement. They urge us to aim for zero harm and zero worker injury by embracing a culture of high reliability, one whose values and norms are embraced by leadership and frontline personnel alike. They urge us to foster teamwork and strong team cultures, and to push ourselves every day to improve what we do.

Another theme of Confucius's teaching present in this book concerns the use of ritual. Life is complicated, and we often don't know quite how to behave. Happily, rituals serve us as frequent, predictable moments in which we can behave "as if" we are actualizing our best selves. An older person enters the room, and you stand up—as if you were respectful. A colleague does you a small favor, and you say, "Thank you"— as if you were grateful.

Using ritual to behave "as if" we were good is not hypocritical, any more than everyday manners are willfully deceptive. Performing rituals conforms to clinicians' common understanding that they are "on stage" every time they begin a patient encounter. And rituals also have important implications for safety. Regular, ritualistic behaviors allow us to anchor ourselves, making desirable behaviors more likely when we really need them. One ritual that appears on the surgical checklist used at many institutions calls for everyone to pause and introduce him- or herself prior to the procedure. Doing so consistently affirms everyone's status as an equal member of a team, which in turn helps nonphysicians feel comfortable speaking up when they see something going awry. The more often they speak up, the more likely it is that teams will prevent potentially deadly errors.

I first connected Confucius's teachings about ritual with my clinical work when I encountered data showing that clinicians should sit down in a chair when talking to hospitalized patients who were lying in bed. This recommendation forms part of the work that defined Press Ganey's Compassionate Connected Care framework, as described in Press Ganey chief nursing officer Christy Dempsey's recent book *The Antidote to Suffering*.[1] As I began presenting these data myself and making that recommendation nationally, I knew I had to adopt it in my own clinical work. When I walked into patients' rooms to find that family members were using every chair, I made myself pause and say, "Let me find a chair so we can talk." Often, someone from the family would offer me his or her chair, and I almost always took it—I'm not a saint. But I compelled myself to communicate at the same level as the patient, behaving *as if* I was respectful, genuinely wanted to understand the patient's opinions, and wouldn't be hurried. I don't know for sure what impact this new habit had on my patients, but I do know that behaving "as if" allowed me to feel better as a physician and as a person.

Confucius's thinking about rituals conforms well with the recommendations for specific, daily "habits" sprinkled throughout this book. At the same time, I hope readers won't get so lost in the specificity that they miss the loftiness of the book's ambitions and implications. Its authors seek nothing less than the transformation of healthcare's culture, so that individuals and teams can deliver care that is reliably safe, empathic, and technically excellent. As we all improve, and as our organizations grow closer to zero harm and zero workplace injury, we'll gain satisfaction in knowing that we are not just serving patients better and keeping them safe, but are ourselves noble, and becoming more so every day.

Acknowledgments

THIS BOOK DELIVERS a powerful approach in reducing harm to both patients and caregivers. The approach has been piloted, tested, and refined over 15 years to the success it is today because of the 1,200 clients and the thousands of caregivers who used it to improve. Thank you so much for the privilege of partnering with you on your journey to zero harm, and to better serve your patients, families, and caregivers.

Great companies require great vision and leadership. Pat Ryan, our chief executive officer, and Joe Greskoviak, our president and chief operating officer, provide both the vision and the leadership that have allowed us to be innovative and successful. They are both experienced healthcare leaders who not only have a deep passion for improving healthcare but the courage and determination to allow us to be bold in helping to transform it. Our work and this book is possible because of their encouragement, mentoring, and support

This book would not have happened without Gregg DiPietro, a senior vice president with Press Ganey. He moved mountains to get the manuscript ready in finished form, and his incredible insight and understanding of the healthcare landscape made the work coherent and better. Our editor, Seth Schulman, brought clarity and cohesion to the manuscript. It's surprising that Seth has no experience in safety, because from the way he tackled this project, one would have thought him an absolute expert. When we first pitched the idea of a book on healthcare safety to Casey Ebro, our editor at McGraw-Hill, she immediately saw the topic's importance and potential impact. She believed in us from the start and encouraged and supported us every step of the way.

The editors have a special thank you to **Kerry Johnson** and **Gary Yates**, two of the four founders of Healthcare Performance Improvement (HPI). Both are retiring this year. We began this journey in 2002 with a Zero Harm mission that remains resolute today. This book is a waypoint in the never-ending journey of making reliability a reality in healthcare. Kerry and Gary, your contributions to "making a dent in healthcare" will long be remembered.

Working with so many talented people who authored chapters for this book is a serious undertaking. Jim Merlino and Carole Stockmeier want to provide special recognition to our coeditor, Craig Clapper. When we first committed to this project, Craig jumped in with both feet and brought determination and focus to the manuscript that provided the glue that holds it all together. He provided coaching, guidance, and occasionally soothing reassurance to all involved. This book would not have come together without Craig's leadership. We also wish to acknowledge the following individuals:

Chapter 1: Thank you to the many thought leaders and patient advocates who started the modern safety moment, most notably Dr. Lucian Leape, Dr. Don Berwick, and Drs. Mark Chassin and Jared Loeb. Because of them, our trail was easier to travel.

Chapter 2: Thank you to Dr. Lee Sacks, Dr. Rishi Sikka, and Kate Kovich of Advocate Health Care for openly sharing your stories and insights. We also acknowledge Alan Stolzer's book

Implementing Safety Management Systems in Aviation, which has served as a useful guide to healthcare safety. Michael Laign of Holy Redeemer shared his story and insights, as did Scott Jones of Cancer Treatment Centers of America (CTCA). Thank you, both.

Chapter 3: We wish to acknowledge Dr. Gene Burke, formerly of Sentara, and Christine Sammer, formerly of Adventist Health System, for graciously sharing their time, experiences, and ideas.

Chapter 4: Thanks go out to Ellen Crowe, director of clinical excellence and care redesign for the Connecticut Hospital Association (CHA), and Dr. Mary Cooper, also of CHA, for sharing their story and, in general, for their invaluable work. Bill Corley, formerly of Community Health Network, John Duval of VCU Medical Center, and Dr. Steve Linn of Inspira Health Network also shared their stories and experiences. Thank you, Bill, John, and Steve.

Chapter 5: We wish to acknowledge the lifework of James Reason, for without it, there would likely be no safety science. We also thank HPI for sharing its large datasets of safety events from HPICompare. A special thank you goes to Joan Wynn, chief quality and patient safety officer of Vidant. Joan and her team have long committed themselves to zero harm and were eager to share their work with others.

Chapter 6: We wish to thank Laura Cooley, senior director of education and outreach at the Academy of Communication in Healthcare, and Kate Kovich of Advocate for providing compelling data and insights.

Chapter 7: We wish to acknowledge Dale Harvey of VCU Medical Center, who was kind enough to provide us with a detailed case study in just culture. We again acknowledge James Reason for pioneering Just Culture and giving it a name.

Chapter 8: The authors of this chapter wish to thank Nationwide Children's and Sentara Healthcare for providing data and insights, and Carole Stockmeier, Press Ganey-HPI partner, Cheri Throop, senior manager for Press Ganey-HPI, Cathy Corbett, our former partner, with Chong Chiu, Craig Clapper, and Kerry Johnson, for published work that we found extremely helpful. Last but certainly not least, we acknowledge and thank Shannon Vincent, a manager in Press Ganey consulting, for lending her work in engagement strategy.

Chapter 9: Thank you to Glenda Battey of Providence Health & Services for sharing materials and insights, and to the people of Dianne's organization (you know who you are!) who courageously shared their story of failure and redemption in an anonymized case study.

Chapter 10: We wish to thank Don Goble and Rob Douglass, both consultants with Press Ganey-HPI, for sharing their industry experience and expertise in workforce safety. Thank you as well to Judy Geiger of Intermountain Health, Ken Smith of Sisters of Charity of Leavenworth Health, Alan Bennett of Riverside Health System, and Anne Davis of Sharp HealthCare for sharing their stories of improvement so that others may learn and improve. Last, a special thanks to Crissy B for sharing her very personal story in an anonymized case study.

Chapter 11: We wish to acknowledge the pioneering work in measuring healthcare quality of Drs. Irwin Press and Rodney Ganey, founders of Press Ganey. Without Irwin and Rod, none of this would be possible. Thank you as well to the Institute for Innovation at Press Ganey for freely sharing its large datasets and analysis.

Our biggest acknowledgment of all goes to our family and friends, who encouraged our patient safety and workforce safety improvement efforts over these many years, endured the writing process over these many months, and consoled the authors during the editing. Thank you!

Introduction

Craig Clapper, PE, CMQ/OE

Too many patients are harmed each year in US healthcare settings. The numbers vary, but they're all frightening. According to the 1999 IOM report *To Err Is Human*, errors and omissions lead to 98,000 patient deaths every year—one patient death every five minutes 22 seconds.[2] A more recent (2016) estimate of patient harm found that errors and omissions were the third leading cause of mortality in healthcare, accounting for 251,000 deaths each year, or one every two minutes, six seconds.[3] The highest estimate, published in 2013 in the *Journal of Patient Safety*, ascribed 440,000 patient deaths per year to errors or omissions, or one every one minute, 11 seconds.[4]

It's not just patients who suffer from accidental harm, but employees. The Bureau of Labor Statistics (BLS) reports the illness and injury data that healthcare administrators submit to the Occupational Safety and Health Administration (OSHA).[5] The best measure of workforce safety is the Total Case Incident Rate (TCIR), defined as the number of OSHA recordable injuries for every 200,000 hours worked. For hospitals in 2016, the mean TCIR was 5.9—that is, about 6 of every 100 full-time employees were injured on the job that year (assuming that the typical full-time employee works 2,000 hours annually). In long-term care settings, about 6.4 out of 100 employees were injured, while ambulatory care was safer, with only 2.3 percent of employees injured.[6] These numbers might not sound large, but consider this: between 1985 and 1995, when I worked in the US nuclear power industry, our TCIR was only 0.3—*20 times lower* than healthcare today. The costs that accrue due to poor workforce safety are also staggering—in 2011, healthcare organizations suffered some $13.1 billion in losses and more than two million lost workdays.[7]

Money is important, but we should also remember that injuries and harm produce pain and suffering for large numbers of people. Patients suffer directly when they experience harm, and also when errors or omissions prevented them from obtaining positive outcomes they otherwise would have experienced. As Christy Dempsey relates in her book *The Antidote to Suffering*,[8] patients suffer even when they do receive a positive outcome if their care was neither compassionate nor connected. Caregivers and providers also suffer when their organizations don't respect them for the contributions they make, when they don't feel engaged in meaningful work, and when they're injured on the job. Our work now as healthcare leaders is to dramatically reduce this suffering. But how?

Aim for Zero Harm

This book argues that healthcare organizations should adopt *zero harm* as their goal, and that they should apply proven principles of safety science to make that goal a reality. Zero is the only acceptable number in safety. Leaders, administrators, clinicians, and employees can and must work tirelessly and in the best interests of our patients and workforce until we have zero preventable harm and zero injury.[9]

A number of healthcare executives have rallied behind the cause of zero harm. In 2011, Dr. Don Kennerly, then at Baylor Health Care System, argued for three zeroes—zero preventable deaths, zero preventable injuries, and zero preventable risks. Likewise, James Skogsbergh, chief executive officer of Advocate Health Care, along with Drs. Lee Sacks and Rishi Sikka, physician executives at Advocate, observed the critical role that mindful leadership plays for organizations pursuing zero harm.[10] Most safety leaders in the Healthcare Performance Improvement (HPI)/Press Ganey client community have signed on to the *Zero Harm Commitment*, a Press Ganey movement launched by Jack Lynch, chief executive officer of Main Line Health, to organize the patient experience around safety and the goal of zero harm.

And yet, some healthcare leaders continue to resist the notion of zero harm, perceiving it as an unrealistic goal. They observe that even if an organization reduces the incidences of harm by 50 percent every two years, it might get close to zero, but it will never quite reach it. It's simple math—zero is an asymptote. Or is it? Safety science holds that zero *is* possible. As an organization reduces harm and injury, the numbers get increasingly small. First, the organization achieves zero harm for a day. Then it goes an entire week without an injury or incidence of harm. Then an entire month. And finally, at some point, it reaches zero for a year. Doug Cropper, chief executive of Genesis Health System in the quad cities of Iowa and Illinois, led his system to zero. Genesis defined "patient harm" as preventable harm greater than or equal to "moderate temporary harm." A patient who experienced a mild and temporary skin reaction as the result of a medication error wouldn't have reached the threshold of "moderate temporary patient harm" under this definition, but one who experienced a wrong site surgery resulting in loss of organ function or a medication error requiring supportive care in the intensive care unit would have. Genesis measured harm at any point in time by counting the number of qualifying incidents that had occurred over the preceding 12 months. When the organization achieved 12 consecutive months without serious preventable harm, it arrived at zero—for now.[11] If and when another harm occurs, Genesis will no longer be at zero.

Some healthcare leaders argue that even if zero harm is realistic, organizations can't afford to aim for this goal. Here again, the naysayers seem to have mathematics on their side. If you treat safety improvements as a set of external rules or processes an organization tacks on to patient care, the work system becomes more complex and costs increase as you move to improve safety. Unfortunately, harm and injury will also usually increase as a work system becomes more complex, leading to failure all around. But when you approach safety as a means of also increasing a work system's reliability, you wind up *simplifying* the work system and making it less prone to errors. Harm and injury decline, and so does cost, because the work system becomes more efficient. Safety doesn't mean more controls in a work system. It means *better* work systems.

We've seen other industries become more reliable—and less costly—as they've increased safety. As Dempsey notes in *The Antidote to Suffering*, the nuclear power industry saw the number of safety events decrease by 70.6 percent over the years 1995–2005. But the costs of production fell as well, by 28.7 percent. The industry didn't pay more for safety. Rather, safety allowed the industry to operate more efficiently. Data about cost savings in healthcare are equally compelling.[12] Studies of return on investment in the HPI client community show companies reaping value that outpaces costs by factors ranging from 2:1 to 5:1 over three years, with most of the real savings coming in the form of lower costs related to insurance, claims and settlements, and the treatment of hospital acquired conditions (HACs).

How quickly might other healthcare organizations hope to see significant improvements by applying safety science? The answer might surprise you. I trained in safety science and High Reliability Organizing while working for Dr. Chong Chiu at Failure Prevention Inc. (FPI) in San Clemente, California. Trained as an engineer at MIT, Chiu was an innovator in nuclear power safety and safety culture (and he was also quite a character). He theorized that complex systems such as manufacturing operations, chemical plants, and nuclear power plants could reduce loss events by 80 percent every two years (two years is an average improvement cycle for transformational cultural change in a large organization). A nuclear power plant that formerly suffered 100 precursor safety events each year would experience only 20 per year after an improvement cycle of two years. After a second two-year improvement cycle, it would experience only five per year. That's a 95 percent reduction over four years. In reality, we achieved reductions of 75 percent over four years—not too shabby!

Kerry Johnson was my longtime partner with Chong Chiu and later at HPI before its acquisition by Press Ganey. We applied the same safety science/High Reliability Organizing methods to companies in power, transportation, manufacturing, and for the last 18 years, healthcare. Whenever we brought safety science to a new industry, we encountered skepticism. How did we know that what worked in a nuclear plant would work at a coal plant? How did we know that what worked in power generation would work in power transmission and distribution? What evidence did we have that we could apply aviation safety practices in railroads, shipping, or trucking? How did we know that what worked for safety in power and transportation would work in heavy manufacturing? In each new industry, we answered such skepticism by producing results—on the order of an 80 percent reduction in safety incidents every two years.

In 2015, when HPI joined forces with Press Ganey, the two organizations shared a common vision. Under the leadership of CEO Patrick Ryan, Press Ganey had committed itself to an ambitious project of transforming multiple facets of healthcare, including safety, clinical quality, and patient experience. Meanwhile, we were a small Virginia Beach, Virginia–based healthcare consulting group dedicated solely to the first of these goals: reducing patient harm and workforce injury by applying safety science/high reliability principles. As Pat clearly saw, healthcare had impeded progress by reducing the measurement and improvement of patient experience to the measurement of "satisfaction." Calling patient experience "satisfaction" diminished the importance of the patient experience, and it also failed to engage clinicians, since they wanted to improve the *quality* of patient care. To spur change, Ryan assembled an impressive group of thought leaders, including Dr. Thomas Lee, Christina Dempsey, and Dr. James Merlino. I invite you to learn more about the patient experience in Jim Merlino's book *Service Fanatics*, and about the broader changes required in Tom Lee's book *An Epidemic of Empathy in Healthcare*.[13]

Today, we know that safety science is universally relevant, not limited to a particular industry, company, or location. We also know that it works in healthcare. Over 80 healthcare systems currently deploy our approach to safety culture transformation, including 1,200 hospitals as well as post-acute care, home health, physician practice sites, and other facilities. Figure I.1 shows a sampling of the results they obtained. The numbers, I think, speak for themselves.

These organizations haven't achieved zero harm yet, but with continued diligence, they very well could. Bear in mind, though, the point is not simply to reach zero once. It's to reach it for a period of time before faltering, and then to reach it again, and then again, staying at zero for progressively longer periods. If we experience one patient death every 7 days, let's improve that to one death every 30 days. Then let's improve that to one death every 365 days. Likewise, if your organization is experiencing three

	Patient Safety (reduction in safety incidents)	Workforce Safety (reduction in safety incidents)
1	Sentara 80% reduction over 2 years, reported in 2005	-
2	Vidant 83% reduction over 4 years, reported in 2013	-
3	Nationwide Children's 83% reduction over 3 years, reported in 2013	Nationwide Children's 50% reduction over 2 years, reported in 2013
4	WellStar 90% reduction over 4 years, reported in 2014	WellStar 84% reduction over 4 years, reported in 2014
5	Main Line 88% reduction over 3 years, reported in 2014	-
6	Sisters of Charity 62% reduction over 3 years, reported in 2016	Sisters of Charity 58% reduction over 3 years, reported in 2016
7	Signature 88% reduction over 3 years, reported in 2016	Signature 76% reduction over 3 years, reported in 2016
8	Advocate 58% reduction over 3 years, reported in 2017	-
9	Sharp 64% reduction over 2 years, reported in 2018	Sharp 48% reduction over 2 years, reported in 2018
10	Riverside 53% reduction over 4 years, reported in 2018	Riverside 25% reduction over 4 years, reported in 2018

Figure I.1   Safety Improvement Among Selected Healthcare Organizations

worker injuries per day, aim to get that down to one per day. Then improve that to one per week. Perhaps one day you'll see zero worker injuries for an entire month or year. It's a realistic goal, and the effort you make to attain it will improve your organization's financial performance in the process.

About This Book

Zero Harm provides a comprehensive overview of safety science as well as frameworks for reducing safety incidences to zero in your organization. We've written this book for anyone in healthcare interested in safety, including safety experts, quality experts, leaders, caregivers, patients, and their families. The chapters that follow provide a comprehensive guide to building a safety strategy, but readers can also consult them separately as handy references on specific safety topics. For readers looking simply to learn the basics of patient and workforce safety, we hope *Zero Harm* will serve as an accessible introduction both to safety culture and its transformation.

The book's first three chapters lay the foundation for readers' safety improvement efforts. In Chapter 1, Dr. Gary Yates, an HPI/Press Ganey partner and former physician executive with Sentara Healthcare, offers a brief but essential history of the modern patient safety movement in healthcare, describing both the general trajectory and watershed events. Carole Stockmeier, also an HPI/Press Ganey partner and a former safety and reliability leader from Sentara, goes on in Chapter 2 to provide an overview of safety management systems (SMS). Several published works describe safety management systems in other industries, but no safety management system book currently exists for healthcare. Healthcare systems are complex, so much so that we can't achieve safety improvements without a formal management system in place.

I proceed to further lay the foundation for safety improvement efforts in Chapter 3 by discussing safety science and High Reliability Organizing (HRO). Safety science comprises the knowledge and practice of system controls to prevent harm and injury. High Reliability Organizing is a body of knowledge describing the attributes of organizations that achieve strong safety records under very trying conditions. As we'll see, the key principles of safety science and High Reliability Organizations will inspire the practical methods for improving safety surveyed in subsequent chapters.

In Chapter 4, Steve Kreiser, also an HPI/Press Ganey partner and a former naval aviator with commercial aviation experience, begins the work of putting principles into practice. He discusses several high-leverage leadership skills that your organization will need in order to make progress on safety, drawing examples from healthcare as well as naval aviation. Culture is the shadow cast by leadership—so if you're a leader or manager, this is the chapter you'll want to know, speak to, and live.

Shannon Sayles, a nurse and senior managing consultant with HPI/Press Ganey, continues the work of putting principles into practice in Chapter 5 with a discussion of universal skills for preventing harm. Universal skills are nontechnical skills or behaviors shared by all caregivers and providers, and indeed, among all job functions in all industries. They include attention, thinking, communication, and compliance skills, as well as the ability to use guidance documents effectively. As you might be surprised to discover, consistent application of these skills could prevent roughly three out of every four acts, leading to serious preventable harm.[14]

David Varnes, also a senior managing consultant and a former naval aviator, will continue the discussion of universal skills in Chapter 6 with an eye toward communication, collegiality, and teaming. To think together as a care delivery team, team members must deploy universal relationship skills so as to tame the distancing effects of power inequalities on the team. Dave will discuss relationship skills as companion skills to the universal skills Shannon covers.

We return to the topic of leadership in Chapter 7. Judith Ewald, also an HPI/Press Ganey senior managing consultant and a former safety and quality leader from Inova Health System, argues that a strong safety culture cannot exist simply by articulating cultural norms. Leaders must also hold people accountable and create a learning environment so that caregivers and providers can improve the larger systems in which they work. Safety leaders should always support team members who make honest mistakes, and they should save those who choose at-risk behaviors by meting out progressive discipline. Isn't that an odd turn of phrase, "save" team members with discipline? Too often, healthcare leaders would rather ignore poor practice until it's too late to save the job of a caregiver or provider. As safety leaders, we can save caregivers from their own poor practices by holding them accountable proactively with "just culture" principles.

In Chapter 8, Cheri Throop, a nurse and HPI/Press Ganey senior managing consultant, and Martin Wright, director in workforce solutions with Press Ganey Strategic Consulting, describe the importance of measurement and control loops for patient safety and workforce safety. Healthcare leaders understand measurement quite well, and Cheri and Marty will provide a sound system of leading, real-time, and lagging measures for both patient and workforce safety. Control loops are management systems that monitor for deviation in a measure, prompt us to solve for system problems leading to the poor performance, provide a countermeasure to improve performance, and allow for continued monitoring. It's the strength of the control loop that dictates performance, not the strength of the measure.

Tamra Strong, a director in HPI/Press Ganey and a nurse, continues in Chapter 9 with a detailed treatment of learning systems—processes or procedures for discerning and addressing errors. Safety culture requires mechanisms for learning because all complex systems operate in a degraded mode, with problems lurking beneath the surface. Healthcare likely puts too much emphasis on achieving big performance improvements (a small number of large changes), and too little emphasis on small performance improvement via daily, informal problem solving on the part of teams ("local" learning systems). As Tami urges in Chapter 9, we should put more energy into local learning, mindful of the old bromide, "Improvement by the yard is hard, improvement by the inch is a cinch."

So far, the book has focused on patient safety. In Chapter 10, Emily Halu, a staff consultant with HPI/Press Ganey and also a nurse, and Joseph Cabral, Press Ganey's chief human resources officer, offer a stand-alone primer on workforce safety, describing the powerful connection that exists between workforce safety and engagement. Emily and Joe provide a compelling case for taking action and then go on to discuss the solutions available to organizations. It turns out that the safety culture, leadership skills, and universal skills prescribed by Emily and Joe are the same as those for patient safety. The big difference is the use of safety action teams to identify and correct system problems for five types of workforce injury.

Deirdre Mylod, executive director for the Press Ganey Innovations Institute, Stacie Pallotta, formerly of the Cleveland Clinic and now a partner in Press Ganey consulting for patient experience, and Dr. Thomas Lee, Press Ganey's chief medical officer, go on in Chapter 11 to share our latest thinking on High Reliability Organizing (HRO) for the patient experience. Patient experience comprises patient safety, clinical quality, and experience of care. Safety—and the high reliability demanded to keep people safe—has a profound effect on patient experience. Deirdre, Stacie, and Tom provide a short history of patient experience measurement and improvement and a case study on leading practices. Finally, they help us "see around the corner" to the next wave of innovation in patient experience.

Dr. James Merlino, Press Ganey's chief transformation officer and also formerly of the Cleveland Clinic, discusses transformational change in the Epilogue. Tying the book together, he provides a blueprint for change across the entire healthcare enterprise.

All of the authors recognize that no doctor, nurse, administrator, technician, or other provider or caregiver ever wants to cause harm, see a patient or colleague harmed, or become involved in an incident of harm. But many of us still haven't dedicated ourselves, our teams, and our organizations to safety. If you fall into this group, I hope you'll become a true safety zealot after reading this book. Understand that safety is not just inherently valuable, but also the best possible producer of quality, patient experience, workforce and physician engagement, and efficiency. Know that if some safety is good, more of it is even better, and total safety—zero harm—is the ultimate goal.

If you're already a safety zealot, I hope reading this book puts you in a better position to improve safety at your organization, and that you'll feel even more emboldened in your efforts. Think of it: the insights contained in *Zero Harm* are based on learning that occurred as a result of the deaths of an estimated 4,600,000 people in healthcare, power, transportation, and manufacturing. Please don't waste lessons so costly learned. Just a single framework or tactic presented in *Zero Harm* can create a ripple effect in your organization that might save 60 lives over two years. And that's only the beginning. Rededicate yourself to eradicating errors and injuries entirely. The chapter authors in this book and I desperately want your organization to experience zero harm. And that's what *you* should want, too—for the patients you serve, their families, and the caregivers and providers who have devoted their lives to serving others.

The History of the Modern Safety Movement

Gary Yates, MD

Although healthcare leaders first began focusing on patient safety during the 1980s and 1990s, concerted efforts to improve safety remained few and far between. In 1999, a courageous group of healthcare quality leaders decided to "go public" with the issue, sparking a dialogue that continues to this day. Unfortunately, almost 20 years later, despite well-intentioned efforts by hospitals and health systems and over $1 billion in financial support from CMS, the rate of patient harm remains unacceptable. Our patients and communities deserve better.

MY INTRODUCTION TO medical error came in 1979, during my fifth week as a newly minted, third-year medical student. A resident physician and I were making rounds on a relatively quiet Saturday morning when we encountered a patient who had received the wrong dose of a medication, likely because of poor communication between our service and one of the other surgical teams. When I asked my intern about it, he suggested that we ignore the incident and move on, lest we risk embarrassing the clinicians involved. "Gary," he said, "this kind of thing happens."

Avoiding open discussion of safety issues was an unfortunate part of the culture of healthcare back then, and patients and caregivers paid an enormous price. In the decades since, we've seen the birth of the modern patient safety movement in the United States, as well as the erosion of the "culture of silence." Hospitals, health systems, and other healthcare providers have all taken important steps to eliminate unintended harm. Still, progress has been disappointingly slow. In a 2017 survey of 2,536 adults, 21 percent of respondents reported having personally experienced a medical error, while 31 percent reported that someone else whose care they were involved with experienced an error.[1] As survey respondents confirmed, harm often had a lasting impact on patients' "physical health, emotional health, financial well-being, or their family relationships."[2] Those who provide the care also suffer harm. As we saw in the Introduction, the Bureau of Labor Statistics found that in 2016, hospital employees experienced six cases of injury and illness for every 100 full-time workers, much more than in industries like manufacturing and construction.[3] Clearly, unintended harm is still affecting unbelievably large numbers of people.

Patient safety experts generally agree that we'll have to make fundamental and wide-ranging changes before we achieve the ultimate goal: zero harm for patients. But why hasn't healthcare yet managed to "solve" the problem of patient harm? And what will the future likely hold?

Origins of the Modern Safety Movement

For decades, clinicians involved in harm events generally suffered in silence or quietly shared stories with one another. Hospital and health system leaders, along with the attorneys with whom they worked, knew of allegations of harm thanks to the lawsuits and claims filed by patients and their families. Occasionally, a case would break through into the news media, focusing the general public's attention on safety issues in healthcare. In 1966, the popular weekly magazine *Look* ran a lead article with the cover headline "Our Hospitals Are Killing Us: An alarming report on conditions in many American cities" (Figure 1.1). The article, entitled "Dirt, Infection, Error and Negligence: The Hidden Death Threats in our Hospitals" described potentially harmful conditions that routinely existed in hospitals, along with observations from physician leaders about deficiencies in hospitals and care and the need to correct them.[4]

Figure 1.1 "Our Hospitals Are Killing Us," *Look* magazine cover, 1966

Stories like these didn't provoke a strong public reaction or widespread calls for change from within the medical community. To most people, instances of patient harm seemed uncommon and idiosyncratic. Within the medical community, some viewed errors as the price to be paid for technological advances, while others regarded them as an unavoidable part of delivering care. Many viewed errors as reflecting the personal failings of the caregivers involved rather than the limitations of the healthcare system as a whole. Lucian Leape, MD, MPH, regarded by many as the father of the patient safety movement, once observed that, "Physicians are expected to function without error, an expectation that physicians translate into the need to be infallible. One result is that physicians, not unlike test pilots, come to view an error as a failure of character—you weren't careful enough, you didn't try hard enough."[5]

By the 1980s, a few visionaries within the medical field were beginning to think differently. Dr. Leape, for instance, served as lead author on a series of influential research articles about safety. Evaluating care at 51 New York State hospitals, his group found that 3.7 percent of the 30,195 randomly selected patients sustained an injury that resulted in a clear disability or a longer hospital stay. They also found that errors in management contributed to 58 percent of the instances of harm, and that the rates of adverse events rose with a patient's age.[6]

In 1991, Leape and his colleagues published similarly unsettling findings from a study of the Harvard Medical Practice in the *New England Journal of Medicine*. Predictably, the medical community's response was muted. Many physicians and healthcare leaders couldn't believe that preventable patient harm could occur so frequently in what many regarded as the world's highest quality healthcare system. Undeterred, Leape continued to study medical errors, publishing the landmark article "Error in Medicine" in the December 1994 edition of the *Journal of the American Medical Association* (*JAMA*). Leape argued that healthcare should look to other industries that had been able to significantly reduce errors, and that healthcare would need to take a preventative, systemic approach in order to significantly improve patient safety. "Accident prevention has not been a primary focus of the practice of hospital medicine," he observed, noting that, "the most fundamental change that will be needed if hospitals are to make meaningful progress in error reduction is a cultural one. . . . Errors must be accepted as evidence of systems flaws not character flaws. Until and unless that happens, it is unlikely that any substantial progress will be made in reducing medical errors."[7]

By the mid-1990s, public pressure for change was beginning to mount, thanks in part to media coverage. In September 1993, Betsy Lehman, the Boston Globe's chief medical reporter, a mother of two, and the wife of a cancer researcher, was diagnosed with breast cancer. With standard treatment only partially effective, she elected to undergo an autologous stem-cell transplant, an aggressive but promising treatment at the time. In November 1994, she sought care at Dana-Farber Cancer Institute. Despite early signs that her malignancy was beginning to respond, she passed away in the hospital, presumably due to complications of her disease. Several months later, a routine data check of the experimental protocol in which she had participated revealed that Betsy had received four times the intended dose of Cytoxan, a powerful chemotherapy agent. Her death likely occurred thanks to the overdose, not her disease itself.[8]

The media picked up Betsy's story, raising disturbing questions: How could such an error occur at one of the world's finest cancer centers? If it could happen to the wife of a cancer expert, what risks did patients with relatively limited medical knowledge bear? In its April 1995 piece entitled "The Disturbing Case of the Cure That Killed the Patient," Time magazine described Betsy Lehman's case as well as other horrific incidences from around the country in which patients had the wrong leg amputated, had the wrong breast removed, had their breathing machine inadvertently turned off, or had died after undergoing a routine tonsillectomy. As the article noted, "Three large studies over the past 30 years have documented a distressingly consistent rate of medical mishaps in the U.S. . . . That toll is a sign to some critics that improvement is needed in the systems that hospitals use to catch errors and review doctors' performance."[9]

By 1996, the healthcare profession was beginning to take such criticism seriously. In October of that year, the American Medical Association, The Joint Commission, the American Association for the Advancement of Sciences, and the Annenberg Center for Health Sciences sponsored one of the first conferences to publicly acknowledge the issue of harm and discuss ways to deal with it. The Annenberg conference program's opening sentence stated, "Despite remarkable advances in almost every field of medicine, an age-old problem continues to haunt medical care—the occurrence of errors."[10] It was a remarkable and courageous statement by this group. The conference led to the creation the following year of the National Patient Safety Foundation (NPSF), one of the first organizations that focused on safety. The NPSF was designed to be a collaborative body, a kind of "Switzerland" that convened and coordinated efforts to accelerate improvement in patient safety. Through sponsored studies, white papers, and other thought leadership activities, NPSF has gone on to provide significant support for a number of important patient safety initiatives. In 2007, the NPSF's Lucian Leape Institute was created to provide a national vision for improving patient safety.

By the late 1990s, others within the healthcare profession were becoming similarly emboldened. Harvard-trained pediatrician Don Berwick, MD, had become a student of modern industrial quality improvement, looking to W. Edwards Deming, Joseph Juran, and others for approaches that would reduce errors and improve the quality of care. As part of his pioneering work, Berwick founded the Institute for Healthcare Improvement (IHI), which continues to serve as a leader in improving healthcare quality and patient safety. In 2017, the organization merged with the NPSF to form a single, powerful organization dedicated to this cause.

As Berwick has related, his thinking about patient safety evolved based on the care his wife, Ann, received in several leading US hospitals. In 1999, he noted that he had "seen [safety problems] firsthand . . . sitting by Ann's bedside for week after week of acute care. The errors were not rare; they were the norm." Although Ann began to recover, the experience was eye-opening. "Before this I was concerned," Berwick said. "Now I am radicalized. If what happened to Ann could happen in our best institutions, I wonder more than ever before what the average must be like."[11]

At about this time, the Institute of Medicine of the National Academies launched the Quality of Health Care in America Project (now the National Academy of Medicine). The project convened a number of distinguished members, including Drs. Leape and Berwick, and was charged with devising strategies that would result in major improvements in care quality.[12] Members of the group had grown frustrated that few organizations had moved to improve patient safety, despite clear evidence that significant problems existed. The group issued a general report highlighting significant opportunities to improve healthcare quality, but failed to garner much attention in professional circles. The group therefore made the courageous decision to "go public" with the problem, seeking to use public interest and concern as a lever to spur healthcare leaders to take action.

In late 1999, the group released a report exclusively focused on patient safety and medical errors called *To Err Is Human: Building a Safer Health System*. The report became national news, appearing on the front-pages of the *Washington Post*, *Wall Street Journal*, *USA Today*, and other publications. Journalists were especially interested in the report's assertion, based on data from a Harvard Medical Practice study and a Utah and Colorado study, that medical error led to the deaths of between 44,000 and 98,000 Americans each year.[13] That was about as many as would die if a fully loaded Boeing 747 aircraft were to crash each day. The IOM report and the subsequent public reaction stimulated a flurry of activity in the medical community to acknowledge and address the patient safety issue. For this reason, many today regard the report as marking the beginning of the modern safety movement in healthcare.

The same committee produced a second report in 2001, *Crossing the Quality Chasm: A New Health System for the 21st Century*, which looked more broadly at improvements needed in the health system. As the committee asserted, the system should aim to produce care that is safe, effective, patient-centered, timely, efficient, and equitable.[14] This report received more attention within the healthcare community than among the general public, providing a valuable framework for improving not just safety, but other key elements of patient care. In particular, the report's concept of becoming "patient-centric"—placing the patient and his or her family at the center of care—was provocative at the time, and has since become a primary focus of many health organizations.

As the safety movement gained momentum, another patient story rocked the industry and one of its most highly regarded institutions. In 2001, 18-month-old Josie King was brought to Baltimore's Johns Hopkins Hospital for burn care. During her hospitalization, her family became concerned that Josie wasn't doing well and that her caregivers weren't listening to their concerns as attentively as they might have. Despite warning signs of clinical deterioration, Josie passed away due to dehydration that was possibly exacerbated by side effects from pain medications.[15] Afterward, hospital officials reached out to the family to admit that caregivers had erred. Eager to assure that Josie's death led to improvements in the healthcare system, the family partnered with the hospital to create the Armstrong Institute for Patient Safety and Quality, which aims to support improvement in quality and patient safety at Johns Hopkins and across the industry.[16] Working together with a leader of the Institute, Peter Pronovost, Josie's mother, Sorrel King, became a passionate, articulate, and influential advocate for improving patient care and taking steps to reduce harm to patients. "Josie's story" has been heard by many, if not most healthcare providers, along with the plea that they listen to and partner with patients and their families.

Several organizations such as The Joint Commission, the American Medical Association, and the American Hospital Association began to provide important support for the growing safety movement. One organization that emerged as an industry leader was the Institute for Healthcare Improvement (IHI), under the direction of Don Berwick and his successors as CEO, Maureen Bisognano and Derek Feeley. In 2004, IHI unveiled one of its most visible initiatives, the "100,000 Lives" campaign. Utilizing principles derived from successful social change initiatives and political campaigns, the initiative sought to establish a clear goal for preventing harm as well as a target date by which change would occur. It lobbied health systems and hospitals to commit to adopting six evidence-based interventions, including the deployment of rapid response teams at the first indication of a patient's decline; the "delivery of reliable, evidence-based care for acute myocardial infarction"; the "prevention of adverse drug events"; the "prevention of central line infections"; the "prevention of surgical site infections"; and the "prevention of ventilator-associated pneumonia."[17] Although some questioned the extent of its impact, the campaign did lead to improvements in care, and it energized the healthcare community around quality improvement and patient safety. IHI followed this initiative with others such as the 5 Million Lives Campaign, in which it asked participating hospitals to implement a set of specific evidence-based interventions to prevent 5 million patient harms from 2006 to 2008.

Berwick went on to serve as the Obama administration's administrator at the Centers for Medicare and Medicaid Services (CMS) between 2010 and 2011, spearheading the $1 billion Partnership for Patients program (PfP), a public-private partnership designed to improve healthcare's quality, safety, and affordability. When launching this program, the Department of Health and Human Services incorporated elements of the previously successful IHI campaigns in its design, and in particular targeted a specific set of hospital-acquired conditions for reductions. Nearly three-quarters of all US hospitals participated in the PfP-funded initiative in 2012–2013, implementing specific tactical initiatives to improve 11 types of patient harm events.[18] The initial program evaluation published in 2014 found "decreased rates of harm in five of the eleven" targeted areas, including readmissions, early induced labor, medication errors, pneumonia for vented patients, and bloodstream infections in patients with central-line catheters.[19]

At around this time, government and private payers were also beginning to explore ways to incent providers to reduce harm events and the costs associated with them. The CMS and several insurers began offering "pay for performance" plans (which they continue to expand and refine to this day). These plans provided financial incentives as well as penalties based on safety performance for hospitals and other healthcare providers. These plans have garnered outsized attention from leaders relative to the size of the dollars involved, partly because the results are publicly available and could affect an organization's reputation. Organizations like the Leapfrog Group have also helped support safety improvement by publishing periodic grades and rankings of hospitals based on safety performance.

Looking Beyond Healthcare

Despite these various initiatives, a number of healthcare leaders still felt that progress in improving safety was occurring too slowly. Much of the improvement seemed to occur one disease or condition at a time as hospitals and healthcare systems focused on improving specific processes to reduce harm. In addition, frustration was mounting that certain types of events, such as operating room fires and procedures on the wrong patient or body part, seemed "resistant" to change efforts and were continuing to occur at alarming rates.

Eager for new ideas that would help accelerate safety improvement, concerned leaders sought out models from organizations in other industries that maintained remarkable safety records, including nuclear power plants, commercial aircraft operators, and aircraft carrier flight deck operations. Scholars such as Karl Weick, Kathleen Sutcliffe, Rene Amalberti, Karlene Roberts, and Sidney Dekker had studied these so-called High Reliability Organizations (HROs), theorizing about key characteristics and operating principles that contribute to their success. Healthcare systems and hospitals now began to examine the "high reliability" principles for possible adaptation to healthcare.

In a landmark 2013 article in the *Milbank Quarterly*, Mark Chassin and Jerod Loeb at The Joint Commission proposed a prescriptive model for healthcare, positing three changes that healthcare organizations needed to make in order to become highly reliable. First, leaders needed to explicitly focus on the goal of high reliability. Second, organizations needed to implement a culture that supported high reliability. And third, organizations had to deploy robust process improvement tools.[20] The authors also emphasized the difficulty of these changes, stating that "achieving high reliability in healthcare will require hospitals to undergo substantial changes that cannot take place rapidly."[21]

As a result of this focus on HROs, healthcare organizations have recognized the central role safety culture plays in creating highly reliable performance. Organizations such as IHI/NPSF, The Joint Commission Center for Transforming Healthcare, Johns Hopkins's Armstrong Institute, and others have supported cultural change efforts and continue to provide thought leadership for the industry. Over the past 5 to 10 years, a number of hospitals and health systems have begun to undertake a journey toward high reliability. These organizations are providing second-order learning as they gain practical experience from which other organizations can benefit. One encouraging example is the Children's Hospitals Solutions for Patient Safety (SPS), a network of 130 children's hospitals across North America that work together to implement best practices to improve pediatric care. Growing out of successful initiatives at Cincinnati Children's Hospital Medical Center and the Ohio Children's Hospitals Solutions for Patient Safety, SPS employs high reliability concepts and quality improvement science methods to prevent readmissions, serious safety events, and 10 hospital acquired conditions (HACs). Between 2012 and 2017, this effort kept 9,361 children from experiencing grave harm, saving approximately $151 million in healthcare expenses.[22]

Limited Progress

Overall, healthcare's efforts to improve patient safety since the IOM report in 1999 confront us with a thoroughly mixed picture. On the one hand, patient safety experts generally believe that healthcare is safer than it was 20 years ago. However, they also believe that significant challenges remain, and that the industry still has far to go before reaching what should be its ultimate goal: zero harm for patients.

A series of studies of patient deaths illustrate these challenges. As we've seen, the IOM's 1999 *To Err Is Human* report estimated that between 44,000 and 98,000 patients died in the United States every year from medical error. In September 2013, John James published an updated—and much higher—estimate.

Using a weighted average of four studies published between 2008 and 2011 that deployed the IHI Global Trigger Tool, a method of searching patient charts for signs and symptoms of harm so as to identify possible events, James estimated that preventable harm in hospitals led to between 210,000 and 440,000 deaths per year.[23] Likewise, in May 2016, Martin Makary and Michael Daniel at Johns Hopkins calculated that 251,454 deaths related to medical error occurred each year in the United States, making it the country's third leading cause of death overall.[24] They based their estimate on new research following the 1999 IOM study, modifying those results to encompass the total number of US hospital admissions in 2013. Clearly the progress that has taken place in safety remains grossly inadequate.

Other studies have confirmed that despite significant improvements America still has a big health safety problem. Each year, the Agency for Healthcare Research and Quality (AHRQ) releases a report on the progress made in reducing hospital acquired conditions (HACs). As AHRQ's 2016 report showed, HACs declined by 17 percent from 2010 to 2014, and subsequent data released in June 2018 showed a further 8 percent decrease between 2014 and 2016. Comparing the 2015–2016 HAC reductions with those of 2014, AHRQ estimated a reduction of 350,000, which corresponded to a savings of some $2.9 billion as well as 8,000 fewer hospital deaths. The 2016 report estimated that between 2010 and 2014, "HAC reductions totaled 2.1 million," resulting in approximately "$19.9 billion in cost savings and 87,000 fewer HAC-related inpatient deaths." Still, as of 2016, HAC's were still occurring in 90 out of 1,000 discharges.[25] That rate is far too high, suggesting that additional improvements are sorely needed.

We might wonder why so much remains to be done after nearly two decades of serious attention paid to patient safety. Cultural barriers have certainly impeded progress. At many organizations, clinicians and employees persist in regarding errors as inevitable given healthcare's complexity. Organizations like CMS, The Joint Commission, and state agencies have provided only partially effective external accountability, and hospitals and health systems still lack the kind of comprehensive internal oversight present in other industries. Healthcare has also been relatively slow to introduce high reliability principles. In many healthcare organizations, unfortunately, people still fear retribution if they report errors and near misses. Further, they continue to perceive personal failure as unacceptable and standardization as a burden.[26]

Organizations also struggle to measure patient harm accurately. As multiple studies have shown, incident reports and other event reporting systems record a small percentage of actual harm events, as do reported lawsuits and claims filed. Hospitals and healthcare systems have resisted the use of more comprehensive approaches such as the IHI Global Trigger Tool, regarding them as too time- and resource-intensive. Instead, many hospitals and health systems have contented themselves with tracking a handful of discrete types of harm (such as falls with injuries, number of healthcare associated infections, and so on) to assess their patient safety performance. Identified retrospectively, these harm types have provided only a partial picture of the harms suffered by patients, since many harm events elude these categories. As a result, organizations have made incremental, year-over-year improvement in a few categories of harm rather than pushing for breakthrough improvement across all types of patient and workforce harm.

Perhaps most important, few organizations have taken a comprehensive, strategic approach to improving patient safety, preferring instead to rely on a series of isolated tactics to address the issue. Well-intended hospitals have implemented evidence-based programs such as team training, only to see them falter because employees viewed them as "flavor of the day" and disconnected from the organization's strategy. Leaders and boards have been slow to declare patient safety as a "core value" of the organi-zation rather than just another priority. Of course, priorities can change, while core values do not. Organizations can only accom-plish the kind of transformational change required to significantly improve safety if leaders drive it, and if clear support exists among board members as well as among operational and clinical leaders.

Toward a Brighter Future

As unsafe as US healthcare remains, a number of signs as of this writing point to a brighter future. Leaders are increasingly call-ing upon healthcare systems to refocus and accelerate their efforts to improve patient safety, starting by setting an explicit goal of "zero harm" for patients. Whether or not it's possible to completely eliminate harm, setting zero as the goal energizes the industry to take bold action. Healthcare organizations have also increas-ingly accepted the need to expand patient safety efforts beyond the hospital environment to encompass the full continuum of care. A 2015 expert panel convened by the NPSF advocated looking beyond the inpatient setting, pointing out that "roughly 1 billion ambulatory visits occur in the US each year," as compared with only about "35 million hospital admissions."[27] Healthcare leaders have likewise begun to pay more attention to the safety of health-care workers, not just patients—an important trend that should help improve safety across the board.

Many leaders are also now turning to high reliability orga-nizing as the most promising approach to significantly improve patient safety in a complex, adaptive system like healthcare. As health systems begin to learn from their experience actu-ally implementing high reliability principles, they are poised to identify even more effective ways to incorporate high reliability organizing. Across the United States, organizations are working to better understand what strong safety cultures look like, and how key components of such cultures—such as "fair and just" response, trust and respect, collegial interactive teamwork, and a personal commitment to safety, all described elsewhere in this book—contribute to creating a robust culture of safety. A number of organizations have also begun to look upon high reliability organizing as a way to improve the broader patient experience in general, not just safety. Published survey data suggest that powerful links exist between safety, quality, the patient's experience of care, workforce engagement, and efficiency. In particular, it appears that safety strongly correlates with worker engagement, and vice versa.[28] Understanding that patients want care that is reliably safe, high quality, *and* patient-centric inspires healthcare leaders to deploy high reliability organizing in hopes of improving performance across the entire patient experience. Interest in high reliability as a generalized operating system or "chassis" is an important, relatively recent development in the field of healthcare safety improvement, one that sets the stage for future successes.

Although safety has gained momentum, we must remain ever-vigilant. In 2015, the National Patient Safety Foundation issued a disturbing report, noting that, "although our understanding of the problem of patient harm has deepened and matured, this progress has been accompanied by a *lessening* intensity of focus on the issue . . . the healthcare system continues to operate with a low degree of reliability, meaning that patients frequently experience harms that could have been prevented or mitigated." The group called for identifying patient safety as a public health issue and for a shift in approach to accelerate the pace of improvement, stating that "advancement in patient safety requires an overarching shift from reactive, piecemeal interventions to a total systems approach to safety."[29] It's tempting to celebrate local successes as they occur and conclude that we've "solved" our safety problem, but such complacency will only impede our efforts to achieve zero harm.

The time has come for healthcare organizations to accept nothing less than breakthrough improvement. A road map to high reliability has emerged based on successful healthcare initiatives and the experience of other industries, and a growing number of hospitals and health systems have implemented improvement efforts based on this road map. What the industry needs is additional engagement from boards, senior leaders, and physician leaders. As more leaders become personally invested in driving the journey toward high reliability, progress in individual organizations will accelerate, and the industry as a whole will become safer. The foundations for safety in healthcare exist. With aligned, focused, and personally engaged leadership, we can move much closer to the goal that remains at once essential, noble, and elusive: zero harm.

IN SUM

- Clinicians involved in harm events have long suffered in silence or quietly shared stories with one another, while their organizations have done little to address harm at the systemic level.
- The landmark 1999 IOM report finally prompted members of the medical community to acknowledge and address the patient safety issue.
- To hasten progress, a number of healthcare leaders have sought out models from organizations in other industries that maintain remarkable safety records.
- Healthcare's efforts to improve patient safety since the IOM report confront us with a mixed picture. The industry has made progress, but still has far to go.
- Leaders are increasingly calling upon healthcare systems to refocus and accelerate their efforts to improve patient safety, starting by setting an explicit goal of "zero harm" for patients.

CHAPTER

2

Introduction to Safety
Management Systems

Carole Stockmeier, MHA

Most healthcare organizations haven't seen rapid improvements in safety because they've tended to deploy disconnected, localized tactics. This chapter outlines four elements of a comprehensive safety management system, providing an overview of subsequent chapters.

DR. LEE SACKS, chief medical officer of Advocate Health Care, Illinois' largest healthcare system with 12 acute care hospitals, can trace his personal commitment to improving safety to a situation he experienced back in 2004. At a meeting in San Diego, Dr. Sacks lined up with other healthcare quality leaders to accept an American Hospital Association (AHA)—McKesson Quest for Quality award (honorable mention) on Advocate's behalf. He smiled for the photo op and waited patiently as other award winners spoke of their experiences improving safety and quality. Listening to their uplifting stories, it struck him that each quality leader had described an episode of tragic harm, naming the patient affected and describing the organization's subsequent redemption through an improvement effort. What nobody seemed to recognize was that even one harm incident was too much. Dr. Sacks decided that he would never return to receive an award granted on the heels of an Advocate patient's tragic death. Instead, he would transform Advocate's safety culture before he had that tragic story to share.

That goal proved to be more elusive than Dr. Sacks had ever imagined. In 2006, he formally began his organization's journey to zero, supported by his chief executive officer, James Skogsbergh, his chief operating officer, William Santulli, and his sage medical director of patient safety, Dr. Donald Aaronson. The three executives believed wholeheartedly in their goal of zero harm, and they followed "best practices" in organizing their efforts. They set clear expectations for their organization, trained leaders and staff on safety behaviors, and put measurement processes in place, including a balanced scorecard for harm events and an overall measure of serious preventable harm.[1] By 2010, they had managed only a modest decrease in the most severe patient harms—a hugely disappointing record, to Dr. Sack's mind. Further, the leadership and staff safety behaviors that Dr. Sacks and his team had introduced hadn't "stuck" among the workforce, taking root as strong daily habits. If Advocate were to have any hope of ever attaining zero harm, it would need to step back and make a whole new attempt at building its safety culture.

Why didn't Advocate's initial efforts succeed? First, the organization took a piecemeal approach to safety. "Our approach was very reactive at both the strategic and operational level," Dr. Rishi Sikka, formerly Advocate's vice president of clinical transformation, explained. "We would react to individual safety events after they occurred; we would react to initiatives and programs after they were announced by regulators or payers; we would react to trends and news in our environment. I remember one of our senior leaders saying to us: 'I know safety is important—and I say it is important—but I don't know what else to say and I don't know what else to do.'"[2] As Dr. Sacks remembers, the organization missed "an overall strategy focused on high reliability that would ultimately lead to true change. This required education and buy-in from the board, the CEO, and the executive leadership team before moving across our large organization."[3]

Advocate's efforts also yielded disappointing results because Dr. Sacks and his leadership team lacked a structure and a discipline for managing the system and keeping it "top of mind" for leaders. As Kate Kovich, Advocate's vice president of high reliability innovation, remembered, "Harm was thought to be the cost of doing business in healthcare—nothing could be done. Our lack of transparency left safety largely invisible as one of many important objectives."[4] To give safety a higher profile and allow the organization to advance toward zero harm and zero injury, Advocate needed a road map—a more strategic approach—as well as safety leaders at each of its sites, not just at the system office. Most important, it needed the mutually reinforcing system of a safety goal, safety measurement, and high reliability leadership skills.

Many organizations make the mistakes that Advocate made. The solution, as this chapter argues, is to implement what safety experts call a safety management system (SMS). Similar to quality management systems, SMSs organize leadership activity, safety programs, and improvement programs under one overarching framework, allowing an organization to muster consistent safety efforts, performance, and improvement over time. Like quality management systems, SMSs establish, maintain, sustain, and improve an organization's change efforts. But while quality management systems are often used in healthcare, safety management systems are few and far between. Let's review the key components of such systems, including the frameworks on which subsequent chapters will elaborate. The result will be a road map both for this book and for structuring your own organization's efforts to reach zero harm.

Committing to Safety

Drawing on Alan Stolzer's brilliant guide for safety management systems in aviation,[5] we can identify four key components of a well-defined SMS. First, such systems include formal statements of the organization's commitment to patient and workforce safety. Often these statements read as extensions of the organization's mission, vision, and values statements, but some healthcare organizations go so far as to make safety a core value. Holy Redeemer, a healthcare organization north of Philadelphia with one acute care hospital and large post-acute care and home care operations, adopted its own safety statement as a faith-based organization in articulating its commitment to safety: "We are called to care, comfort, and heal those who entrust us with their lives and the lives of the ones they love. They come to us with faith that we will restore health, heal wounds, or, even, bring happiness. When errors and mistakes result in harm, we fail in our mission, and we fail those we serve. Harm turns *care* to *careless*, *comfort* to *discomfort*, and *heal* to *hurt*. Our patients take it for granted that we will heal without harm. We cannot take it for granted. Our commitment is to care, comfort, and heal . . . without harm. The only acceptable goal is zero events of harm."[6]

In expressing safety as a core value, Holy Redeemer is sadly in the minority among healthcare organizations. In 2015, we reviewed the websites of 54 healthcare organizations, including some of the largest and most highly respected in the United States. Only five organizations—or 9.3 percent of the total—mentioned safety in their mission statements. By contrast, 25 organizations (46 percent of the total) listed safety among their organizational values, with 5 of those listing it as their first value (2 of those organizations also mentioned safety in their mission statements). Seven organizations articulated a zero-harm commitment on their websites: Carteret Health Care, Catholic Health Initiatives,

Cincinnati Children's Hospital Medical Center, Genesis Health System, MedStar Health, Nationwide Children's Hospital, and Vidant Health. This is a good start, but shouldn't all healthcare organizations publicly state their commitment to zero harm, or at the very least, to safety and high reliability?

As some leaders might find, adopting a zero-harm goal takes courage, since colleagues inside and outside the organization might not understand its purpose. At a major healthcare conference held in 2012, Holy Redeemer's CEO Michael Laign described his organization's progress toward zero preventable harm, including the number of lives Holy Redeemer's initiatives had saved. Standing beside him on stage was Kate Flynn of the Health Care Improvement Foundation (HCIF), a nonprofit dedicated to improving healthcare across the five counties of the greater Philadelphia area. In 2010, harm events claimed the lives of 251 people across the hospitals working with Kate at HCIF, including Holy Redeemer's facilities. In 2011, that number was 183, for a difference of 68 lives. When Mike paused for questions, a healthcare executive commented that 68 lives didn't seem that much given the number of hospitals working with Kate Flynn's foundation. "Well," Mike replied, "I am sure it made a big difference for those 68 people and their families." The questioner couldn't grasp the concept that even one preventable patient death was too much. To him, Mike's quest to eradicate safety lapses seemed a bit odd, and perhaps even misguided. Thankfully for those 68 families, Mike and Kate saw it differently.

As we at Press Ganey advise our clients, leaders should articulate their zero harm goals in writing, communicating them to the governing board, leadership team, and medical and non-medical staff. They should also take a number of supportive steps to articulate the organization's deep commitment to safety. First, they should make harm visible by transparently communicating safety events. Best practice here is implementation of an "all-cause" harm measure, such as Serious Safety Event Rate (SSER) for patient harm and Total Case Incident Rate (TCIR) for workforce safety. Leaders should share these measures with caregivers, providers, and board members, and they should also put a human face on safety, telling stories about patients who have been harmed and caregivers who have suffered illnesses or injuries on the job. In addition, leaders should consistently praise and reward any progress made toward zero, adopting intermediate goals, such as a 50 percent reduction in patient harm or workforce injury over a two-year period. Of course, leaders must be clear: the journey is not over until the organization reaches zero. Even then, the organization will continue to work to sustain zero harm.

Leaders committing to safety should also formally articulate what we might call a "just culture." This is a set of organizational values and beliefs that enable safety culture by encouraging the safest possible practice habits and discouraging the punishment of workers who make mistakes on the job. Since human error causes harm to patients, administrators and colleagues have traditionally reacted by inflicting harm on the people making the error. Punishing people for their honest mistakes causes errors and defects to go unreported, preventing organizations from learning from experience and improving practice habits. In just cultures, people feel more comfortable speaking up about errors they've witnessed or committed themselves, positioning the organization to make more rapid and meaningful progress on safety.

Just cultures don't simply happen. Leaders have to work at creating them, and the first step is to issue formal statements defining what such a culture looks like for the workforce. Here's an example of one such statement:

We believe in treating people with dignity and respect. A just culture is important to human dignity and mutual respect.

And a just culture is important to safe care for every patient every day and for improving patient care delivery processes every day. We will always support those people who experience honest human error. We will consistently provide corrective action to maintain safe practice habits. And we will apply our just culture principles to the facts in each instance to know the difference between honest human error and unsafe practice habits.

All healthcare systems have made some efforts to institute a just culture, but none has done nearly enough. Healthcare leaders often apply just culture principles after a harm event to a few individual caregivers, but fail to embed these principles deeply into the organization's daily operations. At one organization, for instance, the leaders were trained in how to apply just culture principles to individual harm events, and that was it—no change in practice or culture. The algorithm for applying the principles sat idle on the back credenza, and their culture survey continued to show non-punitive response to error as the weakest domain of their safety culture. Ideally, just culture principles would figure in an organization's mission, vision, and values. Leaders and staff would personally promote the notion of "mess-up, fess-up" as a cultural norm in their daily interactions, and they would incorporate just culture principles into learning systems such as event cause analysis and peer review. Only with constant care and attention will just culture principles come to define the general climate that prevails in our healthcare organizations.

Building a Culture of Safety

To bring their commitments to safety and reliability to life, organizations should strive to create a culture of safety (the second step in creating a safety management system). Specifically, organizations should provide training in the specific leadership behaviors required to build high reliability organizations (HROs). Sometimes called leadership tools or methods, these behaviors are usually few in number (between 3 and 12) and designed for everyone occupying a leadership role (defined as anyone who is supervising one person or more) to perform daily.

Safety ultimately boils down to individuals' daily actions. If leaders talk about safety and safe practice, their teams will likely practice safely as caregivers and providers. If they don't talk about safety and safe practice daily, teams probably won't practice safely. Leadership behaviors that make a difference include starting meetings by delivering a safety message, teaching safety every day by rounding with caregivers and providers, and leading daily safety huddles. For best results, organizations should codify the desired leadership behaviors into a toolbox, train all leaders on the behaviors, and foster consistent practice using leader-to-leader accountability. Healthcare systems practicing the Lean methodology of process improvement often include these behaviors in their "leader standard work," a daily management system guiding leaders to consistently perform key leadership activities every day. We'll talk more about these behaviors in Chapter 4.

Organizations can also help build a strong safety culture by training all leaders and employees in what we might call "reliability skills" (also known as error prevention techniques, safety behaviors, safety tools, or nontechnical skills). Safety experts tend to group these together with relationship skills, calling them both *universal skills*. When practiced consistently and habitually, reliability skills work to prevent human error even when another system-related cause exists, such as time pressure or interruption. Attention, communication, compliance, and thinking skills are essential reliability skills for organizations, as they can prevent nearly three out of every four acts (73 percent) that lead to harm.[7] The best organizations codify reliability skills into a formal "toolbox," training every caregiver and provider on the skills and fostering consistent practice using both the aforementioned leadership skills and peer-to-peer accountability. We'll describe these skills in greater detail in Chapter 5.

In Chapter 6, we'll describe the other type of universal skills organizations need—relationship skills. Safety practitioners sometimes call relationship skills *tones*, as they tend to be simple and even nonverbal. The most frequently used relationship skill is "smile and say hello," while the best relationship skill for a provider to use with his or her care team is "explain the positive intent of your actions." In addition to making the workplace more pleasant, such courtesies flatten differences in perceived power between people, leading members of care teams to communicate more frequently with one another—behavior that greatly enhances safety, clinical quality, and the care experience. Marci Vanderbosch, the high reliability transformation lead for Sacred Heart Medical Center and Children's Hospital and Providence Holy Family Hospital in Spokane, Washington, could not overstate the importance of relationship behaviors on her hospital: "The impact tones had on safety has been one of the surprise 'aha' moments for many of our caregivers, and not just clinical but nonclinical caregivers. I have personally witnessed how tones quickly reduce power distance, and team members feel safe to discuss their safety concerns and make recommendations for improvement."[8] Again, the best organizations codify these skills by presenting them as a formal "toolbox," training every caregiver and provider on the skills, and fostering consistent practice using HRO leader skills and peer-to-peer accountability.

A final step organizations can take to build safety cultures is to have individuals and teams perform personal safety assessments. Individuals or teams should pause before beginning work to consider environmental hazards and the risks inherent in the tasks they're performing. It's risky, for instance, to administer medications in a dimly lit room. A safety assessment would identify the risks of administering the incorrect medicine or dose to the patient, compared with the risks of turning on lights and waking patients who might be asleep. The assessment could also identify workforce safety risks such as performing procedures in cramped spaces, where staff might trip over cords and tubes. Once an individual or team has identified specific risks, teams can remove the hazards, minimize them, or use the aforementioned reliability skills to prevent harm or injury caused by the hazards.

Organizations can and should use personal safety assessments to anticipate both workforce injury and patient harm, as doing so can sometimes mean the difference between life and death. An 84-year-old patient named Alice was visiting the clinic at one organization to obtain treatment for chronic magnesium deficiency (Alice went weekly for these treatments). Her nurse was busy as usual preparing infusions for several patients. The nurse stopped before accessing Alice's venous access port, implanted just under her skin on her left side, to think, and specifically, to perform her personal safety assessment. Did the patient look okay? Were her labs correct? Had the physician ordered the correct meds? Actually, the nurse noticed, Alice didn't look right. She hadn't touched the turkey sandwich and lime-green Jell-O she had ordered for lunch—usually she gobbled it up. Also, Alice seemed withdrawn when answering simple questions. The nurse stopped to consult with Alice's physician, and Alice was eventually admitted to the hospital to resolve a life-threatening kidney condition linked to her chronically low magnesium. In this instance, one nurse's personal safety assessment helped Alice survive many more months longer than she would have if the acute kidney condition had gone unnoticed and untreated.

Reinforcing and Promoting Safety Culture

Once an organization has mechanisms in place for training care-givers, leaders, and healthcare providers in desired behaviors, it can take additional actions to reinforce the culture (the third step in building an SMS), ensuring that everyone—the govern-ing board, senior leaders, operational leaders, staff, and medical staff—are working consistently and intensely to bring the culture to life.

First, organizations can define what we call *safety absolutes*, key actions that are absolutely critical to maintaining a safe environ-ment. They can also enshrine these actions in policy and protocol as work rules. Sometimes called "red rules," "cornerstone safety behaviors," or simply "safety behaviors," safety absolutes work best when they are few in number, discrete, and action-oriented. In the HPI client community, organizations routinely define patient identification, time-outs before invasive procedures, and checks for high-risk medications, blood, and blood products as safety absolutes. Organizations should treat safety absolutes as a commu-nications tool to promote safety, not as elements of a zero tolerance or escalated enforcement scheme. Whenever a caregiver or other staff member appears to have broken a safety absolute, leaders and managers should evaluate the action using just culture principles and take appropriate action.

Organizations can also reinforce their budding safety cultures by communicating lessons learned to leaders, staff, and medical staff, reinforcing safe practices and correcting mistakes that result in near-misses. To create systems of safety, organizations can't just ask leaders to frequently discuss lessons learned with their staff. They have to create an ongoing program of learning that involves leaders and safety specialists and that uses diverse communication channels, both written and spoken. Leading-edge organizations implement weekly or monthly harm reports, send out frequent safety alerts or advisories, publicize the safety "catch" of the day, and leave time for safety messages at the beginning of meetings. Carolinas HealthCare in Charlotte, North Carolina (now called Atrium), has a well-designed SAFER program to communicate lessons learned from events within the system and emerging safety issues identified outside of the system. "SAFERs" are one-page documents that convey lessons from other people's failures, including the causes of the problems and steps employees can take to prevent the failure from occurring in their team environment. In its highly effective and well-regarded "good catch" program, MedStar Health in Washington, DC, disseminates shorter lessons about harms that team members prevented, celebrating the catch, teaching the workforce how harm and injury can occur, and describing how MedStar's safety culture works to prevent those events.

A final way that organizations can reinforce their safety cultures is by deploying artifacts related to the culture in the care environment. Artifacts are objects that carry important meanings inside of organizations, conveying to employees, managers, and caregivers "who we are" and "who we want to be." If safety really is the most important priority, then people need to see this message. Leading-edge companies deploy an array of artifacts that people encounter every day, including posters, signs, screen savers on computers, badge cards with safety statements, displays of safety data such as "days since last safety event," and patient stories. Memorial Hermann Health System in Houston, Texas, began its safety culture transformation by creating a series of edgy posters to catch employees' attention. In one of these, the organization encouraged employees to pause and cast a critical eye on their activities on the job, with the tagline reading: "Your most important step is a stop." Novant Health in the Carolinas used an even edgier poster to stop healthcare acquired infection by promoting flawless hand hygiene. "This nurse can kill you with her bare hands," read the tagline.

Scott Jones was part of the executive team at Vidant Health (formerly University Health Systems of East Carolina),[9] an eight-hospital system centered in Greenville, North Carolina, that reduced serious preventable harm by 83 percent, winning the Eisenberg Quality Award in 2013. Later, Jones helped Cancer Treatment Centers of America (CTCA), Chicago reduce patient harm by 93 percent over the three years ending in 2016. As part of its safety efforts, CTCA, Chicago created a set of illustrated superheroes to represent each of its safety behaviors. One employee favorite, *The Clarifier*, modeled the safety culture by asking good questions, while another, i*Wonder Woman*, exemplified a "questioning attitude"—the safety practice of wondering why before deciding what constitutes the best care for a patient and the safest for workers. Scott and his safety heroes presented these superheroes in a CTCA safety culture comic book (Figure 2.1) as well as a video.

Figure 2.1 Safety Superheroes at Cancer Treatment Centers of America, Chicago

Building a Learning Organization

A fourth component of safety management systems is the implementation of organizational learning systems that allow leaders to monitor performance, and in turn improve care delivery. In our experience working with healthcare organizations, learning systems comprise 10 discrete elements:

- **Patient harm measures.** Organizations should measure all causes of harms, not just a few types, and count each instance of harm, not merely indicate how frequently a particular kind of harm occurs relative to the overall harm rate. They should also use scorecards of harm measures. The Serious Safety Event Rate (SSER) used in and developed by the HPI client community fulfills all of these requirements. We will discuss harm measurement in more detail in Chapter 8.
- **Workforce injury measures.** Standard measures already exist in this area, including Total Case Injury Rate (the number of workforce injuries per 200,000 staff hours worked) and Days Away Restricted and Transferred (DART), a more severe subset of the Total Case Injury Rate (TCIR). We'll cover workforce injury measurement in Chapter 8 as well, while Chapter 10 details a safety management system dedicated to workforce safety.
- **Safety culture measures.** These are leading indicators of safety performance, and as such provide an early warning system alerting organizations to declines in safety performance. Since we define culture as shared values and beliefs, we can best measure it using psychometrics, such as surveys. The best safety organizations combine safety culture measurement with measures of caregiver engagement.

- **Safety climate measures.** These measures are similar to safety culture measures, in that they are psychometrics as well as leading indicators. However, while safety culture comprises the shared values and beliefs that shape behavior, safety climate captures the prevailing work environment created by those behaviors. Safety culture and safety climate continuously reinforce one another. Organizations should measure both, creating a balanced scorecard for safety.

- **Workforce engagement measures.** We define engagement as the commitment that caregivers and providers have to the organization's overriding mission. Engagement is another leading indicator: when engagement improves, so does safety, because the workforce works harder to achieve outcomes and improve work systems. Engagement, culture, and climate are all mutually reinforcing, for better or for worse. Organizations thus do well to measure them all together.

- **Cause analysis programs.** Organizations must investigate safety lapses to understand why they happened. Cause analyses study single events (and in some cases, multiple events) that resulted in serious consequences or that constituted "near misses." Each analysis identifies systemic causes leading to the harm or injury, an improvement action for each cause, and a plan to implement those improvement actions. We'll offer a more detailed treatment of cause analysis in Chapter 9.

- **Common cause analysis programs.** Organizations have to step in and analyze situations in which multiple failures occurred. In these analyses, the organization aggregates each patient harm or injury into a single dataset. The bigger the dataset, the more effective the learning. Leading-edge organizations usually perform common cause analyses annually or biannually, although organizations can perform them at any time.

- **Self-assessments of safety programs and affiliated care delivery systems.** How good are safety programs themselves? Leading-edge organizations undertake periodic internal audits of these programs, querying employees, managers, and caregivers in a given unit for feedback, and also calling upon peers from other teams or units in the organization. Self-assessments should study how the programs look both on paper and in practice.
- **Independent assessment safety programs and affiliated care delivery systems.** To achieve a more objective evaluation, organizations should ask outside experts to review safety programs periodically.
- **Operating experience.** These learning initiatives study failures in other healthcare delivery systems, looking for lessons to apply inside the organization. Due to the vast amount of data available, such initiatives can often yield faster improvement. Organizations query whether the causes of harm present in other systems exist inside their own system. If they do, organizations can create action plans to address these causes and reduce instances of harm.

As we advise clients, organizations should judge their learning systems by the pace of improvement, not by the volume of learnings they publish. The components of a complete safety management system are outlined in Table 2.1. Healthcare today has no trouble with ideation, but rather with execution. We study many improvements in theory, yet move painfully slowly to put them into practice. Mary Ann Hilliard, chief risk counsel for Children's National Medical Center in Washington, DC, highlighted the need for quicker learning, asking: "What is our tolerance for accepting time lag in adopting best practices?" With Mary Ann's courageous impatience, Children's National reduced patient harm by 70 percent using its version of learning systems and safety culture.[10] Children's National estimates that it saved $35 million by preventing 28 serious harms to children over three years.[11] It really is true: you don't pay for safety. Rather, safety pays you.

Table 2.1   The Components of a Safety Management System

Commitment	Safety Culture	Safety Promotion	Learning Systems
Safety Statement	HRO leader skills	Safety absolutes	Harm measures
Zero Harm Goal	Reliability skills	Lessons learned	Injury measures
Just Culture	Relationship skills	Artifacts	Culture measures
	Personal safety assessment		Climate measures
			Engagement measures
			Cause analysis
			Common cause analysis
			Self-assessment
			Independent assessment
			Operating experience

Source: Figure borrowed from Press Ganey's "Safety Management Systems in Healthcare."

Zero Harm in the Healthcare Industry: What Will It Take?

In 2010, aware of the lack of substantial, measurable improvement in safety, Advocate's Dr. Lee Sacks resolved to redouble the organization's safety efforts. Aware that Advocate needed more leadership focus, he bolstered the talent devoted to the project, bringing in Dr. Rishi Sikka as vice president of clinical transformation reporting to him, and Kate Kovich as a new system administrator of patient safety working for Rishi. He also put much more emphasis on training leaders to drive patient safety efforts. Whereas most healthcare systems invest four or eight hours in training leaders, Advocate put all leaders through a series of 12 two-hour modules led by senior Advocate leaders. The added time allowed them to better communicate expectations and promote daily use of leadership tools.

Advocate also reorganized its safety management efforts under four clear strategies. Advocate would "position safety as the foundation for care," implementing a communications campaign and mobilizing site patient safety committees aligned to a system safety council. It would charge leaders to "lead to patient safety," mandating daily safety briefings, just culture, executive safety rounds, disclosure of harm to patients, and robust safety metrics. It would "enable the front line to address safety issues" by promoting safety event reporting, educating caregivers and providers on safety science, launching a safety coach program, providing care for the caregiver in the wake of safety events, rolling out safety metrics for staff to see, and standardizing work so as to improve reliability. Finally, the organization would "engage patients and families in patient safety," giving patients a chance to collaborate in the redesign of care protocols, placing patient and family representatives on the organization's safety councils, creating means by which patients and their families could report safety events, and educating patients and their families about their role in assuring safety.

With more structure behind it, and more support from leaders throughout the organization, Advocate's second wave of safety efforts finally succeeded in moving the system forward. In 2017, Advocate reported that it had reduced serious preventable harm by 58 percent over the preceding three years—more than halfway to zero. At the 2016 HPI Safety Summit in Chicago, which the organization hosted, Jim, Lee, and Rishi shared their progress and urged others to intensify their own organizations' harm reduction efforts. And yet, when it was Jim's turn to speak, the audience learned in dramatic fashion that Advocate's progress was hardly an unmitigated success. Jim's voice faltered, and he hung his head, trying to keep himself from losing his composure, as he revealed that despite the organization's gains, a newborn had recently died in one of the best Advocate hospitals because of medication error.

Zero harm won't come easy. But leading-edge healthcare organizations are making a dent by adopting and embedding sophisticated safety management systems. What if all organizations took that step? And what if all organizations worked together to espouse a *shared* safety management system? Such industry-wide collaboration has enabled aviation and nuclear power to achieve incredible safety outcomes, and it can work in healthcare, too. We must create a shared language of safety across all delivery systems and care settings, as well as a common structure of improvement processes based on leading practices. Just as safety culture within an organization is a team sport, achieving safety culture in an industry requires a broad commitment from industry players. If nothing else, we hope that this book will spur exactly such a shift in both mindset and practice.

IN SUM

- Without an overarching strategy or set of strategies in place, organizations might make modest progress in their safety efforts, but they'll never come close to zero harm.
- Develop your own safety management system. Healthcare systems are far too complex for us to manage without help, even for the most heroic safety leaders.
- Build your safety management system to include all four domains of a robust management system: commitment, safety culture, safety promotion, and learning systems.
- The healthcare industry should come together to espouse a shared safety management system, just as companies in nuclear power and aviation have done.

CHAPTER 3

Safety Science and High Reliability Organizing (HRO)

Craig Clapper, PE, CMQ/OE

> *This chapter provides a basic introduction to safety science and high reliability organizing (HRO), serving as an all-in-one reference for the busy healthcare professional.*

FOR MEDICAL DOCTORS, the job suddenly becomes "real" on a single day—the day they transition from interns to resident physicians. Dr. Gene Burke's day was July 1, 1976. Sadly, on this very same day, Dr. Burke inadvertently harmed his first patient. At around 10 a.m., a patient under his care slipped into septic shock, leading to an emergency code. The team transferred the patient to the intensive care unit (ICU), and Dr. Burke started him on large doses of gentamicin, a powerful antibiotic known to harm the kidneys. Despite Dr. Burke's expert knowledge and honorable intentions, the changes in dosing he ordered failed to keep pace with the patient's worsening kidney function, and the drug further damaged his kidneys. A pharmacist later commented that Dr. Burke had "likely set the record for the highest gentamicin level ever recorded for a patient in that teaching hospital."

The patient quickly fell into multiple organ failure, and members of the medical team judged him unlikely to survive. They consulted with the family, stopped heroic treatments, and began to deliver comfort care. Surprisingly, the patient improved in the ICU over the next few days. Thinking that he might recover from multiple organ failure, Dr. Burke restarted aggressive treatment, including broad-spectrum antibiotics, pressors, and anti-arrhythmics. All this was in vain. The patient's condition worsened again, and two days later, he was dead.

Modern systems of safety didn't exist back then in healthcare. Instead, as we've seen, the industry attributed safety to the individual practitioner's own personal competency. A clinician was either well-trained and safe, or poorly trained and unsafe. Well-intentioned leaders worked to offer the highest quality training possible, but they paid no attention to broader processes or technology that might minimize human error, nor did they encourage and train care teams to function well together. Such a narrow approach might have made more sense at a time when healthcare delivery systems were simple, with fewer handoffs to other clinicians, fewer devices, fewer and less powerful medications, and many fewer treatments of all kinds. Today, however, systems are so complex that a single clinician never sees the entire picture of care, nor can he or she possibly handle all aspects of care competently. In this context, safety is no longer a competency of the individual, but a property of the care delivery *system*. Subsequent chapters will explore in more detail how to build and shape this system to improve safety, but first let's take a moment to examine safety systems and safety science in general, including the concepts of safety culture and high reliability organizing (HRO).

Safety Science and Systems

We can define safety science as the knowledge and practice of safety,[1] including the knowledge of systems, event models (conceptual frameworks that describe how errors occur in complex systems and combine to form harm), and system-based solutions to prevent harm and injury. Put simply, safety science comprises all the knowledge and practice needed to keep people safe. In healthcare, that knowledge encompasses five distinct groupings of factors, including those related to organizational structure, which defines job functions; processes, which define work and its coordination; protocol, including job aids such as checklists; technology and the care environment, including equipment, medical devices, and the physical plant; and people, including their knowledge, skills, and attitudes.

Taking all of these groupings of factors together, we can speak of safety as an "emergent property" of the complex system that exists in healthcare organizations. That is, safety doesn't owe to any one or more of these specific factors that make up the system, but rather emerges from the effective *interaction* of these factors. A system is safe when organizational structure, processes, protocols, technology and the care environment, and people all work well together without creating a large number of errors, omissions, and defects.

As this definition suggests, when we speak of systems, we're denoting socio-technical systems—people, processes, and technologies that come together for the purpose of performing specific tasks. In general, people are slow and a little sloppy (they make mistakes and drift in practice), although they can think consciously. Technology, by contrast, is lightning fast and very accurate, but unlike people, it cannot think. Safety in healthcare and other industries arises from the right combination of the system's human and nonhuman components, and leading for safety requires an accurate mental model of a socio-technical system.

Several such models for safety systems currently exist. One model known as the *domino effect* conceives of harm and injury as arising out of a direct, cause-and-effect relationship in which a single systemic problem causes a human error, resulting in harm or injury. This model helps us understand some, if not most, workforce injuries. When a healthcare provider sticks herself with a needle, the absence of a safety device on the needle coupled with inattention on the provider's part might add up to harm in the form of exposure to a blood-borne pathogen. But this model doesn't begin to help us understand patient harm, which might reflect several human errors caused by the system.

Let's say a patient dies because he didn't receive necessary treatment in time, even after he complained multiple times of worrying symptoms. We might wonder: why didn't the nurses caring for him notice that he was in distress? If one of them did, why did it take her too long, and why didn't she take appropriate action? Why did the doctor on service at the time initially refuse to deliver treatment, brushing off the nurse's insistence that treatment was necessary? Might the hospital have avoided this death by keeping more staff on duty, so that the nurse taking care of this patient could have paid more attention to him? Might it have trained nursing staff on how to listen better to patient concerns? Might it have developed a better protocol for treating this specific condition? Might it have trained nurses and doctors to work better together as a team? Might it have put processes in place to ensure that doctors on duty had a better grasp of patient developments that occurred during the previous shift? Patient care is neither simple nor linear, as the domino effect model presumes.

Another model for systems of safety, the *Swiss cheese model*, also doesn't perfectly describe safety in healthcare. Under this schema,[2] harm results when an active human error coincides with latent system-wide problems, allowing the error to continue unimpeded and cause harm to the patient or injury to the care delivery team. As suggested in the Figure 3.1, these latent problems amount to "holes" in an otherwise solid system into which caregivers and patients might fall—hence the use of this dairy-based metaphor.

The Swiss cheese model describes safety in complex, linear systems—but again, healthcare is not linear. Some patients make their own way through the system without staying on a standard clinical pathway. A gunshot victim, for instance, might contract

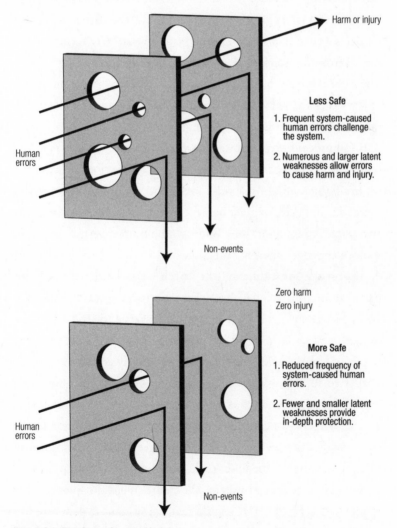

Figure 3.1 The Swiss Cheese Model

an infection during surgery, requiring both a postsurgical pathway and an infection-control pathway. A fragile patient in intensive care may be too unstable to reposition in bed, thereby interfering with a standard skin care protocol. A patient undergoing a triple bypass might have an unrelated lung ailment that requires special measures outside the standard protocol.

The *sharp end model*[3] enhances the Swiss cheese model by incorporating the notion that the human errors that trigger the Swiss cheese effect are also *caused* by the system. *Sharp end* in this model is a term that safety experts generally use to describe behaviors of frontline workers shaped by a larger system, with the term *blunt end* referring to the system itself. Problems at the blunt end of the system can place mental and physical stress on people working at the sharp end, making human error more probable (Figure 3.2). To prevent errors from occurring, we can take action at the blunt end. When caregivers sense time pressure, for instance, the brain's fight-or-flight response kicks into motion. Attentiveness increases, but the caregiver becomes more likely to make a cognitive error. A blunt end solution might be to change the system to remove or reduce the time pressure.

Safety experts have put forth still other models to better approximate the realities that exist in healthcare contexts—Rasmussen's *dynamic safety model*, for instance, or the colorfully named *bow tie model*.[4] But to make the journey to zero patient harm and zero workforce injury, we need only concern ourselves with two models: sharp end and Swiss cheese. The sharp end model describes how we as safety leaders could and should manage the tendency of care delivery systems to cause the human error that triggers the Swiss cheese effect. Safety leaders can improve safety by changing the blunt end, providing for a more reliability focused socio-technical system. We can then use the Swiss cheese model to describe how we should manage systems to contain error and prevent the resulting harm and injury. Leaders can find and

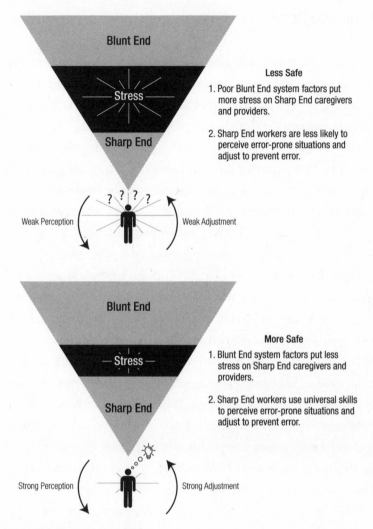

Figure 3.2 The Sharp End Model

fix the latent systemic problems, represented as holes in the cheese. Together, these two models allow us to understand how systems might prevent the relatively few errors that lead to harm events, and also stop those errors, once they occur, from causing harm and injury. Deploying these two models, organizations can realize an 80 percent reduction in harm each two-year development cycle, as theorized by safety science.

Safety Culture

How do leaders enhance safety on the level of the system? They use learning systems to change *culture*. Defined as people's shared values and beliefs, culture is central to systems of safety. It is especially important in healthcare; here, systems are built around people to a far greater extent than systems in the power, transportation, and manufacturing industries. Culture comprises the single most important behavior-shaping factor in the blunt end of the system, binding together all of the other behavior-shaping factors. A safe surgery checklist in an operating room doesn't prevent harm—the people in the operating room who think together as a care delivery team using a checklist do. Barcode scanning for medication administration at the bedside doesn't prevent harm. People who scan the medications and think about the signals from the computer do. Something similar holds true for workforce injury. Lift equipment doesn't prevent injury in patient handling. Proper use of lift equipment does. Likewise, proper use of gown and gloves prevent spread of infection. Behind each part of the systems of safety, there is always a person who is thinking, choosing, and doing, which means that culture comes into play.

Safety culture is a nexus of commonly held values and beliefs that prioritizes safety. We can think of safety cultures as cultures in which people regard safety as more important than any other consideration, practice at every moment as if safety was the most important consideration, and seek to maintain and improve work systems so that they can practice in this way. But what composes safety cultures exactly? Thought leaders have set forth a number of specific frameworks. Christine Sammer, for instance, has identified the following seven domains or subcultures of safety cultures:[5]

1. **Leadership**, starting with the chief executive officer and permeating the entire organization

2. **Teamwork**, a multidisciplinary and multigenerational approach across all levels of leadership, teams, and organizations

3. **Evidence-based clinical care**, delivered using best-practice delivery systems, including checklists

4. **Communications**, which create shared situational awareness and organizational learning

5. **A learning environment**, which is created using structured learning systems (performance improvement methods)

6. **Just culture,** a strong, blame-free regime of accountability for safe practice

7. **Patient-centered care**, marked by compassion, a patient focus, and collaboration with patients and their families in the making of care decisions

To these seven domains, we can add the five characteristics of safety cultures set forth by Ronald Westrum and Patrick Hudson, principal developers of Shell Oil Company's Hearts and Minds campaign, a successful and large-scale safety culture transformation:[6]

1. **Communication**, with high frequency and closed loops for vertical information flow and lateral integration

2. **Organizational attitudes** based on respect that allow leaders and staff to partner in fixing system problems

3. **Health, safety, and environmental (HSE)** programs owned by staff, with a few safety professionals in advising roles

4. **Organizational behavior** that prioritizes safety as much as production, engenders trust among leaders and staff,

and enables frequent dialogue on the importance of
working safely and improving work systems

5. **Working behavior**, with staff providing the safe
environment and leaders sharing lessons learned among
staff members

We might also point to a framework from the nuclear power
industry and the Institute of Nuclear Power Operations (INPO),
an industry group dedicated to creating and maintaining the highest possible safety standards. INPO has prepared several standards
for safety culture, the most recent dating from 2012. These standards contain both principles and traits. Replace the word *nuclear*
with *patient* in the following statements, and the standard is quite
consistent with best practice in healthcare:

- "Everyone is responsible for nuclear safety."
- "Leaders demonstrate commitment to safety," specifically
  by adopting "leadership safety values and actions."
- "Trust permeates the organization," with a culture that
  is marked by "effective safety communication, respectful
  work, and environment for raising concerns."
- "Decision-making reflects safety first."
- "Nuclear technology is recognized as special and unique."
- "A questioning attitude is cultivated."
- "Organizational learning is embraced" through "continu-
  ous learning and problem identification and resolution."
- "Nuclear safety undergoes constant examination," again
  through "continuous learning and problem identification
  and resolution."[7]

This framework seems especially relevant when we consider
that the nuclear power industry has a very strong safety record
to date,[8] and that it bears strong resemblance to healthcare. A

nuclear power plant is very complex (although perhaps not as complex as the human body and healthcare delivery systems). The people operating the plant mostly care for the plant while it operates, just as clinicians care for or support the patient while the patient's body heals itself (in extreme cases, of course, such as cardiopulmonary bypass, clinicians "operate" on a patient rather than simply caring for him or her). Likewise, nuclear power plants and hospitals are both stationary and mostly operate for extended durations, whereas in air, rail, and ship transportation teams operate vehicles in motion for a fixed duration. The people operating a nuclear power plant spend their time monitoring plant operations, diagnosing malfunctions in the making, performing procedures to repair and replace failing components, and very occasionally rescuing the plant from a safety event. Caregivers and providers diagnose disease, provide treatments, and occasionally rescue a patient. Given all of these similarities, we would do well to look to nuclear power and other industries for inspiration when conceptualizing strong safety cultures in healthcare. And this observation in turn brings us to our next topic.

High Reliability Organizing

To improve safety on a systems level, organizations must aim for something besides safety: high reliability in the system's performance. We can define reliability as the system's capability to correctly perform its intended functions. A perfectly reliable system would function correctly 100 percent of the time, and a perfectly unreliable system would never function correctly (reliability would equal zero). Some modicum of safety can exist without high reliability, but in the presence of systemic dysfunction, human errors will inevitably occur, resulting in harm and injury. Organizations can never hope to reach zero harm without focusing both on safety and high reliability. On the flip side, organizations that achieve high reliability can use it to improve much else, including clinical quality, patient experience, workforce and provider engagement, and efficiency.

Let's delve a bit deeper into how to describe levels of reliability in an organization. Consider the following equation:

$$\text{Reliability} + \text{System Error (unreliability)} = 100\%$$

Working with this equation, we find that a system with 90 percent reliability has a 10 percent system error rate. When we improve system reliability to 99 percent, system error falls to 1 percent. When we further increase system reliability to 99.5 percent, we further reduce system error (unreliability) to 0.5 percent. When reliability numbers rise to 99.9 percent or above, we do better stating system error as an error rate—in this case, 1 error out of every 1,000 attempts. Typically, safety experts express error rates using scientific notation: 1 error in 1,000 = 10^{-3}, 1 error in 10,000 = 10^{-4}, 1 error in 100,000 = 10^{-5}, 1 error in 1,000,000 = 10^{-6}, and so on.

Blood banking and anesthesia already have high reliability: the probability of unexpected patient death is less than 1 in 1,000,000 (i.e., reliability rates in both exceed 10^{-6}). In both cases, we find strong systems of safety. Blood banking is safe because it boasts a reliable combination of people with safe practice habits, standard processes and protocols, and technology. Have you ever heard the expression "check it like a hard-nosed blood banker"? That statement testifies to the reliability of blood bank personnel. Anesthesia is safe because it boasts a reliable combination of people, standard process and protocol, and an excellent interface between humans and the anesthesia machine. Indeed, this interface is so strong today that people tend to think of the anesthesiologist and the machine as composing a single entity. The journey to zero will require that we achieve reliable combinations such as these in many more healthcare micro-systems. Overall, the probability of unexpected patient death is 10^{-3} per hospital admission—one death for every 1,000 admissions. By comparison, the probability of unexpected death in commercial aviation is 10^{-7} per departure—one death for every 10,000,000 airline departures.

A reliability of 10^{-3} represents the frontier of human reliability. Left on their own, people can only perform routine tasks in familiar work environments to a reliability of 99.99 percent. Every 1,000 actions will contain some error, omission, or defect. The lesson: don't leave people to work on their own. Surround them with systems of safety. James Reason, the safety thought leader and developer of the Swiss cheese model, observed: "We cannot change the human condition, but we can change the conditions under which humans work."[9] Systems of safety lower error rates and improve system reliability to 10^{-4}, 10^{-5}, and below. As system reliability increases, the numbers of patient harms and workforce injury steadily decrease and eventually approach zero.

High reliability, like safety, is an "emergent property," brought into being by the combinations of behavior-shaping factors in the socio-technical system. When systems provide reliable combinations at the blunt end, practice at the sharp end becomes safer. When systems provide poor combinations, practice becomes more dangerous. Organizations that seek better safety and reliability must use learning systems to change the combination of shaping factors. Specifically, organizations should follow principles learned in other organizations that have achieved very high levels of reliability.

A discipline called high reliability organizing has arisen to describe very advanced differences between high reliability organizations and less reliable organizations. Operating within this discipline, a number of experts have contributed descriptive theories of safety and high reliability, including Karlene Roberts, founder of the Berkeley school of high reliability; Karl Weick, founder of the Michigan school of high reliability; and Kathleen

Sutcliffe, also of the Michigan school.[10] The focus of theorists and the discipline itself have evolved over time. (See Figure 3.3, which identifies specific thought leaders and depicts the chronology of their scholarship from left to right.) Prior to 1980, most safety thought leaders considered how to prevent individual people from committing errors in their work. After 1980, focus shifted toward systems of safety. The discourse of safety culture thought leaders (shown upper center) and high reliability organizing (HRO) thought leaders (middle lower center) merged into a single subdiscipline. A new subdiscipline called resilience engineering (upper right) merged safety culture's emphasis on preempting harm (by aiming for zero defects at the outset) with high reliability organizing's emphasis on compensating for and adjusting to existing defects so as to prevent harm.

The best-known descriptive theory of high reliability organizations is the five characteristics of high reliability set forth by Karl Weick and Kathleen Sutcliffe.[11] These five characteristics are so well known that many HRO practitioners perceive them as the *only* characteristics of high reliability organizations. The first three of these characteristics allow systems to *anticipate* failures and thus avoid their attendant harms. High reliability organizations are: (1) preoccupied with failure and constantly looking for its early signs; (2) resistant to simple, easy, or noncritical interpretations of failure; and (3) sensitive to operational reality—that is, these organizations maintain dynamic, nonlinear systems so that leaders can provide direct oversight and adjust to unpredicted interactions.

The final two characteristics identified by Weick and Sutcliffe help organizations *contain* failures once they occur. High reliability organizations are: (4) committed to resilience, focused on preserving function even during high-demand periods and after failures have occurred, and on learning and growing after harm or injury events and near misses; and (5) deferential to expertise, seeking experts with knowledge and experience, regardless of rank or status.

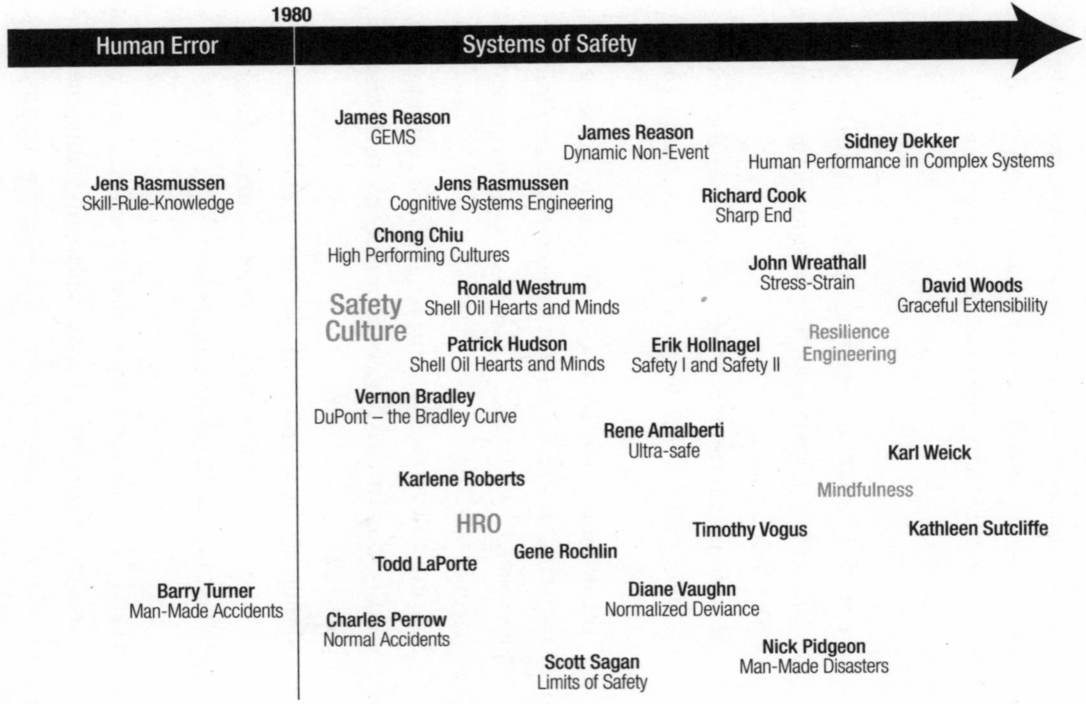

Human Error | 1980 | Systems of Safety

Jens Rasmussen
Skill-Rule-Knowledge

James Reason
GEMS

James Reason
Dynamic Non-Event

Sidney Dekker
Human Performance in Complex Systems

Jens Rasmussen
Cognitive Systems Engineering

Chong Chiu
High Performing Cultures

Richard Cook
Sharp End

John Wreathall
Stress-Strain

David Woods
Graceful Extensibility

Ronald Westrum
Shell Oil Hearts and Minds

Safety Culture

Patrick Hudson
Shell Oil Hearts and Minds

Erik Hollnagel
Safety I and Safety II

Resilience Engineering

Karl Weick

Mindfulness

Kathleen Sutcliffe

Vernon Bradley
DuPont – the Bradley Curve

Rene Amalberti
Ultra-safe

Karlene Roberts

HRO   Gene Rochlin

Todd LaPorte

Timothy Vogus

Diane Vaughn
Normalized Deviance

Charles Perrow
Normal Accidents

Scott Sagan
Limits of Safety

Nick Pidgeon
Man-Made Disasters

Barry Turner
Man-Made Accidents

Figure 3.3 Thought Leadership in Safety and Reliability

As useful as Weick and Sutcliffe's framework is, it doesn't probe the relationship between the system and the people working inside it as closely as it might. Approaching safety from that angle, Rene Amalberti, a professor of medicine who studied human factors in aviation and later in healthcare, identified five additional characteristics of safety cultures and reliability, sets of behaviors that when practiced tend to enhance safety across a system. These behaviors include:[12]

- **Accepting limits** on discretionary action, whether by deferring to expertise, adhering to protocol, or complying with safety limits
- **Abandoning autonomy** by becoming mindful of others and coordinating with people, activity, processes, and systems
- **Transitioning away from a "craftsperson" mindset** and embracing that of the "equivalent actor" (i.e., embracing standard work practices based on evidence-based best practice)
- **Sharing risk vertically** in the organization, communicating problems to leaders both retrospectively and proactively
- **Managing the visibility of risk** using visual management techniques and information systems to predict failure, make adjustments, and prevent harm

In general, HRO theory assumes that a number of key parts of a complex system of safety are already in place, including the competency of caregivers and providers, the reliability of processes, and the reliability of equipment, devices, and technology. If any of these assumptions don't hold true, organizations will first need to take remedial action according to an evidence-based performance improvement model. Once the organization has progressed in these areas, it can then deploy a cultural transformation model to advance safety and high reliability. Such models seek to establish a target behavior, usually framed as a tool, and reinforce that target behavior until it becomes a practice habit among employees, managers, and others within the system. Organizations can deploy any of the available evidence-based change management models to pursue culture transformation, as all of these share three fundamentals: they establish a target behavior as a performance expectation; they enable people to perform to that expectation by providing the necessary knowledge and skills; and they align measurement, reward, and accountability systems so that the target behavior becomes a strong habit.

These models often group behaviors together as "bundles" or sets of skills, one for leaders and one for everyone—leaders, caregivers, and providers. In practice, organizations would start with one of the characteristics defined in a safety science or high reliability organizing framework—for instance, Weick and Sutcliffe's notions of preoccupation with failure or sensitivity to operations. Organizations would then identify a leadership skill or behavior that when regularly practiced helps to nurture these characteristics, such as a daily, hospital-wide check-in or safety huddle.[13] Such a huddle would uncover the information needed to deliver safe patient care, providing a daily forum for leaders to listen for faint signals of harm in the making.

An HRO leadership skill such as "daily check-ins" also helps organizations manage the visibility of risk, as in Amalberti's model. Team members report problems at the check-in meeting. Leaders attending the meeting now know about these problems and can shift resources to keep patients and caregivers safe. More generally, organizations can deploy several of the safety culture and HRO practices by adopting just a few leadership skills bundled together. There is no need for a separate skill for each practice. Most healthcare systems using this approach, including early adopters such as Memorial Health University Medical Center in Savannah, Georgia, and Cincinnati Children's Hospital Medical Center, have deployed bundles of three to five leadership skills and five to six universal skills. Organizations can use a change management model to deploy the bundles of leadership and universal skills, cultivating several of the safety science and HRO characteristics at once.

How should organizations select which bundles of leadership and universal skills to deploy? The answer is to perform a systematic study of existing practices within the healthcare system. Leaders should study organizational performance, performing a safety culture survey, an assessment of system capability, and a common cause analysis of harm events. Safety culture surveys are psychometrics that quantify the organization's potential to work safely. System capability assessments gauge a socio-technical system's ability to translate that potential into safe performance. The Reliability Governance Index (RGI), for instance, is a tool that comprehensively gauges system capability, assessing 40 critical "success factors" in high-reliability including leadership, strategy, operational systems, operational leaders, and practice habits of staff and medical staff. The tool, which also includes 10 modes for performance improvement, serves as both a snapshot of existing performance and a blueprint for future improved performance.

The third component of a study of organizational performance, common cause analyses, assesses past harm events in the aggregate to identify system causes of error leading to harm and injury. Leaders should also create an inventory of leadership and universal skills, assessing each for efficacy, and form a culture design group composed of leaders, caregivers, and providers. This group should choose skills that are indicated by the study and also evidence-based. It should likewise select methods for educating leaders and the wider employee population in leadership and universal skills, respectively. Finally, the group should identify accountability systems to help leaders, caregivers, and providers practice those universal skills as habits.

All of the approximately 80 healthcare systems in the HPI client community have used this approach, each adopting its own combination of HRO leadership and universal skills based on its respective diagnostic study. HRO leadership and universal skills turn out to be the missing piece in every healthcare system of safety. In effect, our healthcare facilities are far more dangerous than they should be because leaders and the workforce at large haven't adopted the right behaviors at the right times. When organizations close that gap by adding necessary skills, they can truly start the journey to zero patient harm and zero workforce injury.

Advocating for Safety

If we can discern a silver lining in the horrible tragedy that started on Dr. Gene Burke's first day as a resident, it was the power of that tragedy to galvanize change in some small way, nudging healthcare closer to systems of safety. During his subsequent career as a physician and physician executive, Dr. Burke sought to reduce and ultimately eradicate the harms that patients suffered and the injuries that caregivers experienced on the job. And eradicate them he did. Dr. Burke served as physician champion when Sentara Healthcare, located in Virginia and North Carolina and one of the top integrated healthcare systems in the United States, launched the electronic intensive care unit (eICU) to remotely monitor and manage its most critically ill patients. He was present when Sentara articulated its version of universal skills for safety culture and promoted those skills among the workforce. And he was present for Sentara's articulation and promotion of HRO leadership skills. In fact, he was one of several safety and reliability leaders who developed Sentara's systems of safety. In 2004,

Sentara reported an 80 percent reduction in serious preventable harm during its first 18 months of focusing systemically on safety. In recognition of its safety improvements, Sentara received the American Hospital Association (AHA) Quest for Quality Award in 2004 and The Joint Commission (TJC) Eisenberg Quality Award in 2005.

As we've seen, organizations like Sentara don't achieve safety by focusing on individuals, but rather by drawing on safety science to create systems of safety and high reliability. Half of an organization's improvement will emerge from efforts to shape internal processes, the other half from efforts to shape the culture and make leadership and universal skills common practice within the organization. To put your organization on the path to zero harm, become a student of safety science and high reliability organizing, shape processes in your organization to make your system more reliable, and undertake initiatives to teach leaders and the workforce as a whole new safety-related skills. With sustained effort, you can help ensure that your newly minted physicians won't experience the horror that Dr. Burke did—not on their first days at work, nor on any days thereafter.

IN SUM

- Organizations achieve zero harm by deploying systems of safety consistently over time. Safety is an emergent property of a complex system, not a competency of the individuals practicing within the system.
- Safety science provides safety leaders with the organizational structure, processes, protocols, environment of care, and technological interfaces necessary for safety.
- Culture is often the missing piece in systems of safety. High reliability organizing (HRO) provides us with a theory of this missing piece, while

HRO leadership and universal skills provide us with the daily practices we need to fill in the gap.

- Design HRO leadership skills and universal skills by studying the causes of your own patient harm events and workforce injuries. Choose five leadership skills and five universal skills. Make sure that each skill is evidence-based and indicated by your study.

An Introduction to HRO Leadership Skills

Steve Kreiser, CDR (USN Ret.), MBA

What do leaders in high reliability organizations (HROs) do to obtain such outstanding outcomes? As this chapter argues, the answer is fourfold. Leaders focus on communicating safety principles and organizational commitment, building engagement and accountability, supporting operations, and nurturing learning efforts among frontline staff.

LIKE MANY ADMINISTRATORS, "Jill Cruze," the semi-fictional chief executive officer of a 300-bed hospital on the East Coast of the United States,* felt intense pressure to maintain market share and revenue while also containing costs and meeting productivity goals. At the same time, she had to build and maintain positive relationships with the medical staff, and also ensure that they delivered on safety and quality measures. Physicians regularly voiced concerns about one aspect of care or another. Recently, a surgeon had complained about the overhead lullaby played after a mother delivers a baby. Patients loved this feature, but

---

* "Jill Cruze" is not a real person, but rather a composite of several actual healthcare leaders. Her situation is representative of many we've encountered.

the lullaby woke up the surgeon while he was sleeping on-call, creating, in his opinion, a safety issue (he wasn't able to rest and perform at his best). Another physician complained about inadequate staffing levels in the ICU. True, the hospital had experienced an exceptionally high patient load over the past two months, and the ICU had seen an elevated, three-to-one patient-to-nurse ratio at times. Yet Jill's chief nursing officer assured her that overall, the staffing levels in the ICU were well within national benchmarks and certainly enough to assure safe outcomes.

Organizations like Jill's are incredibly complex, filled with interconnected departments that often are quite siloed. How can leaders lead and manage such organizations effectively? With so many distractions and demands, how can they keep the organization aligned around the three big priorities of keeping patients and staff safe, delivering high-quality clinical outcomes that attract patients and drive revenues, and ensuring that patients have an exceptional experience?

High reliability organizations (HROs) in other industries manage complex, high-risk work environments while also successfully minding costs, budgets, and finances. In these complex systems, unlike in most healthcare organizations, leaders are constantly intervening to drive results. Scott Snair, an associate dean with the Henley-Putnam School of Strategic Security at National American University, observes that, "A well-led institution has predictable leadership. . . . You can conjecture what its managers are doing and what they are likely to do next."[1] In healthcare, Howard Kern, CEO of Sentara Healthcare and a former member of HPI's executive committee, has called upon the industry to codify "best practices" for leaders seeking to build HROs. Evidence-based, standard work for leaders reduces variation in leadership practice, improving reliability in achieving and sustaining performance expectations. "We have evidence-based clinical bundles," Kern said in 2007. "It's time we have evidence-based leadership."[2]

This chapter seeks to further the cause of evidence-based leadership in healthcare by examining an array of tools and techniques that leaders can use to increase their organizations' reliability (and hence their safety). These HRO leadership skills fall into four categories: messaging on mission, building engagement and accountability, supporting operations, and leading local learning. Let's review each one in turn, drawing on examples from healthcare and other industries in which we find high reliability organizations.

Messaging on Mission

Norfolk Southern is a Fortune 500 company with $35.7 billion in assets, $10.5 billion in revenue, 36,000 miles of railroad track, 67,000 locomotives and freight cars, and 27,000 employees.[3] Although the company has succeeded financially, you won't find "maximizing profits" in the vision statement that Norfolk Southern communicates both internally and externally. Rather, the company seeks to "Be the safest, most customer-focused, and successful transportation company in the world."[4] As this statement suggests, safety isn't just part of the job for Norfolk Southern personnel. It's their top priority. Leaders purposefully incorporated safety into the company's vision statement, seeking to inform employees that despite any financial or production pressures they might feel, leadership was committed first and foremost to providing employees with an injury-free work environment.

Norfolk Southern affords important lessons for healthcare leaders. First, senior leaders must clearly articulate that safety is the organization's core value, the glue that holds the organization together and drives all activities. Put differently, leaders are presenting safety as a *precondition of operations*. Many healthcare organizations proclaim safety as their top priority, but from the perspective of frontline associates, priorities seem to shift during daily operations. Leaders in an HRO want and expect their people to think and act for safety first. They want their people to know that management will support their decisions, even (and especially) if a safety concern didn't turn out to exist after all.

As important as it is to clearly proclaim safety as a core value, leaders' actions in support of safety matter even more. Leaders can take action to support *cultures of safety* composed of certain values, beliefs, and behavior expectations, with such cultures in turn shaping how individuals and teams act and interact. Edgar Schein, former professor at the MIT Sloan School of Management, has described a number of ways that leaders can reinforce and embed a desired culture. These include regularly focusing on it and measuring it; paying attention to their own behavior in times of crisis; allocating scarce resources in particular ways; working deliberately to model, teach, and coach desired behaviors, beliefs, and values; and promulgating formal statements of the organization's philosophy, values, and creed.[5] To increase safety and reliability, healthcare leaders should adopt tactics to reinforce a culture of safety, measure safety on a daily basis, place safety paramount in decision-making, and personally model safe practices.

Healthcare organizations increasingly understand how important culture is to achieving not just better safety, but clinical quality and experience of care. Leaders of these organizations strive to design and manage culture, imparting it to the organization through what we call "messaging on mission." Over time, culture becomes so deeply imbedded that employees feel a sense of ownership over it, driving it in turn. How can you "message on mission" in your team or organization? Here are three powerful techniques.

Technique #1: Start Every Meeting with a Safety Message

Naval pilots conduct preflight briefings before every flight. The first item on their checklists: a safety-related item. Healthcare leaders can borrow this method to reinforce a safety-first mindset in their organizations, and they can inspire leaders and physicians throughout the organizations to do the same. Start by making safety the first item on printed agendas for major meetings, and translate the practice over time to smaller meetings, both formal and informal. Begin at the board and executive team level in quarterly or monthly meetings, and then spread the practice vertically by promoting the inclusion of opening "safety moments" on agendas in meetings of the medical executive committee, shared governance council meetings, the hospital finance committee, and clinical and nonclinical departmental meetings. The box offers 10 ideas for safety starters for your next meeting.

10 Useful Safety Starters

1. Share your convictions on patient or personal safety.
2. Explain how safety contributes to the organization's mission.
3. Tell a story about safety or harm occurring in the organization.
4. Tell a story about safety or harm in another organization.
5. Share a concern about safety that keeps you up at night.
6. Review a reliability skill (see Chapter 5) and talk about how it applies in our work.
7. Relate an example of how you used a reliability skill at work or outside of work.
8. Explain how a policy, procedure, or expectation contributes to safety.
9. Discuss the importance of reporting errors, events, and problems.
10. Thank staff for their personal commitment to patient and employee safety.

Stories are especially important when it comes to safety. Minds wander when overloaded with information, but a well-told story holds people's attention and becomes memorable. Stories also have the power to paint a vivid, stimulating picture of a positive future. Most important, leaders can use storytelling to set expectations and impart lessons, since good stories prompt employees to envision themselves in similar circumstances.

As we've found, the best stories are short—just two to three minutes long. They describe the story's purpose, highlight the protagonist along with some conflict, deliver a hook, include a few telling details to make the story interesting, and then resolve the story's conflict while imparting a lesson. Ellen Crowe, director of clinical excellence and care redesign for the Connecticut Hospital Association, tells the following safety story that includes each of these elements:[6]

I'd like to share a story with you about a seven-year-old boy who lived in a small, rural town in Connecticut. The story demonstrates the importance of communicating clearly, handing off information effectively, and having a questioning attitude.

Benjamin was usually quite active, so when he began to show less interest in his usual activities, his parents noticed. He said he was feeling tired, had been having bellyaches, and didn't feel "quite right." After staying home from school for a couple of days, his energy level remained low, and he started exhibiting behavioral changes, becoming argumentative and short-tempered, behaviors quite different from his usual exuberant self.

His mother brought him to the doctor for testing. After taking a family history, the doctor came to a quick diagnosis of Lyme disease brought on by a Babesia parasite. The doctor prescribed oral antibiotics with a recommendation to switch to IV administration in three weeks via a PICC line if the oral treatments were ineffective.

Several weeks into treatment, the insertion of a PICC line was required and the child was started on the IV antibiotic Rocephin (ceftriaxone), a common antibiotic used to treat Lyme. Ten minutes into his first treatment, Benjamin complained of feeling "itchy." Large welts began to appear on his face, and he developed a severe cough and began gasping for breath. His mother screamed for help as a team of physicians and nurses arrived to administer IV Benadryl to reverse the allergic reaction. His physician made note of the condition in the eMR and changed his antibiotic to ampicillin for home care treatments to begin two days later.

The next afternoon, the mother received a call at work from her husband who had stayed home with the child, stating that the home health nurse had just called to say she would be there in a few minutes for their son's treatment. The mother hung up the phone, and a sinking feeling came over her. Home health should not be coming today, as it had not been two days from the treatment in the hospital as the doctor had prescribed. An internal alarm went off in her head as she questioned why a nurse would be coming by their house a day earlier than was expected. She decided to leave her office and head home to verify the situation, driving as fast as possible, only to see the home health agency's van parked in front of her house as she pulled into the driveway. Without turning off the engine or closing the car door behind her, she ran into her front door to see the home healthcare nurse with her child beginning an infusion of IV Rocephin. As it turned out, the order to discontinue the Rocephin had not been changed and communicated to the home care nurses, despite the allergy having been noted in the record.

The mother's questioning attitude saved the young boy's life that day. When something didn't seem right, she quickly moved to verify the situation. I know she is thankful she did, because that child was my son Benjamin, and that mother was me. I'm the one who raced back home to verify a situation that seemed off track, and it's why we should all have a questioning attitude, being ever-vigilant and on the lookout when things we see or hear don't seem right or fit in with what we would have expected.

Crowe's powerful telling of this story clearly conveys safety as a priority, as well as the importance of good critical thinking skills and healthy questioning. Healthcare leaders everywhere should adopt storytelling and develop their storytelling skills so as to emphasize the importance of safety first.

Technique #2: Support Those Who Speak Up for Safety

William Corley, former president and CEO of Indianapolis, Indiana-based Community Health Network, had made it clear to those around him that if someone made a great catch that preempted a serious safety event, he wanted to hear about it as soon as possible. One Saturday morning, a scrub tech in the operating room spoke up to stop the surgical closing of an emergency C-section patient when a sponge turned up missing on the postprocedure sponge count. The surgeon was certain the sponge wasn't in the abdomen and wanted to continue to close. But the scrub tech insisted they get an x-ray for confirmation. Sure enough, the x-ray revealed a sponge tucked behind a fold in the abdominal cavity.

When notified of the great catch that same afternoon, Bill recognized the impact his response could have. He stopped what he was doing (mowing his lawn) and went directly to that unit to thank the scrub tech for her actions. The tech was surprised to see the CEO of the organization at the hospital in his shorts and running shoes, thanking her publicly for what she thought was "just part of her job." But thanks to Bill's actions, everyone in the department clearly understood that he fully supported a culture of safety, including open communications, the asking of questions, and the voicing of safety concerns.

Dr. Lisa Laurent, a radiologist at Advocate Lutheran General Hospital, tells a similar story about a CT tech in the radiology department who came to her with a concern about a patient with a documented allergy to contrast. When the tech questioned how safe it was for the patient to have a CT studied with contrast, Lisa reviewed the order and told the tech the contrast would not be a problem in this situation. Later that night, however, she had second thoughts about her response. Although it had been medically sound to carry out the study with contrast, Lisa felt that she had missed an opportunity to reinforce the tech's behavior of articulating a safety concern. The next day, Lisa made a special effort to stop by the department and publicly thank the tech for voicing a safety concern. That way, everyone in the department would understand that she fully supported a culture of safety, openness in communications, and the posing of critical questions.

It might often seem easier to thank somebody who speaks up via an e-mail, card, or proxy, but when your direct supervisor, manager, senior leader, or physician colleague thanks you in person, it means something. Such expressions of gratitude matter even when the concern or question at issue didn't ultimately yield a safety improvement. What leaders declare about safety is important, but what they do most influences how others think and act.

Technique #3: Put Safety First in Decision-Making

In commercial aviation, considerations of safety win out at all times, even amidst pressures to maintain speed, efficiency, or margins. Something similar must hold true in healthcare. To come to decisions that serve the interest of patient care and employee well-being, leaders, staff, and physicians should always ask questions such as: How will this decision or action affect patient safety? Will it make the patient more or less likely to experience a good outcome? How with this decision or action affect our people? Will it put their safety or security at risk? What is the best or worst possible outcome if we go ahead with this decision or action—or if we don't?

In many healthcare settings, leaders confronted with difficult decisions or challenging work environments respond with unhelpful statements like, "we will never get more staff or equipment," "we can't afford it," "we don't have time," "we asked before and they said no," and the perennial favorite, "we've always done it this way." Such responses send the wrong message to staff and physicians about the organization's commit to safety. To help keep safety foremost in people's minds, ensure that the first words out of your mouth indicate your true concern: providing safe, high-quality care as part of an overall exceptional patient experience.

You can also make time to teach others this approach to decision-making as well. John Duval, former CEO of Virginia Commonwealth University Health System, was rounding when he overheard a discussion between two physicians who were about to perform a procedure. The physicians were debating whether to perform the procedure in the operating room or in the interventional radiology suite. John could tell that the discussion wasn't focused primarily on the patient's best interest, but what better served the care team's needs. John invited both physicians to his office to continue the conversation. Together, they examined what decision would best assure quality of care and the patient's safety, with the physicians eventually agreeing to this course of action. As Duval attests, this was a moment of truth, one that conveyed important messages about organizational priorities.

Building Engagement and Accountability

Mere mention of the word *accountability* makes many people shudder, conjuring thoughts of forced performance of a task we'd rather avoid or, worse yet, the prospect that some authority figure might *hold us accountable* for failing to follow through. Yet accountability isn't a behavior or action done to us. It's an intrinsic characteristic, a measure of an individual's own motivation to perform at a high level, with due regard for ethics and safety. For most of us, accountability is situation-based. We feel more accountable in situations that we perceive as important, less so in other situations. Accountability reflects our own upbringing, education, or work experience ("intrinsic factors"), as well as external drivers like peer influence ("What will my coworkers think of me?") and the influence of authority figures ("What will my boss think of me?").

Leaders can't do much to influence intrinsic factors, even though these factors constitute one of the most powerful drivers of individual accountability. So what should they do? Hire for it! When holding job interviews, human resource departments should screen candidates using behavioral-based questioning that evaluates candidates' commitment to safe, high-quality, patient-centered care. Questions should also give leaders a sense of how comfortable new hire candidates are asking questions, voicing safety concerns, or prioritizing safety over other work pressures.

Peer-driven accountability amounts to a commitment between coworkers to speak up, point out errors or mistakes, and push hard when confronted with concerns about actions or activities that could harm patients or workers. In many cases, peer-to-peer networks influence personal behaviors most strongly (parents of teenagers know this well). Just as parents must find and develop strong peer networks for their children, so developing strong peer networks in healthcare is first and foremost the job of leaders. Leaders should identify early adopters or "safety champions" whom colleagues respect and who will lead from the front line, behaving in ways that others will follow. As it becomes easier and more culturally acceptable for peers to speak up and point out errors and mistakes, momentum grows and a culture of safety takes hold.

Leader-driven accountability entails setting clear expectations linked to an organization's mission, vision, and values. In so doing, leaders must ensure their employees possess the knowledge and skill necessary to meet those expectations. They should feel personally responsible for team members' practice habits, and visit the work environment on a regular basis to observe. To reinforce expectations, they should monitor measures of success, providing positive feedback both when performance meets expectations and when it wanes. Here are two specific techniques to consider.

Technique #1: 5:1 Feedback

During the 1970s, Dr. John Gottman, a marriage researcher from the University of Washington, and his colleague Robert Levenson conducted a classic study in which they videotaped 700 newlywed couples holding 15-minute conversations. Counting the number of verbal and nonverbal interactions that made up the conversations, Gottman and Levenson could predict which couples would still be married 10 years later with an accuracy of over 90 percent.[7] As the two researchers found, the primary factor that led couples to stay together was the ratio of their positive to negative interactions, especially during times of conflict. The closer the couples got to a ratio of five positive interactions for every one negative interaction, the more likely their relationship was to remain strong and intact.

Healthcare leaders can easily incorporate 5:1 feedback into their daily practice. Increase the amount of positive feedback by recognizing, encouraging, and reinforcing observed desired behaviors. Praise using the "lightest touch" possible, saying "thank you" and "nice job" or using nonverbal mechanisms like smiles and head nods. Leaders often feel they shouldn't give positive feedback when an employee is "just doing her job," but as a recent study of 22,000 leaders found, when a leader was ranked in the top 10 percent among his or her peers in giving feedback, his or her team was ranked in the top 23 percent for engagement. Likewise, low team engagement ratings correlated with low leader performance in feedback.

Positive or encouraging reinforcement makes individuals more likely to repeat a behavior, while negative or discouraging reinforcement renders them less likely to do so. Most people are more socially conditioned to give others negative or corrective feedback. While both types help, positive feedback shapes behavior more powerfully, building a relationship of trust and respect between coworkers or between coworkers and supervisors. To maximize employee performance, provide the optimal ratio of positive to negative feedback over time: five positives for every one negative.

Technique #2: Rounding to Influence

In high reliability organizations, leaders feel personally responsible for their teams' practice habits, acting on a daily basis to build situational and operational awareness at the front line. In particular, leaders want employees to understand three threats to reliability: mismatches between workload and resources, complex or infrequently performed tasks, and deficiencies in employees' competence. These conditions can all increase the potential for human error or render an error's consequences much more severe.

When events do occur, HRO leaders tend to engage more directly in managing the consequences. They maintain channels of open communication so that employees can send concerns rapidly up the organizational pyramid, allowing HRO leaders to stop small problems from ballooning.

In addition to daily unit-level huddles, interacting with front-line staff during so-called "structured rounds" help leaders manage safety threats. Rounding alerts leaders to issues that confront staff every day, and they also give leaders a chance to model behavior and convey messaging. Leaders should think carefully about how they use their time spent on rounds, considering whether they're truly embracing the opportunity to create connections with staff, discuss specific work expectations, collect safety-related concerns, and ask for employees' personal commitment to achieving organizational goals.

We give rounding with this specific set of priorities in mind a special name: *rounding to influence* (RTI). Rounding to influence is not a rounding program, but a skill leaders can use while rounding. In the future, leaders should conceive of their rounding as all-inclusive, rounding on both patients and teams and covering all the key topics of interest, including safety, quality, experience, engagement, and efficiency. We cannot afford to maintain separate rounding programs for each and every desired outcome inside of an organization.

Dr. Steve Linn, chief medical officer of Inspira Medical Center Vineland in New Jersey, is especially adept at rounding to influence. When talking to nursing staff and providers about safety culture, Steve conveys that culture's importance by sharing staggering figures about harm in US healthcare. He talks about effective strategies for preventing human error using Inspira's safety behaviors, and he asks each member of the care team if she or he could practice those safety behaviors. To keep the conversation focused and on track, Steve structures his conversation around four important areas, what we call the 4 Cs. First, he "Connects" with the team by sharing data. He then reviews what team members "Can Do" to reduce harm, and asks if they have any "Concerns" about the expectations he is outlining. Then he specifically asks for their "Commitment." All leaders should mobilize these 4Cs while on rounds to support specific behaviors among team members while building and reinforcing accountability. "Rounding to influence with the team has made a huge difference for our patients and our people," Steve says. "They see us out in the patient care areas, sharing our commitment to patient safety, and listening to ideas on how processes could be improved to decrease serious preventable harm, so they know that our commitment as leaders is there for them."[8] Thanks to Steve at Vineland and his counterpart at Inspira Medical Center Woodbury, Dr. Scott Wagner, Inspira Health Network has reduced serious preventable patient harm by 64 percent over two years, more than halfway to zero harm.

Supporting Operations

William ("Bill") Edwards Deming was an engineer and statistician whose quality improvement work in post–World War II Japan transformed the country into one of the world's most formidable economies. It took 20 more years for organizations in the United States to seek out lessons from the "Japanese miracle." Working with Ford Motor Company, an organization struggling with massive corporate losses and declining sales, Deming questioned the culture and the way leaders were managing the organizational system as a whole. As he told them, 85 percent of their problems in building high-quality automobiles owed to management failures and the problems those failures created at the front line.[9] As a result of applying the quality principles Deming championed,

Ford by 1986 had become the most profitable American auto company.

In healthcare, designing and managing the system is one of leaders' primary roles. As mentioned briefly in Chapter 3, we can think of the system as comprising the following five broad categories:

- **Structure.** This comprises the resources, oversight, job descriptions, and training required by the organization. The more specialized jobs become, the more employees have to disseminate information and work activities.
- **Work processes.** This comprises the workflow—the series of discrete activities designed to provide a product or service for the end user or customer. Good processes are efficient and effective, neither missing key steps nor requiring too many steps.
- **Policy and protocol.** Good formal policy and protocol design makes inherent sense from the standpoint of frontline workers. It includes simple job aids in the environment of care that employees can find and use when and where the work needs to be done.
- **Technology and the environment of care.** This encompasses the machines, tools, equipment, materials, and work environments that employees encounter, as well as how they are integrated at the front line. These elements should always add value and make the integration of man and machine intuitive from the standpoint of frontline employees.
- **Culture.** The single strongest factor in any system, culture defines practices that are good and safe, as well as those that aren't. A strong culture will send powerful signals to its members about acceptable behavior, allowing organizations to overcome many other shortfalls in the system.

These five systemic factors are always interacting with one another. If nurses who are feeling stressed and rushed due to a staffing shortage (a structural problem) feel a need to short-cut the labeling of a specimen in front of the patient (an element of formally defined work processes), a strong safety culture will encourage them to take an extra few seconds and do it the right way, even when no other coworkers are around to observe. If specimen labels have not printed properly, or the printers are on the other side of the unit, an added systemic problem (related to technology and environment of care) has arisen for the nurse to overcome.

How might organizations alert healthcare leaders to these systemic problems and their causes so that leaders might fix them? Recall the Weick and Sutcliffe principles of HRO leadership from Chapter 3, and three of these principles in particular: preoccupation with failure, sensitivity to operations, and reluctance to simplify. In HROs, leadership teams create structures that allow team members to identify big and small problems daily. Leaders themselves remain proactive and preemptive in how they respond to those problems. They always want to learn more about the system in which they work, looking for nuances that affect daily operations. They create communication channels and conduits so that they can hear about problems, and they ensure that action is taken to address these problems according to how critical and urgent they are relative to safety.

One highly effective technique that HROs use to support operations is the holding of daily safety check-ins at both the leadership and unit levels. In a nuclear power plant, safety hinges on a precise understanding of plant operations and the quick recognition of problems. At the beginning of each day, plant leaders usually meet to discuss the "Plan of the Day." The meeting's agenda might include a review of emerging safety issues, a status check on the plant's top 10 problems, routine reports, and other concerns. This meeting allows leaders to update themselves on operations, identify problems, plan their resolution, and ensure that everyone understands the day's focus and priorities.

After safety and quality leaders at one healthcare organization learned about this nuclear power practice from HPI, they implemented a 15-minute "Daily Check-In for Safety" meeting. The Daily Check-In is a structured conversation about safety that involves senior leaders and department leaders from across the organization. The group first *looks back* on important safety or quality concerns that arose over the previous 24 hours. Then it *looks ahead* to potential safety or quality issues that might arise over next 24 hours. Finally, the group *follows up* by hearing status reports on issues identified that day or previously. The box gives some tips for running a daily check-in.

Tips for Running Daily Check-Ins

Follow a strict roll-call agenda. Start the same time every morning, allowing leaders to first get to their work areas to build situational and operational awareness that they can then share during the huddle. As many leaders as possible should attend the huddle, with 40 to 50 at most given speaking roles.

Clarify expectations around reporting. Leaders should prepare to participate by looking back at the previous 24 hours of operations in their work areas. This "Look Back" report should include any harm, significant near misses, quality defects, patient experience concerns, equipment issues, process problems, and so. In the "Look Ahead" part of the report, leaders anticipate failure by reporting issues that could affect their ability to create a safe day, including staffing issues, equipment issues, unusual conditions, and so on.

Ensure that senior leaders are present and engaged.
As Ronald Heifetz of the Center for Public Leadership at Harvard University has observed, "Attention is the currency of leadership."[10] If others see senior leaders attending and paying attention to the Daily Safety Check-In, then the meeting will add value. Otherwise, the meeting will wither and die. Senior leaders should ask provocative questions designed to encourage critical thought.

Ensure that senior leaders create a safe environment for reporting. Senior leaders should first thank managers and directors when they report errors, issues, or problems in their departments. They should handle fears of reprisal on the part of fellow leaders adeptly and tactfully, requesting that teams work together to solve safety issues and report back on clearly specified dates.

While the daily check-in for leadership serves to build situational and operational awareness on the part of leaders at the "blunt end" of the healthcare delivery system (see Chapter 3), the unit-level daily check-in builds shared awareness among staff at the "sharp end." As busy as they are, clinical and nonclinical caregivers should pause for 5 to10 minutes at the beginning of each shift, huddling with colleagues to focus on protecting patients and staff from harm. These huddles should share lessons learned from previous shifts, build awareness of current work activities, and discuss threats that might arise during the coming shift. A well-designed unit-level safety check-in should occur within the first two hours of every shift. A manager, supervisor, or unit coordinator should lead it, following an agenda designed to spur critical thinking and to display measures of success (including safety, quality, and experience of care metrics). The box offers a sample agenda for a unit-level daily check-in for a nursing unit. Agendas will vary slightly depending on a department's structure. In all cases, managers should design them with input from front-line staff.

Unit-Level Daily Check-In

1. Recent safety event reports, great catches, rapid responses. or falls
2. Patients of focus—sickest, most "care intensive," highest acuity
3. Hospital acquired condition concerns
4. 1:1 patients—reasons
5. IV drips, high-risk meds, blood transfusion patients
6. Equipment issues or concerns
7. Name alerts
8. Patients on isolation
9. Nurse aide assignments and concerns
10. Nursing concerns

Leading Local Learning

Leaders can also enhance operational safety by leading local learning. In most healthcare organizations, teaching and learning takes place away from the workplace in classrooms, training labs, or staff meeting rooms. While offline learning can introduce employees to new concepts and allow for intensive skill development, high reliability organizations complement it with routine, on-the-job learning, creating a continuous *learning culture*. High reliability leaders are adept at leading such frontline learning. They deploy two key approaches, real-time simulation and local learning boards.

Real-time simulation is, in essence, "on-the-spot" teaching. Leaders can conduct "worst-case scenario drills" that help team members understand policies and protocols for handling difficult situations, as well as the resources available to them. They can conduct "everyday scenario drills" that sharpen team and individual responses to common operational issues and problems. And they can conduct "stump me" sessions in which leaders challenge team members to come up with situations that defy the leader's knowledge or expertise. Real-time simulation allows teams to improve their ability to "manage the unexpected" (as per Weick and Sutcliffe's five-part framework), promoting a healthy preoccupation with failure (considering how operations could fail) and a commitment to resilience (honing the team's ability to respond to unexpected situations). Real-time simulation also accelerates the learning curve among new team members, counters the complacency that sets in following long periods of strong performance, and prompts employees to embrace constant learning. The box gives some tips for real-time simulations.

Tips for Real-Time Simulations[11]

Keep it short—30-, 60-, or 90-second scenarios are best.

Maintain a list of worst-case and everyday scenarios for quick reference.

Pick your spots—take advantage of a momentary break in the action to engage with team members.

Incorporate simulations into start-of-shift huddles.

Give 5:1 feedback.

Encourage team members to suggest scenarios.

Encourage (and reward) organic, independently initiated real-time simulation among team members.

Leaders can also lead local learning by establishing local learning boards. Muhammad Ali once said, "It isn't the mountains ahead to climb that wear you out; it's the pebble in your shoe."[12] Unfortunately, in many organizations frontline employees don't have a single pebble in their shoes that wears them out as they go about their work day, or even two. They have gravel—dozens of problems that burden them every day and prevent them from performing effectively. If organizations don't address such "gravel" in a meaningful way, persistent problems can lead to process, policy, or procedural workarounds that compromise patient care or worker safety.

Local learning boards (Figure 4.1) are large displays put up in high-traffic public areas of a unit. Leaders use these boards to identify systemic, safety-related issues at the local level and to provide a mechanism for unit leaders and staff members to implement solutions together. Implemented properly, a local learning board helps employees move from viewing problems as barriers to seeing them as opportunities for improvement. These boards are divided into three parts: new problems, problems that the team is working on, and problems the team has solved. Leaders encourage team members to use the learning board by recognizing issues on the "New Problem" portion as good news, thanking staff members for bringing the problems to management's attention. Leaders and staff can then collaborate to prioritize problem solving, moving

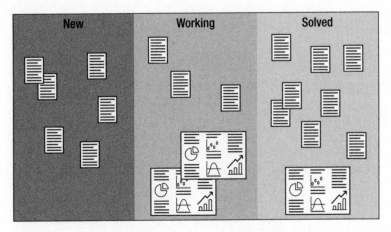

Figure 4.1 Local Learning Board

select items to the "Working" category by forming teams and creating action plans to track problems as they are resolved.

As a learning board becomes part of a unit's daily routine, teams can detect potential problems early, avoiding them before those problems have a chance to compromise patient care. The team then celebrates problems and issues they have fixed, placing them on the "Solved" portion of the learning board and delivering positive feedback to those involved. Combining a learning board with daily, unit-based safety check-ins and publicly posted departmental measures of effectiveness, leaders can create a full-fledged "local learning system" (Figure 4.2) that engages staff within an environment of transparency. Team members openly share data around safety, quality and experience, creating a "burning platform" that supports change efforts. As they huddle around the local learning system on a daily basis to conduct the unit-level safety huddle, all team members can spot gaps that exist between current and desired performance. The shared understanding of problems and the presence of experts at the front line helping to generate solutions creates ownership, spurring the team to continue its problem-solving efforts.

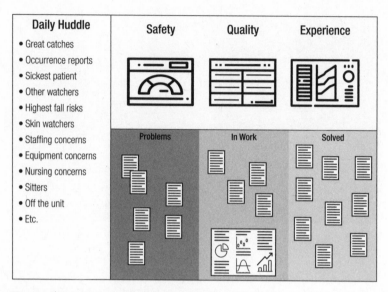

Figure 4.2 Local Learning System Comprising the Local Learning Board, Display of Outcome Metrics, and Huddle Agenda

High Reliability Leadership Skills

Remember Jill Cruze, the semifictional CEO we met earlier? In 2002, she was working as a bedside nurse in the ICU. One of her patients that year had suffered an anoxic brain injury during elective foot and ankle surgery. Simple human errors had caused the injury, forever changing that patient's life and those of her family and caregivers. As Jill moved into nursing leadership and then into higher administrative roles, she resolved that no other patient would ever again experience a harm event like that in her hospital. But as a senior leader, she also felt pressured to improve quality, experience, and financial outcomes. Her solution was to implement lessons from HROs: structured leadership skills built around messaging the hospital's mission of safe care; finding and fixing system problems; and building and reinforcing accountability.

Today Jill leads her hospital's daily safety check-in and rounds numerous times every week. She focuses on influencing the behaviors of staff, physicians, and leaders, and on keeping abreast of systemic factors affecting safety. She looks for opportunities to recognize good performance and isn't afraid to correct poor practices, although she tries to adhere to the five-to-one rule. Like most hospital senior leaders, she pays close attention to the hospital's balanced scorecard, but makes sure to prioritize measuring and discussing preventable harm above all else. She recognizes great catches and safety success stories, and has also worked with risk management to ensure that the lessons learned from safety events spread across the organization. As others throughout the hospital have embraced these HRO leadership skills, Jill has found to her surprise that quality, experience of care, and financial measures have improved as well as safety. HRO leadership skills have helped to create an "operating system" for leadership, one that in Jill's mind has enabled the hospital to become a more successful organization all around.

IN SUM

- HRO leadership skills fall into four categories: messaging on mission, building engagement and accountability, supporting operations, and leading local learning.
- What you declare about safety is important, but what you do about safety influences how others think and act.
- HRO leaders feel personally responsible for their teams' practice habits, and are constantly monitoring those practices, employing 5:1 feedback, and rounding to influence behaviors.
- Put structures in place like a daily check-in of leaders and unit-based huddles conducted before local learning boards. These will help to develop real-time intelligence about potential harm while fostering operational and situational awareness among leaders, staff, and physicians.

Universal Skills for Preventing Harm

Shannon M. Sayles, MS, MA

Universal skills are behaviors that, when practiced by the entire workforce, can prevent the human errors that lead to safety events. In fact, research shows that universal skills might prevent roughly three out of four actions that result in serious preventable harm. This chapter describes the kind of human errors that typically compromise safety in healthcare settings, and presents a number of evidence-based universal skills that organizations can preventatively deploy.

WHEN LEADERS AT healthcare systems contact us about providing consulting support, they often tell us more or less the same story. Their quality indicators have improved tremendously in recent years, as well as their rate of readmissions for patients with congestive heart failure. Still, they're disappointed to see other indicators, such as serious patient falls and deaths related to unrecognized sepsis, trending in the wrong direction. These leaders don't understand why. As they tell us, they've put in place evidenced-based care bundles (care expectations for specific diagnoses) in these areas. They've educated members of the care team in these protocols. They've improved the processes that support these care bundles, such as establishing checklists and putting tools in their electronic health record to remind the care team of the protocols.

Investigating the causes of weak safety performance, these leaders have found that communications issues persisted among team members. In some cases, a caregiver erroneously assumed that a colleague would handle an identified problem. In others, newer nurses and physicians didn't understand the details of the care bundles, having joined the organization after its focused educational efforts. Also, resident physicians have ordered incorrect medications or treatments but didn't feel comfortable asking questions of the attending physician. "These errors seem so basic," the executives tell us. "What are we missing?"

As subsequent analysis typically reveals, these organizations usually have failed to build so-called "universal skills"—all-purpose behaviors that, when practiced in the workplace, prevent the human errors leading to poor safety, quality, efficiency, and patient experience. In Chapter 3, we encountered the "blunt end–sharp end" model, which distinguishes between people operating in layers of the organization removed from the actual provision of care (the blunt end), and people on the front lines (the sharp end). As our clients discover, and as we'll explore in this chapter, how people behave at the sharp end matters, ultimately shaping outcomes. Human error isn't the cause of harm events, but rather a symptom itself of underlying, systemic causes influencing people's behavior. By adopting the right behaviors, we can prevent errors even as we work in imperfect systems. In fact, studies have shown that we might prevent approximately three of every four (73 percent) acts that lead to serious preventable harm.[1]

To improve reliability and safety, organizations should focus on improving systems and processes that affect general frontline behaviors. Specifically, they should set behavioral expectations, provide the necessary skills and knowledge training, and build accountability to assure the formation of practice habits. The last of these in particular can help many organizations reach the next level of reliable performance.

Human Error 101

Noted safety expert James Reason once stated that a need exists on the front lines for "error wisdom"—an understanding that even competent, well-trained human beings can experience errors due to systemic issues.[2] Reason proposes that three kinds of factors render errors more or less likely: the individual's own physical or mental condition (for instance, whether the caregiver is fatigued, inexperienced, or fearful); the environmental context (for instance, the presence of distractions, the need for frequent care handovers, the unavailability of equipment, or the lack of time); and factors related to the task at hand (for instance, the need to perform complicated tasks or those that lack cueing or forcing functions, such as computer alerts when a drug dose is out of normal range). Clearly, systemic factors including structure (people, resources, or organizational arrangements), protocols, work design, and technology should make it easy for employees to work accurately and difficult to make an error. A culture focused on safety and reliability will also greatly reduce the potential for error.

Before we examine how organizations can prevent errors, let's take a closer look at errors themselves. Human beings experience three types of errors: skill-based, rule-based, and knowledge-based.[3] These categories reflect the nature of a person's cognitive functioning at the time he or she experiences an error. Across these categories, people differ in how familiar they are with the task being performed and the extent to which they are applying conscious thought when performing the task.

In *skill-based performance*, a well-developed skill pattern exists in our brain, developed through practice and repetition. When we experience a skill-based error, we have an unintended slip (we do the wrong thing), lapse (we forget to do something), or fumble (we mishandle the task). When we inadvertently lock our keys in the car because we are rushing, or when we forget to move medical equipment out of the way and subsequently trip over it, we experience skill-based errors. Typically, we engage in thousands of skill-based tasks every day, but as research has shown, we typically perform these routine, familiar tasks well, experiencing only one error for every 1,000 of these tasks. Usually, these errors only occur when we are distracted, fatigued, and failing to pay enough attention.

In *rule-based performance*, our brain scans for an operating principle or rule to apply as we engage with a task, usually a rule that we've learned through education or experience. Rule-based errors tend to occur in one of three ways: we apply the wrong rule, misapply a rule, or choose not to follow a rule. We might encounter a physician order for our patient that seems unusual, but decide not to question the physician, assuming that she knew what she was doing. Or we might not check a patient's ID before giving medications, because we "know who the patient is"—he's been coming to our clinic every week for the past six months. In healthcare, most errors tend to occur in rule-based mode. We make these errors more readily than we do skill-based errors—one for every 100 tasks we perform. Also, most healthcare work tends to be rule-based. As we care for patients, we are constantly applying protocols and rules so as to standardize care and improve its quality.

In *knowledge-based performance*, we find ourselves in a new or unfamiliar situation where rules do not exist or are unknown to us. So we enter a kind of problem-solving or "figuring-it-out" mode. Simply put, we wing it. Not surprisingly, studies show that our errors when acting in this mode are quite frequent, affecting between 30 and 60 percent of the tasks we perform. Nobody said learning was easy! As such mistakes teach us, we probably should make more effort to obtain help from someone more experienced than we are when we encounter unfamiliar situations.

Data collected during a review of 1,910 patient safety events from 120 organizations in the HPI client community allow us to distinguish in even more detail the modes of human error that exist among caregivers and other frontline staff. As Table 5.1 shows, we can discern 20 modes of individual failure, grouped into the five categories. Note that these categories describe not *what* the error was, but *how* the individual experienced the error. In the table, errors in the *competency* category are knowledge-based: individuals aren't sure what action to perform or how to do it, yet they proceed anyway (for example, a caregiver might incorrectly program a new and unfamiliar type of IV pump). *Consciousness* errors are typically skill-based failures owing to inattentiveness to the task (for example, a pharmacist might "click through" a series of familiar medication orders on the computer without realizing that she's clicked away from a drug alert message). Errors in the *communication*, *critical thinking*, and *compliance* categories are sometimes knowledge-based, but more often rule-based. To save time, two nurses might decide to double-check units of blood at the nurse's station as opposed to at patients' bedsides, inadvertently swapping the units of blood. This constitutes a rule-based error (a shortcut) that would fall into the compliance category.

Table 5.1 Individual Failure Modes

Category	Percent
Competency (knowledge & skill)	15.1
Consciousness (attention on task)	11.4
Communication (information processing)	9.6
Critical Thinking (cognitive processing & decision-making)	39.7
Compliance (including normalized deviance)	24.1

These aggregate data mirror the results individual health systems have captured when performing baseline diagnostic assessments of their safety events. Many organizations are surprised to find that errors in the communication category aren't the most frequent. After all, aren't most on-the-job problems caregivers experience rooted in poor communication? Indeed, they are—the *action* caregivers are engaged in when committing an error often involves coordinating or communicating about care. But these data describe *how* the error occurred—in other words, what occurred in the mind of the person as he or she experienced the error.

Let's suppose a nurse doesn't consult a physician in the middle of the night as he was supposed to, failing to inquire about a patient's blood pressure that has dropped slightly over the past three hours. Superficially, that seems like a communication error—the nurse didn't communicate. But *why* didn't he? To answer that question, we would need to interview the nurse and ask him what happened. Perhaps he didn't know he was supposed to call the physician for that blood pressure change (competency). Perhaps he intended to call the physician, but was distracted while caring for another, very sick patient (consciousness). Perhaps he asked another nurse to call the physician, but didn't clarify to the other nurse how important the call was (communication). Perhaps he reflected that this particular physician didn't like being disturbed in the middle of the night, so he held off calling (critical thinking). Perhaps he didn't contact the physician because he thought it wasn't necessary—he could handle the situation by himself until the morning, even though policy clearly required him to call the physician (compliance).

Universal Skills for Error Prevention

To prevent these human errors, organizations can build habits in two distinct types of universal skills: *relationship* skills that flatten hierarchies and allow for better teamwork among caregivers, and *reliability* skills that prevent human error. Chapter 6 discusses relationship skills in more detail. As for reliability skills, HPI has outlined five major types of such skills (Table 5.2) along with techniques team members can use to exhibit these skills effectively.

Table 5.2 Reliability Skills and Related High Leverage Techniques

Universal Reliability Skill	Examples of High Leverage Techniques
1. Attention on Task	Self-check
2. Communicate Effectively	Communication techniques for clarity and understanding Structured problem communication
3. Think Critically	Exhibit questioning attitude and intelligent compliance
4. Protocol Use and Adherence	Tool designation as continuous use or reference use
5. Speak Up for Patients and Teammates	Risk awareness and escalation Peer checking & peer coaching for habit formation

We at HPI have used versions of this toolkit over the more than 15 years that we've spent guiding healthcare organizations. Initially, we blended activities from other industries with those that healthcare organizations were beginning to deploy. As time has passed, we've found that organizations progress more quickly toward the goal of zero harm when the techniques they employ connect as closely as possible to the actual experience of human error in the healthcare environment. Human error is the same everywhere, but we must tailor prevention techniques closely to the organizational context. Let's examine the specific tools healthcare organizations have used to build universal skills, avoid error, and improve safety.

Attention on Task

As researchers have documented, the human brain can perform two tasks at once, so long as these tasks don't engage the same areas of the brain.[4] A person can listen to music and read at the same time, since music requires auditory processing, while reading requires visual processing. However, when we ask our brain to focus on two or more similar tasks at the same time, we force our brain to "switch-task"—repeatedly stop and start each of the tasks, pinging back and forth between them. Switch-tasking is less efficient and makes us prone to error. Imagine that a busy housekeeper is cleaning a large patient care unit (her usual assignment) when a supervisor asks her to drop what she is doing to quickly clean a room being prepared for an admission, or that a surgeon is performing back-to-back cases while also worrying about making her 2 p.m. office hours. Add in other sources of stress, fatigue, and time pressures, and you have a recipe for catastrophic safety failures.

We can deploy universal skills to prevent the unintended slips and lapses that occur in the course of daily work, especially when we perform familiar, routine acts unthinkingly. The key is to add *intention* to safety-critical tasks—to slow down and let our head get ahead of our hands. A self-checking tool called STAR (Stop-Think-Act-Review) can help us here. Caregivers pause for one second before taking action (stop). They consider the task they are about to perform, confirming that they are about to perform it correctly (think). They perform the task (act), and then confirm that their action had the intended result (review). STAR dates from the early 1970s, when the Jefferson Center for Character Education in Pasadena, California, developed it to help prevent school children from acting impulsively.[5] Two professional groups, aircraft pilots and nuclear power operators, subsequently adopted the tool to enhance safety on the job. In these professions, pressing the wrong button without thinking could result in in a serious safety event. Taking just a couple of seconds to perform this simple tool can make all the difference.

People who habitually employ STAR use the technique as many as 500 times per day. While humans perform, on average, over 10,000 skill-based acts each day, using STAR for the most important tasks adds just minutes overall to a person's daily workload, and it can improve performance, mitigating the effects of the time pressure people feel. One anesthesiologist described an incident in which he was preparing medication for a patient in advance of a surgery. Rushing because the team had fallen behind schedule, he grabbed what he thought was the proper medication. He was about to inject it into the patient's IV when he remembered the STAR tool. "I looked more closely at the vial," he said. "I thought I had looked at the label, but in retrospect I just looked at the shape and color of the label. I didn't know that the hospital had recently changed suppliers for this medication. I didn't have the anesthesia drug . . . I had a vial of epinephrine! Thank heavens I used STAR! I didn't think those tools we learned in our safety class were necessary, because Anesthesia already had a lot of technology safeguards built in to prevent errors. But we can also make a mistake without intending to."

Although STAR has gained traction in healthcare contexts, many organizations initially resisted it, unhappy about the prospect of injecting yet another acronym into an already "acronym-heavy" environment. Leaders at one organization told us that the acronym STAR already meant something else at the time to their workforce and hence invited confusion. Rather than abandoning the tool, they created another acronym—SAFE (Stop, Assess, Focus, Evaluate) and deployed it with teams. They soon discovered that many staff members found SAFE confusing and hard to remember. So, the organization went back to using STAR. Magically, it seemed, staff began to avoid more skill-based errors.

Communicate Effectively

Caregivers and others in healthcare communicate a great deal of information verbally. While such communication doesn't represent the largest source of error (see Table 5.1), it is still significant. Universal skills for communication help assure that team members transmit information clearly and accurately, and that listeners understand it. These skills include a number of simple but effective tools. With the three-part communication tool "Read and Repeat Back," a sender provides the information, the receiver repeats it back (or writes it down and reads it back), and the sender confirms that he or she received the correct information by saying "that's correct." Individuals might also ask one or two clarifying questions to confirm expectations (for instance, "Doctor, when would you like me to start the new medication?" or "Do I need to reboot the computer after installing the program?") and use phonetic and numeric clarifiers to ensure accuracy ("That's B as in Bravo," or "That's fifteen—one five.").

Communication errors frequently occur when individuals hand over tasks or information to colleagues. One tool that helps in this situation, SBAR (Situation-Background-Assessment-Recommendation), was first introduced to healthcare at Kaiser Permanente in 2002.[6] Based on a communication strategy used in the US Navy, the tool enables individuals to format their communications in a coherent way, focusing first on identifying the problem or challenge at hand, then offering some background as to what action has already been taken, then providing an assessment of the current situation, then conveying a recommendation for desired action.

Nurses and physicians initially used SBAR to improve patient handoffs, but we've found that anyone in healthcare can use it to assure that someone else performs a critical action correctly. HPI has coached the organizations it works with to add one important action when using this tool verbally: actually saying each word referenced by the acronym when communicating. A worker might contact her IT help desk and say: The *situation* is that my computer keeps getting a blue screen with a message "all data will be lost"; the *background* is that I opened an e-mail and a file from another company outside ours yesterday. I have rebooted my computer twice so far, and the same thing happens; my *assessment* is that if I'm not able to get this fixed I won't be able to get any work done today; my *request* [an acceptable substitution for "recommendation"] is that we take the time now to figure out what the problem is." This approach enables the speaker to communicate more clearly and succinctly, and the listener to more easily understand the problem.

SBAR isn't always the best tool to use in more complicated patient handoff situations, such as those that occur between shifts or when transferring a patient. For these situations, a tool called the "5P Handoff" provides a better mechanism for identifying details of the handoff. Staff identify the *patient*, and then communicate a *plan* for the next step in the patient's care. They convey the *purpose*, or the desired goals caregivers have for the patient. They go on to describe any different or unusual *problems* that are known to exist regarding the patient, as well as *precautions*—elements of the patient's care that might prove different, unusual, or complicating. HPI developed these categories based on existing research regarding the causes of handoff failures, and it has since incorporated the tool into its electronic health record system.

Think Critically

Elizabeth, a nurse at one of our client organizations, was helping an elderly woman into bed when she fell and struck her head on the floor. Elizabeth called the physician on duty, receiving an order for a head CT scan. Although it took some time to do the test, Elizabeth performed frequent neurological checks, finding no causes for concern. The patient went in for her scan, and when the results came back, it showed that she had a large bleed and needed emergency surgery. Later, Elizabeth looked back at the chart and realized that the woman had a history of dementia, a condition that can cause the brain to shrink. With the extra space available in the skull, the woman wouldn't have shown signs of bleeding as quickly as another patient would. Elizabeth remembered thinking how odd it was that this woman didn't exhibit more neurological changes, as she'd hit her head quite hard. "If I had remembered the patient's dementia diagnosis," Elizabeth said, "I would have gotten that CT done much sooner, and she might have gotten treatment sooner than she did."

Elizabeth failed to get her patient the care she needed because she hadn't thought critically enough. As Table 5.1 shows, failures in critical thinking account for the greatest percentage of healthcare errors leading to harm events. When we don't think critically, we assume (often incorrectly), we misconstrue, and we blind ourselves to anomalous or unusual data. Such errors occur especially often in healthcare because caregivers are attempting to manage the unpredictable complexities of the human body and its response to disease. To prevent these kinds of errors, caregivers or others can maintain what we might call a *questioning attitude.* In this crucial critical-thinking skill, individuals stay focused and alert to situations unfolding around them, paying close attention when something doesn't seem right. In the simplest form, a questioning attitude helps detect incorrect information and incorrect assumptions. Housekeepers might question whether doctors are still keeping a patient in isolation because the sign they saw posted an hour ago is no longer there. Likewise, a biomedical engineer might question an abnormal reading on a piece of equipment that appears to be functioning properly.

"Validate and Verify" is the specific tool we use to apply critical-thinking skills. Individuals first validate aspects of a situation, asking: "Does this make sense to me?" or "Does it fit with what I know or what I expected to see?" Validation is an internal check, one that should always remain active, like a smoke detector in your home. If the answer to the above questions is, "No, what I'm seeing doesn't fit with what I expect," then the person's next step is to check out the issue by verifying whether action is required. Here, the individual consults a reliable and independent source, such as a policy manual, a reference manual, or others on the team who possess recognized expertise.

When using Validate and Verify, healthcare workers should understand that receiving an answer to a question from a seemingly reliable source doesn't always suffice. We need to question the answers, not simply ask questions. If the information still doesn't sound right, consult yet another expert to help resolve your concerns. You may need to use the tool in successive cycles until you feel satisfied with the answer. One experienced nurse who had recently started working at a hospital was reviewing a list of medications for her patient when she noticed that the patient was receiving 150 units of insulin. She knew that this represented a very high dose of insulin, higher than she'd ever before given a patient (validate). She checked the chart to see if the order was transcribed correctly (the hospital hadn't yet allowed physicians to enter orders into the system themselves), and found that the order written in the chart was indeed for 150 units of insulin (verify).

Upon reflection, she decided she still wasn't comfortable and called the doctor. He told the nurse that he wasn't the patient's regular doctor but was covering for his partner. Apparently, the patient had informed him that this was the medication he was taking. The nurse hung up and decided she still felt uncomfortable, so she called the pharmacy. The pharmacist responded that it was a high dose, but that if the prescribing physician was okay with it, she could go ahead with the order. The nurse decided to talk to the patient, who confirmed that he was taking that much insulin. Ever diligent, the nurse offered to check with the home pharmacy the patient used. She learned that the patient was taking

15 units, not 150 units. By persevering in her questioning, she had prevented a potential deadly event.

While Validate and Verify clearly helps caregivers avoid common errors, some clients of ours have chosen to adjust the verbiage, observing that people tend to use "validate" and "verify" interchangeably in daily conversations. To assure that all members of their staff understand the actions to be taken, they renamed the tool "Reflect and Resolve" or "Question and Confirm." Whatever the terms, the tool's nature and functioning have remained the same—and thankfully so.

Protocol Use and Adherence Skills

Are caregivers and other staff remembering to adhere to best practices, performing them exactly as they should, each and every time? In many organizations, the answer is no. To improve *adherence skills*, organizations deploy procedures, protocols, and checklists—tools designed to clarify expectations for standard work and to enable compliance without having to rely on one's memory. Unfortunately, providing these tools and teaching everyone how to use them isn't enough to assure error-free performance. To obtain better results, organizations can borrow techniques from other high reliability industries.

In 1935, a Boeing B-17 Model 299 bomber crashed during one of its last test flights before mass production began.[7] Three crew members were badly burned, and two died. At the time, it appeared that the Model 299 program was dead—some newspapers had dubbed it as "too much plane for one man to fly." As the pilots realized, the plane was flyable—they just needed a way to make sure that crews performed all the necessary tasks during flight. They wound up developing four separate checklists for pilots, one each for taking off, flying, the period just prior to landing, and the period that follows landing. These checklists weren't powerful in and of themselves, but rather because using them got pilots in the habit of always pulling out the document and performing each and every check, even though they'd done these procedures hundreds of times and knew them by heart.

Another helpful tool emerged out of the nuclear power industry, which during the 1980s began to develop clear guidelines for using and adhering to procedures in power plants. In providing these guidelines, the industry asked teams to distinguish between "continuous use" and "reference use" protocols.[8] A *continuous use protocol* is one designated for procedures or checklists that are safety critical, complex, and performed infrequently. Users of these protocols should read and understand the entire protocol before taking any action, ensuring as well that the entire team understands all the steps. Most important, they must keep the tool/checklist/job aid at the job site and use it each and every time while taking action, referring to it frequently. The industry urges teams to use simple "place-keeping" techniques, such as keeping a finger or a pen on each item of the protocol as workers are performing it. When an action is completed, employees should keep track of it by checking it off.

A *reference use protocol* is one that is not safety critical, complex, and frequently performed. Here again, users should read the entire protocol or checklist before taking any action, use the checklist to support their work, and maintain a questioning attitude when unusual situations occur.

With HPI's assistance, many healthcare organizations have built these principles into their reliability toolkits. When staff at Providence Health and Services are following a protocol or a checklist, they first use a tool called "Know Why and Comply" (Figure 5.1) to understand whether they are to use the protocol or checklist for reference or continuous use. Know Why and Comply has produced operational improvements throughout the organization, including many that directly affect patient safety.

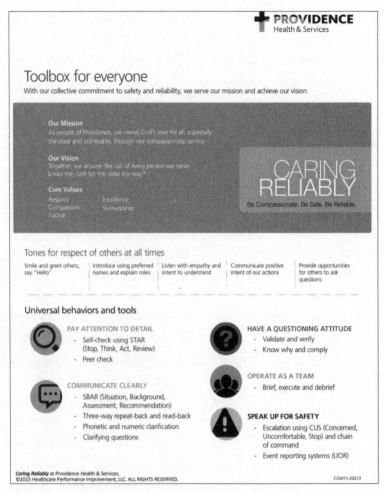

Figure 5.1 Providence Health and Services' "Toolbox for Everyone"

At a large warehouse it operated, the organization had problems keeping restocked items available on the shelves. Employees were scanning the barcode to get the item back in inventory, but not checking to assure that the item was stocked in the correct location. Using Know Why and Comply, the team corrected that problem. More recently, nurses using Know Why and Comply discovered a patient who was barely breathing. Had the tool not existed, the nurses likely wouldn't have entered the patient's room, as the patient was sleeping and they didn't want to disturb him. Thanks to this and other tools, Providence has experienced at least a 48 percent reduction in serious events of harm from its baseline set two years ago.

Speak Up for Patients and Teammates

To create a zero harm environment, organizations must do a better job getting employees to speak up when a concern or issue arises. But how can they embed this behavior? We advise organizations to work toward "200 percent accountability"—the expectation that team members will not only take responsibility for their own work, but look out for colleagues so as to avoid harm-producing mistakes. Organizations can use two kinds of techniques to implement this universal skill: those that enable employees to become more aware of safety concerns and to take action to resolve them, and those related to what we call "peer checking and coaching for habit formation."

The first class of techniques involves various forms of inquiry, advocacy, and assertion. Employees must learn to increase their own situational awareness, enhance someone else's situational awareness, and effectively communicate or "escalate" their safety-related concerns. To escalate concerns, employees can use a number of techniques, including two favored by HPI clients: ARCC (Ask a question; make a Request; Communicate a concern; Use a Chain of command to handle the issue if necessary), and CUS (I'm Concerned; I'm Uncomfortable; This is a Safety issue). Whichever tool an organization adopts, leaders must convey to team members the importance of escalating concerns they might have, and the potentially disastrous consequences that might accrue from saying nothing.

Now, why do employees so often say nothing? The answer, of course, has to do with power. *Power distance*, a term coined by the

Dutch researcher Geert Hofstede, captures the extent to which a less powerful person in an organization expects and accepts that power will be distributed unequally.[9] Measuring power distance in different countries, Hofstede discovered that in countries like Indonesia, the Philippines, and numerous Latin American countries, where power distance was very high, people didn't question superiors, nor did they challenge people who held more power thanks to gender or professional stature. In the United States, moderate levels of power distance exist, but in certain industries and professional groups, including among physicians and nurses, power distance runs quite high. In such contexts, tools like ARCC or CUS are especially effective, granting team members a clear way (in the form of code words) to reach out to authority figures, express their safety concerns, and serve as advocates for patients.

Another class of techniques, peer checking and coaching for habit formation, also encourages team members to speak up more about safety. These techniques embody the same principles described in Chapter 4 for shaping an effective culture of accountability, only translated to the peer-to-peer level. Leaders must pay attention and offer comments that reinforce desired behaviors and discourage unhelpful ones in order to create a solid culture, and so, too, must coworkers. As Dr. Glenn Bingle, Indianapolis-based Community Health Network's former chief medical officer, remarked, behavior change entailed "Hawthorne until habit." Bingle was referencing the well-known Hawthorne effect, which states that people will adjust their behavior for the simple reason that others are observing them.[10]

When practiced effectively, peer accountability activities represent one of the most important tools available for building and sustaining a reliability culture. In the course of daily work, individuals can "cross-check" one another, working together to perform a task like giving medication, with one colleague performing the task and another quickly verifying the first colleague's work. Team members can also offer peer coaching, reinforcing desired behaviors and discouraging unsafe ones. If you happen to overhear a colleague using phonetic clarification in communicating ("The patient's last name is Terry—that's T as in Tango."), you might respond by saying, "Thanks for using communication clarifiers—that's what helps keep our patients safe." Likewise, if you spot a coworker about to use a rolling office chair as a stepladder, you might offer helpful coaching by saying, "Hey, let's find you something safer to stand on." In coaching peers, it's important that team members follow Dr. John Gottman's five-to-one rule described in Chapter 4, offering positive or encouraging feedback five times as often as they do negative or corrective feedback.

One hospital CEO told his team that he would know that their culture had truly changed when he made rounds in departments and units and observed frequent peer coaching. As we've found, organizations that reinforce peer coaching dramatically enhance their ability to maintain safety gains. Community Health Network managed to maintain a rate of zero ventilator-associated pneumonia cases for several years not just because it implemented evidence-based care protocols, but because supervisors encouraged personnel to use peer checking and coaching tools, reminding their coworkers to remember to put the head of the bed up or to wash their hands.[11] Such cross monitoring conveys to coworkers that you've "got their back." To build high reliability safety cultures, we really do have to look out for one another, catching one another's mistakes and expecting everyone to hold him- or herself accountable—even us.

Achieving Zero Harm

In working with the universal skills we've described, leaders should create a comprehensive toolkit of universal skills for error prevention. Leaders should first spend time reviewing past safety events to identify the typical themes or causes of individual errors. Most healthcare organizations will find that the incidence of human error breaks down more or less along the lines of Table 5.1, but it's worth taking the time to confirm whether that's true. Leaders should also assure that behavioral expectations are clear and align with the organization's vision and goals. Merely asking people to "communicate clearly," for instance, doesn't assure that everyone is doing it in the same way. Leaders should convey expectations strategically so as to galvanize all constituencies, including staff, physicians, and leadership. Get as much input as possible before finalizing the toolkit. When possible, incorporate other toolkits that the organization has implemented, such as those designed to encourage effective customer communication.

Does using a toolkit to foster universal reliability skills really work? Two organizations with whom we've worked can confirm that it does. For over a decade, Vidant Health has worked diligently across its health system to achieve zero harm. Adopting principles of high reliability, including a preoccupation with failure, Vidant convened team members and providers to develop a toolkit of safety habits and error prevention tools. Vidant educated all leaders, physicians, team members, and new employees on these tools, reinforcing them and building accountability by making safety a core value, establishing unit- and department-based safety coaches, and focusing weekly and monthly on specific tools or techniques. Leaders have owned this effort, starting at the board level, and they've kept the basic toolkit intact even as the organization has grown and the leadership team has changed. Staying the course and turning skills into habits among all Vidant team members has yielded impressive results. Between 2007 and 2018, the rate of serious events of patient harm has dropped by 62 percent, and in 2013 the organization received a John M. Eisenberg Award for Innovation in Patient Safety and Quality.

As Joan Wynn, the chief quality and patient safety officer, notes, "We are relentless in pursuit of our zero harm goal. Reliably using safety habits and error prevention tools assures that we make progress every day with every patient we serve."[12]

A second organization with whom we've worked, Virginia-based VCU Health, is at its core an academic healthcare setting, which brings challenges of its own for an organization seeking zero harm. In conceiving and executing its safety initiative, dubbed "Safety First, Every Day," the organization made a special point of engaging with its medical school residents and students. In particular, leaders worked to get residents and students in the habit of speaking up for safety and reporting safety events. As a result of their efforts, VCU Health has seen reports of safety events rise from 200 to 1,200 over a three-year period, as well as a 57 percent reduction in serious safety events. In 2014, VCU Health received the AHA-McKesson Quest for Quality Prize in recognition of its efforts to reduce harm. "We have learned so much about the critical role of teamwork, escalation, and effective communication," said Ron Clark, MD, chief medical officer of VCU Medical Center. "Each phase of the journey leads us to a new understanding of what is achievable and that 'zero events of preventable harm' is not just an ideal, but something we can attain if we sustain our efforts."[13]

In virtually all organizations with which we've worked, the creation of a strong toolkit has proven instrumental in reducing the frequency of safety events over the first few years. Leaders at these organizations would tell you that this toolkit should be comprehensive, yet applicable to all layers of the organization, and that it should reflect the organization's unique goals and experiences. Yet they will also note that at the core, the concerns of all safety-focused organizations are the same: to have every team member focus when performing safety-critical tasks, communicate clearly to colleagues, think with a questioning attitude, and adhere diligently to safety-oriented protocols. Finally and most important, leaders agree that a culture where anyone can articulate a safety concern or thank a colleague for doing the right thing is essential. You can do everything else right, but as we saw at the outset of this chapter, it won't stick unless you get everyone to understand universal reliability skills—and to practice them consistently.

IN SUM

- Human error doesn't cause harm events, but rather is a symptom of underlying, systemic causes influencing people's behavior.
- To prevent the key kinds of human errors that exist in healthcare, organizations can build reliability skills across the workforce.
- Organizations lay the foundation for zero harm by creating a clear toolkit of universal skills that everyone in the organization learns and practices to prevent errors.
- The toolkit should include techniques that incorporate task focus, clear communication, a questioning attitude, adherence to protocols, and a willingness to speak up despite power differences.

Communication, Collegiality, and Teaming

David Varnes, CDR (USN Ret.), MSAE

> When team members work poorly together, more mistakes are liable to happen, resulting in more incidents of harm. This chapter provides a comprehensive resource for readers seeking to learn how to help teams better care for patients and their families.

LAUREN WARGO, A teenager from Shaker Heights, Ohio, underwent surgery to extract a mole from her eyebrow in 2006. During the procedure, the cautery caused a supply of pure oxygen to combust, leading to extensive burning on Lauren's face. Four years later, this 23-year-old still covered the resulting scars with a baseball cap and couldn't completely close one eyelid.[1] During a court appearance, Lauren's surgeon claimed he had requested that the oxygen be disabled, as per protocol. An assistant, however, disagreed, claiming in court that the surgeon had done no such thing.

How do harm events like these happen? In this case, multiple failures in communication occurred, reflecting an underlying systemic weakness in communication within Lauren's surgical team. As research has confirmed, harm events don't result from single errors, but rather from combinations of mishaps (see

Jim Reason's Swiss cheese model in Chapter 3). That's because safety-conscious industries and organizations design systems that can withstand individual human errors, implementing defensive barriers such as technology, processes, policies, or other people. This chapter explores how healthcare organizations can mobilize the last of these barriers—people—to prevent system failures, especially when they work in team contexts. Dr. Myles Edwin Lee once characterized good teamwork as a "system of mutual checks and balances" that increases the chances "that every consideration in the patient's best interest has been addressed."[2] If Lauren's surgical team had trained in the universal skills introduced in Chapter 5, including those related to communications and paying focused attention to the task at hand, that system of checks and balances would have been in place, and her accident likely never would have happened.

We can define a team as two or more people who work together interdependently, cooperatively, and collaboratively to achieve a common purpose or goal through open communication, trust, and respect. Based on this definition, we can discern several types of teams at work in the healthcare setting. *Microsystems*, as they are called, are teams in which people know one another and interact with one another frequently. Examples include teams in the emergency department, operating room, labor and delivery, intensive care unit, and settings involving people who participate in shift-to-shift handoffs. *Purpose teams* are groups whose members know one another but interact with one another less frequently. Such teams include code or rapid response teams. Teams whose members don't know one another well but who interact frequently are *ad hoc teams*. They tend to be temporary and to have a specific purpose—like root cause analysis (RCA) teams and rapid improvement teams. In "just-in-time" teams, people don't know one another and interact infrequently. Examples include mass casualty or emergency response teams.

Regardless of the kind of team in question, we know that organizations can't ensure strong teamwork simply by placing people in a group and calling them a team. We also know that building awareness of different team-related social skills doesn't necessarily mean that people know, understand, or practice such skills, or that they practice them habitually. Research has shown that off-site team-building interventions usually have little effect on team task performance, often because leaders don't define clear goals.[3] To see significant safety gains, healthcare organizations must go much further, setting expectations about specific universal skills related to teamwork, training the workforce in these behaviors, and using leader, peer, and intrinsic accountability to reinforce these behaviors (see Chapter 5). Organizations that perform this work see team-related universal skills take root as habits within the workplace, significantly reducing cases of serious preventable harm. Clearly, collegiality and teaming have a vital role to play in any organization's quest for zero harm.

The Role of Teams in Safety

The notion of using other people as a means of catching and "trapping" human error emerged out of the airline industry and its concept of crew resource management (CRM). In 1977, two Boeing 747s collided in Tenerife, Spain, killing 583 passengers and crew, in what remains the deadliest aircraft in commercial aviation history. In 1979, seeking to improve safety in the skies, NASA scrutinized the causes of major aviation disasters. As their data revealed, air crew might have prevented over 70 percent of most accidents were it not for poor communication, decision-making errors, and failures in leadership. NASA resolved to improve teaming among flight crews. Dr. John Lauber, a member of the National Transportation Safety Board (NTSB), defined

CRM's goals as using "all available sources—information, equipment and people—to achieve safe and efficient flight operations."[4]

CRM has evolved considerably since then. Initially, airlines focused on improving interaction among cockpit crew members by training each member individually. Training focused on clarifying forms of cooperation appropriate for various flight phases, identifying leadership styles, and evaluating the crew's performance. Unfortunately, many of the cockpit crews trained didn't take the training seriously, dubbing it "charm school." During the 1980s, the industry began training team members together as a group, and it also now defined the cabin crew as part of the "team," not just those in the cockpit. This change occurred following a lavatory fire incident on an Air Canada DC-9 jet. An NTSB review of the accident revealed that proper and appropriate cooperation had taken place between cockpit crew members, but that the cockpit team had not coordinated well with the cabin crew. During the 1990s, the industry further expanded CRM to include areas like flight operations and maintenance. Cockpit personnel, members of the cabin crews, and flight operations teams would all participate in CRM training together. Additionally, airlines began looking at how corporate culture affected the performance of individuals.

During the 2000s, the airline industry regarded CRM as a means of managing human error, using James Reason's Swiss cheese approach. As Reason emphasized, we might not be able to eliminate human errors, but we can reduce their frequency by adjusting work conditions. CRM effectively functioned as a corrective process, involving prevention, detection, and correction. Today, safety experts in the industry take an even broader approach, holding that CRM should permeate an organization's culture. Instead of consciously pausing and thinking to apply CRM in situations where we perceive its necessity, CRM now comprises the very essence of how we relate, collaborate, and communicate—it's simply the way the industry operates. In the words of psychologists, the industry has become "unconsciously competent" at CRM.[5]

Other industries have also recognized communication, collegiality, and teamwork as essential for achieving safe, consistent outcomes. As recently as May 2015, the Institute of Nuclear Power Operations (INPO) reemphasized its longstanding concern that weak organizations and leadership teams were impeding performance at power plants. After reviewing industry strengths and areas for improvement, assessing the practices of high-performing organizations, and consulting with industry groups and executives, researchers linked five attributes of teams to high performance: whether the team was aligned around a common purpose, vision, or goals; whether team members felt committed to the team's success; the clarity of team members' roles and responsibilities; the presence of mutual trust and respect; and effective decision-making and conflict resolution.[6]

Meanwhile, scholarly publications on collegiality and teaming have referenced case studies in healthcare. Harvard Business School professor Amy Edmondson's intensive research of cardiac surgery teams and over 23 hospital ICUs revealed that teaming—a dynamic activity largely created by the attitudes of team members rather than team structures—led to detectable improvement in patient care, as did learning.[7] In another interesting conclusion, Edmondson discovered that teaming behaviors such as communication, coordination, experimentation, questioning, and listening led to better implementation of newer technology in these cardiac surgery teams than in surgery teams marked by a more hierarchical structure. Further, her research has found that teaming can improve people's perceptions and experiences at work as employees learn from one another, gain better appreciation for their work, and feel empowered to detect and act on improvement opportunities.[8] Other research also documents the helpfulness of good teamwork in healthcare. The Joint Commission, for instance, has stated that, "safety and quality of patient care is dependent on teamwork, communication, and a collaborative work environment. To assure quality and to promote a culture of safety, health care organizations must address the problem of behaviors that threaten the performance of the health care team."[9]

Barriers to Communication, Collegiality, and Teaming

While aviation has long created organizational structures to support collegiality and teaming, healthcare organizations have lagged behind. In many organizations, communication failures, loss of "team situational awareness" (a shared perception existing among team members), failures to speak up, failures in individual and team critical thinking, a lack of team leadership, and entrenched hierarchies reduce the ability of teams to fix safety-related problems. A survey by the Institute for Safe Medication Practices (ISMP) found that out of over 2,000 nurses and pharmacists, 88 percent had experienced condescending language or tone from physicians or other providers. A full 79 percent had encountered physicians or providers who hadn't bothered to answer their questions or return their phone calls, or who had done so only reluctantly, while 48 percent had been subjected to strong verbal abuse.[10] Such behavior denigrates and intimidates subordinates and coworkers, degrades morale, and inhibits information flow, ultimately affecting patient care. The same survey found that 34 percent of respondents had avoided clarifying physicians' orders, and 31 percent had felt sufficiently intimidated that they had allowed a physician to give a medication to patients despite harboring safety concerns.[11]

The Joint Commission describes intimidating and disruptive behaviors as encompassing verbal, physical, and even passive behaviors (like not returning a phone call). Often displayed by physicians and leaders, such behaviors tend to increase what organizational culture theorist Geert Hofstede first described as "power distance"[12]—a dynamic whereby less powerful people manage unequal power distributions. At organizations or institutions with high power distances, people tend to believe that superiors are superior people, that power outweighs judgments of good or evil, and that subordinates should expect to be told what to do. At organizations or institutions with lower power distances, people tend to perceive hierarchy as serving a purpose, rather than as an end in itself. They tend to believe that the wielding of power should be legitimate, and that subordinates should expect that leaders will consult them in decision-making.[13] In healthcare settings, organizations with lower power distances tend to be more consultative, democratic places where people come together as equals. Organizations with higher power distances tend to be more autocratic and paternalistic environments marked by formality and hierarchy. Considerations such as pay, titles, longevity, and perks can all contribute to people's perceptions of power distance.

Large power distances pose an obvious problem as far as safety is concerned. In a team led by a domineering, overbearing, or dictatorial person, it requires considerable courage to pose simple questions or to articulate concerns. Among our client organizations we have found numerous instances in which surgeons have operated on the wrong body part because teams didn't perform the initial portions of the surgery checklist (called the "time-out process"). In many of those cases, individual team members knew that the team wasn't following the rules, but didn't speak up and alert the surgeon because they didn't feel they could. Primarily, these individuals feared that the surgeon would retaliate with an outburst of demeaning or derogatory speech, perhaps even extending into long-term intimidation or harassment.

Of course, most teams require some amount of power distance; otherwise roles become unclear, and teams can't reach decisions in a timely way. To create effective teams, we should seek to minimize power distance as much as possible, "flattening" the sense of authority. Only then can we create an environment in which team members feel comfortable speaking up for safety or cross-checking other team members.

Evidence-Based Training to Enhance Relationships and Communication

Laura Cooley, PhD, Senior Director of Education and Outreach, Academy of Communication in Healthcare

In a recent book, *Communication Rx: Transforming Healthcare Through Relationship-Centered Communication*,[14] the Academy of Communication in Healthcare (ACH) provides an in-depth summary of evidence to support the value of communication skill development among clinicians. Research findings strongly support the link between communication, patient experiences of care, and quality metrics. For example, effective communication is linked to higher patient experience scores, increased empathy scores, reduced costs for diagnostic testing, lower readmission rates, improved retention of patients in outpatient settings, lower risk of litigation and malpractice claims, increased clinician satisfaction, and decreased clinician burnout. The importance of communication has been validated as a significant factor impacting patient health outcomes. For example, clinician-patient relationships are linked to better management of chronic diseases (e.g., hypertension, diabetes, and HIV), enhanced outcomes across cancer patients, improved pain control, improved postsurgical outcomes, reduced risk of coronary heart disease and decreased mortality from myocardial infarction, and reduced hospital readmissions.

Clinicians with more effective communication skills achieve personal benefits that reduce their own suffering. We all face challenges in our daily practices (difficult conversations, dissatisfied patients, conflict among team members) that leave us feeling unsettled and dissatisfied. Learning to communicate more effectively helps us avoid preventable errors, make more accurate diagnoses, and enhance adherence to treatment. It also helps us increase our own well-being and resilience.

Contrary to common belief, communication is not just an innate talent, but a procedural skill set that clinicians can learn, practice, and improve upon. The Academy of Communication in Healthcare (ACH) recommends *relationship-centered communication* (RCC)[15] skills training to establish a foundation for interpersonal relationships that allow patients and clinicians to communicate more meaningfully and reliably. Data on communication skills training sessions show that effective programs typically last for the equivalent of a single day, concern themselves with applying new concepts to clinical practice, and are tailored to learners' goals and needs. "Skills-based exercises, including role-play, in small groups or in individualized coaching are more effective than isolated didactic presentations; specific feedback on communication skills contributes the most to heightened patient experiences of care."[16] The vast majority of clinicians who engage in this style of communication training report the sessions as helpful to their everyday practices and suggest that the training also inspires a renewed dedication and energy to their careers.

Universal Skills for Teaming

We've examined the barriers to strong teaming, but what exactly defines a high-performing, high-functioning team? Harvard's Edmondson identifies four primary pillars. First, team members must be able to converse honestly and transparently, asking questions, giving and receiving feedback, and discussing errors. Second, team members must collaborate well, maintaining a cooperative mindset or approach to the team's goal. Third, team members must experiment freely, reaching out to assess the impact of their actions on colleagues and testing how their ideas relate to what others are thinking. Fourth, team members must have ample opportunity to reflect, assessing performance either in real time or after the fact and uncovering new ideas.[17] As others have noted, a range of other elements contribute to collegiality and high team performance, including clear communications, the competency of individual team members, the presence of a defined team leader, the presence of structures that allow for critical thinking among team members, a shared team goal, a sense of psychological safety, and the tendency of team members to believe in their teams' competence and ability to achieve desired outcomes.

To produce such positive team environments, organizations can take steps to cultivate universal skills, general behaviors that people in all areas and levels can use to improve safety and other aspects of performance. As we saw in the last chapter, we can discern two kinds of universal skills, some bearing on *relationships* and others bearing on *reliability*. Relationship skills are important because they create team environments in which people feel comfortable speaking up. Nonverbal in nature, these behaviors tend to reduce impressions of power distance and render authority figures more approachable. When people smile and greet one another, when they refer to others by their preferred name (or use formal greetings when in doubt), when they listen empathetically, when they communicate their good intent, and when they create opportunities for others to ask questions, they foster mutual understanding and trust, encourage the sharing of information, and make collaborative problem solving easier. They also create an environment in which people feel safe maintaining the questioning attitude so vital for safety, building attentive, respectful, and nonjudgmental relationships.

A number of the reliability skills and tools discussed in the last chapter not only help individuals reduce errors, but allow teams to function better too. To improve communications among team members, for instance, teams can deploy the "Read and Repeat Back" tool (also called "Three-Way Repeat Back") in which the sender initiates communication, the receiver acknowledges its receipt, and the sender confirms the repeat back. The phonetic and numeric clarifications also described in Chapter 5 help ensure the fluid functioning of teams, enhancing safety. Likewise, cross-monitoring among team members helps individuals perform better, while also enhancing team performance. Peers can check the accuracy of one another's work, identifying unintended skill-based slips and lapses and bringing unusual situations or hazards to one another's attention. They can also coach one another, praising safe and productive behaviors and discouraging and correcting unsafe or unproductive behaviors. Finally, the critical-thinking and communication ("speaking up") skills discussed in Chapter 5 also promote safety through strong teamwork, including Validate and Verify and ARCC (Ask a question, make a Request, voice a Concern, use Chain of command).

Let's examine a few additional reliability skills that are especially important to help teams function well and safely. One tool for enhancing situational awareness, "Scan Plus Big Lens/Small Lens," helps teams monitor their environment and maintain a sense of the "big picture" while also performing specific tasks to solve immediate problems. The big picture might be a severely injured patient, a mass casualty situation, or a part of a natural disaster response. The leader will assign one team member the role of "little lens," with responsibility for working on an immediate problem, and another the role of "big lens," with responsibility for the overall situation, including safety, resources, and the patient's progression to the next level of care. "Little lens" team members can attend to the task at hand (monitoring a patient's vitals, for instance, or administering medication), knowing that their teammates have their back. The team leader may rotate the "little lens" and "big lens" roles to suit the skill sets of the team and the challenges of the moment.

To further build situational awareness, teams can employ "Call Outs," verbal communications intended to keep the team apprised of a situation or procedure as it unfolds. Team members can use Call Outs to communicate a notice (of their intended action), an announcement (prior to actually taking an action), a status (of a patient or system), an update (on the patient or system), or an alarm (when something is out of process, procedure, or parameters). During a bypass surgery, for instance, team members might use the following Call Outs: "I am preparing to go to bypass" (notice); "I am now going to bypass" (announce); "Patient is on bypass" (status); "Blood pressure is now 110 over 72" (update); and "Blood pressure is down to 88" (alarm). Code teams also tend to use this approach to maintain a shared situational awareness of the patient's condition as well as of the desired or directed course of action.

Some universal skills important for teaming relate to leadership. As Hofstede noted, "It takes leadership to understand and resolve conflict and to instigate thoughtful conversations about errors. Leadership is needed to help groups build shared understanding and coordinate action."[18] One helpful tool, "Lead the Team," directs leaders through the process of taking the lead, assigning roles, and identifying objectives for the group. Working with this tool, leaders learn to assign the most important roles first, assign "little lens"/"big lens" responsibilities, clearly communicate team goals as well as the plan for achieving them, prioritize actions team members should perform, and control the effort's overall progress.

Another tool, "Brief-Execute-Debrief" (BED), adapted from nuclear power industry, aviation, and the US military, helps leaders communicate an ad hoc plan to all team members, especially when it comes to high-risk, infrequent, and new tasks. In the first step (Brief), the leader presents the upcoming mission or activity to the group, assuring that team members understand the scope of the activity, have an opportunity to discuss the specific tasks involved, and understand relevant hazards, controls, and safety precautions. Following the team's implementation of the plan (Execute), the leader debriefs the team to capture the lessons learned— what went well, what didn't, and what additional, unforeseen resources the team needed to complete the task. Leaders might feel tempted to skip the debrief, especially if an activity went as planned, but they should resist the temptation. Debriefs play a fundamental role in a team's continuous improvement efforts, shaping the way we make sense of experience and consolidate it in our minds.

In addition to the other critical-thinking skills described in this book, healthcare teams can use a tool called STEP (Story, Test, Evaluate, Plan) to assess a situation rapidly and make an informed decision, particularly when the team is under time pressure and might not possess complete information.[19] Whenever a team leader asks, "Does anyone have any ideas?" teams might want to dust off and use this tool. First the team creates a narrative about what has happened, and what will happen (Story). Then the team tests the narrative against the facts, changing it accordingly (Test). The team then evaluates the story, asking whether it truly makes sense (Evaluate). Finally, the team develops an action plan predicted by the story (Plan). Teams treating patients whose health is rapidly deteriorating for unknown reasons could profitably use the STEP framework to arrive at a plan of care that arrests the decline.

Yet another important tool—checklists—can help teams improve critical thinking by freeing up precious cognitive space. We often hear that checklists consume too much time, aren't helpful, or get in the way of productivity and throughput. In March 2014, a *New England Journal of Medicine* study concluded that surgical safety checklists implemented in more than 100 hospitals in Ontario, Canada, failed to reduce complications or deaths.[20] Dr. Lucian Leape, a pediatric surgeon, professor, and patient safety advocate from the Harvard School of Public Health, responded to the *NEJM* article in an editorial to the same, citing four likely reasons why the study failed to show a reduction of complications or deaths. Checklists can be difficult to implement—just copying and distributing them doesn't ensure that people will use them as intended. It's also easy to "game" a checklist, documenting its completion as a matter of course even when the checklist wasn't used. Finally, implementations of checklists take time.[21]

Still, checklists *do* improve safety when properly deployed—and at so many hospitals, they're not. As we saw in Chapter 5, when deploying checklists for procedures that are considered safety critical and complex to perform, organizations should have teams read the entire checklist prior to taking any action, ensure that the entire team understands all the steps, and have the checklist at the job site every time, without exception. For procedures that are not safety critical, complex, or frequently performed, organizations should have teams read the entire checklist and then simply ensure that the entire team understands all the steps before taking any action. At most hospitals, the surgical safety checklist would fall into the category of a detailed procedure requiring verbatim compliance, while the act or procedure of taking standard vitals on a patient is a relatively simple, "common sense" act that requires less reliability and hence no verbatim compliance.

It's not enough for organizations to keep checklists and other tools on hand in order to help teams—they must also train and reinforce collegiality and teaming skills properly. One way to do so is what we call a "Triple Play," three improvements performed together to maximize efficiency. First, the organization trains the team on the desired protocol it is to follow, confirming that it's the best possible evidence-based medicine, that it's a simplified process, and that policies are easy to understand and apply, with job aids (such as a visual sign, checklist, or summary of steps) available to help. Next, the organization trains team members on the universal (nontechnical) skills covered in this chapter relevant to the protocol. Finally, the organization puts teams through on-the-job simulations to ensure that they have practical experience with the skills and that the facilities themselves (including equipment, devices, supplies, and environment) won't cause or contribute to harm events.

The Triple Play is especially efficient for building a high reliability organization and improving collegiality and teaming. One Triple Play event can provide three times the benefit, tackling protocol, universal skills, and facilities testing at once. Conversely, conducting a technical simulation on a particular protocol without including the universal or nontechnical skills creates a divide that would never occur in a real situation. Why wouldn't we want to "fight like we train and train like we fight"? After all, what people do every day is what they are likely to do in an emergency—when it really counts.

Seattle-based InSytu Advanced Healthcare Simulation has partnered on Triple Play events with a number of hospitals, providing on-site simulation expertise, management, training, and facilitation. Organizations select a simulation topic such as adult stroke, postpartum hemorrhage, sepsis, shoulder dystocia, and malignant hyperthermia (among other high-risk, low-volume events) for entire teams to simulate. Over the course of two to three days, teams complete six or more clinically realistic, two-hour simulation sessions, allowing a full rotation of unit personnel and other required participants. As organizations complete the technical portion of the simulation, they are also refining their protocols and learning about the performance of their facilities, equipment, and supplies. Meanwhile, participants use their collegial and teaming skills whenever appropriate during the simulation.

All of this makes a vast difference in how teams actually perform in the field. According to InSytu, members of multidisciplinary teams participating in on-site simulation programs not only become more confident in their technical knowledge—they also display improved communication and clarity about roles and responsibilities, do a better job implementing evidence-based practices, and interact with one another better overall (Figure 6.1).

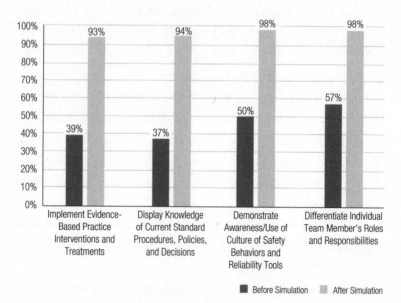

Figure 6.1 InSytu Results from Simulation Training

Miracle on the Hudson—and in Healthcare?

On January 9, 2009, US Airways flight 1549, an Airbus 320 with 150 passengers including five crew members, was cleared for takeoff from New York City's LaGuardia Airport, heading to Charlotte Douglas International Airport. In command was Captain Chesley "Sully" Sullenberger, a former Air Force fighter pilot, glider pilot, and aviation safety expert with a total of nearly 20,000 flight hours, 4,700 of them in the Airbus 320. The first officer was Jeffrey Skiles, who had a total of almost 16,000 flight hours, but only 37 hours in the Airbus 320. The three flight attendants on board had several decades of experience between them. But as is common in aviation, the crew had little experience working together.

The flight was cleared for takeoff at 1524 with First Officer Skiles at the controls. The weather was good, so much so that Sullenberger conveyed to Skiles: "What a view of the Hudson today."[22] Approximately two minutes into the flight, the plane struck a flock of Canadian geese. Passengers and crew reported hearing noises that were later determined to be related to the actual bird strike and subsequent dual engine failure. Captain Sullenberger resumed control of the aircraft, reported a mayday call to LaGuardia aviation control officer Patrick Harten, and instructed First Officer Skiles to work the checklist for an engine restart.

The control tower immediately responded to the mayday call by holding all departures while providing instructions to flight 1549 to return to the runway. After refusing the initial offer of runway 13 at LaGuardia, departure control offered runway 4, which, again, was refused. It was not clear to Sullenberger if the Airbus 320 could make it to either of these runways. Remaining calm, Harten continued to provide options to the struggling crew. Following an offer to land at runway 1 at Teterboro, Sullenberger replied: "We can't do it." Harten followed the third refusal, asking Sullenberger which runway he would like. Sullenberger's response was, "We're gonna be in the Hudson."[23]

Throughout these conversations, Sullenberger and Skiles were also talking continuously about the engine restart and subsequent completion of checklist items, and discussing the airplane landing configuration. This back-and-forth concluded as Sullenberger announced to passengers to brace for impact. Further compounding their dire situation were numerous aural cockpit alerts related to altitude and ground proximity. As flight 1549 descended below radar coverage, Harten suggested Newark airport as one last option to the crew, but never received a response.

As flight 1549 descended near the George Washington Bridge, Sullenberger and Skiles continued to adjust the airplane for its final landing configuration, with Sullenberger even asking his first officer if he had any ideas. The airplane touched down on the water at approximately 3:31 p.m., fewer than four minutes after the initial bird strike.

Following the water landing, Sullenberger left the cockpit and ordered the plane's evacuation. The three flight attendants jumped into action, safely directing passengers to properly functioning exits, away from exits that were either not activating an inflatable raft or were inappropriate for exiting in a water landing. The flight attendants later described the evacuation as timely and orderly. The crew continued to help the passengers out of the aircraft, providing seat cushions or life preservers to those who needed them. Sullenberger and Skiles made two passes throughout the cabin before being the last to exit the ailing aircraft. All told, the incident resulted in zero fatalities and only five serious injuries. For good reason, the event became known as the "Miracle on the Hudson."

Although luck might certainly have contributed to this miracle, it wasn't the only factor. Decades of work on teaming and collegiality in aviation preceded this event, allowing team members to work efficiently and effectively in a time of crisis, even though they hadn't worked together extensively in the past. This is precisely the kind of effort we still need to see in the healthcare industry. To get closer to zero harm, organizations large and small must spread reliability and relationships skills among their workforces, deploying the powerful tools developed by safety science and outlined here.

In essence, organizations must follow the example of Chicago's Advocate Health Care. Between 2015 and 2017, Advocate created High Reliability Units (HRUs) throughout its hospitals, training these teams intensively for three months and providing safety coaches who themselves had trained in reliability science and universal skills. Leaders and coaches also implemented a continuous improvement methodology called "Plan-Do-Study-Act," which helped them resolve local safety issues. The investment paid off. HRUs received higher patient safety culture scores on the AHRQ Hospital Survey across a number of dimensions compared with non-HRUs. These dimensions included "Teamwork Within the Unit or Department," "Organizational Learning," "Feedback and Communication About Error," "Communication Openness," and "Supervisor-Manager Support for Patient Safety." Quite likely, these improved skills led to improved perceptions of safety, and outcomes that really were safer.

How might your unit or organization function if teams underwent such training? How many fewer patients might you harm or employees might you injure if your teams were "in synch," communicating well, speaking up about safety concerns, experimenting freely with new solutions, and assessing failures honestly and thoroughly? "Miracles in healthcare" are possible, up to and including the ultimate miracle of zero harm, but we have to earn them—one extraordinary team at a time. Indeed, given healthcare's increasing complexity, we likely won't see the industry grow appreciably safer unless more individual organizations commit themselves to the exhaustive work of building stronger teams. Here's to hoping that they do.

IN SUM

- Given healthcare's complexity, we must work together to achieve the exceptional performance (zero harm) our patients and their families expect.
- Teamwork isn't innate—it must be taught and practiced.
- Universal skills—both relationship and reliability skills—provide a great foundation for collegiality and teaming, with some—like maintaining situation awareness and leadership—proving especially helpful.
- Use relationship skills to reduce power distance so that employees think together as a team.
- Triple Play is a highly effective way of having teams practice best-in-class universal and teaming skills.

7 Just Culture

Judy Ewald

> *Organizations can't improve unless those closest to the work feel comfortable reporting events and near misses. This chapter reviews the concepts underlying "just cultures," nonpunitive organizational cultures in which leaders mete out culpability more thoughtfully, and people feel empowered to speak out for safety. We describe a series of actions that healthcare organizations can take to create more robust just cultures.*

WHEN ALYSSA SHIN was born during the twenty-fourth week of her mother's pregnancy, she was tiny, weighing just over a pound. Still, her parents had every reason to feel optimistic. Alyssa suffered none of the life-threatening complications that can occur in such preemies, and she had started breathing on her own. She would have to remain in the hospital for a number of weeks, undergoing frequent testing and receiving special nutrition, but doctors had told them that the prognosis was good. And then one morning, Alyssa's mother arrived at the hospital and was shocked to find her daughter surrounded by a cadre of hospital staff as well as the director of risk management. Mrs. Shin learned that staff had prepared

Alyssa's total parenteral nutrition (TPN) solution incorrectly, and that as a result it contained almost 11 times the correct amount of zinc. Too much zinc in the blood impacts cardiovascular function, and in extreme cases can prove fatal. Indeed, Alyssa's heart rate was already plummeting.

The medical team did what they could, including chelation therapy (an attempt to bind and remove the zinc through special IV solutions) and extended attempts at cardiopulmonary resuscitation. But some five hours later, Alyssa passed away. The Board of Pharmacy sanctioned and fined the pharmacy technician who prepared the TPN and the two pharmacists who double-checked the calculations. After the hospital threatened to fire her, the technician resigned.

Months afterward, however, when the case became public, it became clear that Alyssa's death reflected far more than a single technician's incompetence. A myriad of system and process issues came to light, including problems with the compounder (the device that assists in the preparation of TPN), inconsistent practices concerning the writing and checking of TPN orders, and a culture of fear and retribution in the pharmacy. On the very day that the error in Alyssa's calculation occurred, the technician who made the initiating error had been verbally disciplined by her manager because she was wasting time recalculating physician TPN orders—a practice she had implemented because of inconsistency with order writing. Some physicians were specifying the amount of ingredients to include in the TPN solution by the baby's weight, while other physicians were writing their orders based on the solution's total volume.

If the hospital had uncovered these problems before Alyssa's mother had arrived to give birth, Alyssa might still be alive today. But the hospital hadn't, because the very people who were best equipped to spot flaws in the system—frontline staff—felt disempowered to speak out. They noticed the flaws but kept their safety-related concerns to themselves, fearing repercussions from supervisors and others in the organization. After Alyssa's death, the hospital's response of blaming employees instead of investigating possible systemic causes compounded the problem again preventing information about systemic weaknesses from coming to light. Until the story became public, every baby in the NICU at the facility risked suffering the same type of medication error that led to Alyssa's death.

Alyssa's death and the harsh career repercussions experienced by the healthcare professionals involved took place because the hospital lacked what safety experts call *just culture*. This is a nonpunitive culture of "shared accountability" in which organizations bear responsibility for their systems and for treating team members fairly, and team members bear responsibility for speaking out about systemic flaws.[1] High reliability organizations like nuclear power and aviation began advancing just culture principles and practices more than 40 years ago as part of their initiatives to improve reliability and safety.[2] In healthcare, efforts to support these principles began in the United Kingdom around the turn of the century. In 2001, the United Kingdom established the National Patient Safety Agency (NPSA) to support and facilitate patient safety culture and practices across the facilities of Britain's National Health Service (NHS).[3] Concerned that NHS wasn't learning from errors and safety events because managers didn't understand when to discipline staff for their mistakes and when to view those mistakes as an outgrowth of systemic problems, NPSA began working on tools to transmit just culture principles throughout the system, including an Incident Decision Tree that helped leaders evaluate culpability. At the time, approximately 80 percent of NHS employees involved in a serious patient safety event were suspended from duty pending investigation.[4]

Since the advent of the Incident Decision Tree, US healthcare systems have implemented similar algorithms as well as formal just culture programs. Unfortunately, these efforts have delivered mixed results. The safety culture survey from the Agency for Healthcare Research and Quality (AHRQ), used by over 600 hospitals, contains three questions that relate to a just culture: "Staff feel like their mistakes are held against them"; "When an event is reported, it feels like the person is being written up, not the problem"; and "Staff worry that mistakes they make are kept in their personnel file."[5] In 2016, the composite scores from those three questions represented the lowest scoring composite for the entire survey, receiving responses that were only 45 percent positive.[6] Similar results have obtained over a number of years since the survey has existed. Likewise, a 2009 study published by the Department of Health and Human Services estimated that hospital staff report just one out of every seven errors or incidents they observe, and that one of the biggest reasons they don't bring safety lapses to the organization's attention is fear of retribution.[7] When staff fail to report errors, organizations lose the opportunity to take corrective actions. Although further study is needed, the underreporting of unsafe conditions (or "accidents waiting to happen") is also likely quite significant.

To move closer to zero harm, healthcare organizations must commit themselves more fully to developing and sustaining just cultures as part of their broader safety cultures. Let's take a closer look at just cultures as well as at some specific measures organizations can take to root them solidly in place.

Just Cultures and Standards of Culpability

Safety theorist James Reason referred to "just culture" during the late 1990s to describe a prevailing mood of trust in which people

(a) feel free and open to share essential, safety-related information, and (b) can distinguish clearly between safe and unsafe behavior.[8] As Reason noted, a just culture's presence in an organization is closely related to safety culture, as the trust that just cultures generate leads people to identify safety-related issues more readily. But does a nonpunitive culture mean abandoning all punishments, and hence all standards of behavior?

The answer is no. In fact, Reason's definition itself acknowledges the existence of unacceptable behavior. As he recognized, standards for unacceptable behavior, such as a deliberate attempt to cause harm or willful negligence or recklessness, aren't just part and parcel of our duty to the patients and communities we serve. They're implied by the medical profession's most basic tenet: "First, do no harm." "In my view," he said, "a safety culture depends critically upon first negotiating where the line should be drawn between unacceptable behavior and blameless unsafe acts."[9]

To understand better how organizations might establish culpability standards within a just culture, we should remind ourselves of how human beings commit errors. As we saw in Chapter 5, humans experience three kinds of errors caused by systems: skill-based errors that occur when humans are doing rote tasks carried out in "autopilot" mode; rule-based errors that occur when we attempt to solve problems in familiar situations using a set of learned rules or principles; and knowledge-based errors that occur when people are operating in unfamiliar situations and lack internal rules or experience. Skill-based errors amount to slips (doing a task incorrectly), lapses (forgetting to do a task), or fumbles (mishandling a task).

While people tend to regard individuals who commit skill-based errors as blameless, these individuals might well exhibit a degree of intentionality if they knowingly work when unfit for duty or if they pay insufficient attention to the tasks at hand. Rule-based errors involve a higher degree of intent—people might purposefully misapply a rule or decide consciously not to comply.

Knowledge-based mistakes are also considered intentional when the individual fails to seek assistance or expertise required to perform the task correctly. In evaluating culpability, organizations should consider the kind of error a caregiver commits and the extent to which the act was intentional.

Reason also shed light on culpability by distinguishing between outcomes and evaluations of culpability. Consider a situation in which a nurse named Jen has worked for 14 hours straight, even though her shift only called for 12. She has also been caring for twice her usual number of patients because a colleague called out sick. Even though she performed the standard checks, she inadvertently gave the wrong concentration of a drug to a patient, resulting in an intercranial bleed. Another nurse, Ben, made a similar mistake at the beginning of his shift because he was distracted, checking messages on his personal cell phone while passing medications. He self-reports his error of not checking the patient's name and date of birth. His patient doesn't suffer an adverse outcome.

While Ben's actions are clearly more culpable, an organization would punish Jen, not Ben, if it conceived of culpability strictly in terms of the outcome. Jen's error caused her patient harm, while Ben's didn't. The problem with applying such a "no harm, no foul" approach is that organizations might fail to support people who make honest mistakes, to coach and guide people who made poor choices, and to fix the systems causing the errors. Just culture principles require organizations to assess culpability independently of how much harm a mistake caused, thus maximizing the potential to improve safety.

Creating a Just Culture

Determining culpability isn't always a simple task, one that leaders can quickly dispense with by applying an algorithm. Indeed, many healthcare workers probably continue to view their cultures as punitive in part because their organizations have simply created a policy or algorithm to evaluate culpability rather than taking a deeper, more thoughtful approach. In applying the algorithm, these organizations likely miss important nuances in situations, arriving at judgments that offend individual workers' senses of justice and convincing them that just culture is little more than empty talk. To succeed with just culture, organizations must treat it not just as "another program to implement," but as an integral way of thinking that they must apply and live every day. Leaders must exemplify just culture principles in their behavior, and supervisors must incorporate them into their decision-making. Ultimately, organizations must meet four distinct requirements for creating a robust and enduring just culture—requirements that are best implemented systematically as a safety management system (SMS) for just culture.

Requirement #1: Leadership

To help manage implementation, organizations should form just culture steering committees and charge them with overseeing the effort. A representative from the executive leadership team such as a chief nursing officer, chief medical officer, or VP of human resources should chair the committee. Other members should include representatives from departments across the organization, including patient safety, quality improvement, risk management, organizational development, nursing, medical staff, clinical support (lab, radiology, and so on), and nonclinical support (engineering, environmental services, and so on).

Once assembled, the committee should help roll out a deliberate campaign to communicate the organization's just culture principles and practices to the workforce. When the organization unjustly punishes individuals for system-induced errors, it can spur confusion and resentment among the workforce, even if leaders eventually reverse the punishment. Most decisions related to culpability are also confidential human resources or peer review matters (as they should be), so the workforce might not always notice efforts to support a just culture. Leaders can affirm the organization's commitment to a just culture by communicating its definition of this culture, its sense of how the just culture enhances safety, the processes the organization will use to evaluate culpability, and the willingness of executives to manage culpability appropriately and promote a learning environment.

To demonstrate their commitment to just culture principles, leaders should embrace a range of behaviors, including publicly thanking individuals who report events and concerns in good faith; applying just culture practices when a leader or manager is evaluating performance concerns; publicizing actions taken to correct safety-related system or process issues; and immediately acting to stop retribution or gossip about individuals who have spoken up for safety and/or reported events and concerns in good faith. When leaders take these steps consistently, people will know that the just culture is real. Their trust in the system's fairness will increase.

Requirement #2: Policies and Programs

Organizations can also help just cultures flourish by implementing them as policy. Healthcare organizations usually maintain a number of human resource policies related to performance management, including progressive discipline (processes for verbal counseling, written warning, and termination for cause) and guidance for evaluating culpability when a harm incident has occurred. The just culture steering committee should consider creating a separate policy detailing the organization's just culture principles and practices as well as determining how to incorporate that policy in existing documents. Principles and practices should include statements affirming:

- The importance of safety and zero harm
- The organization's desire to create a work environment in which people feel encouraged to raise concerns
- The importance of treating everyone with dignity and respect
- The organization's intention of levying no punishment for honest mistakes and levying progressive discipline depending on the facts of each individual case
- The organization's desire to create a learning culture in which everyone teaches and learns on the job so as to improve performance

Organizations should also consider policies related to physician and nurse peer review. In order to be truly fair, the same principles of just culture must apply equally to all professional groups.

As a part of their just culture policy, most healthcare organizations develop an algorithm to assist leaders in evaluating and managing culpability.[10] Organizations usually include a set of questions in the algorithm to guide users through four categories or "tests" designed to provide insight into an individual's actions, motives, and behaviors (Figure 7.1). The "Deliberate Act Test" questions whether individuals involved in a safety incident had intended to behave correctly. Cases in which they deliberately intended harm represent the highest degree of culpability and often result in the intervention of law enforcement and licensing boards. The case of physician Michael Swango, who intentionally poisoned or overdosed as many as 60 patients in US hospitals during the 1980s and 1990s, exemplifies such culpability.[11]

If an employee intended no harm, the next question to ask is whether he or she was suffering from an incapacity that might have negatively impacted performance (the "Incapacity Test"). Incapacity can include illness, reactions to prescribed medications, or substance abuse. Sometimes an illness or disability can develop subtly or gradually, and the individual might not understand its impact on his or her performance. A diet clerk might deliver the wrong tray to a patient on a restricted diet despite stating that she checked the name and date of birth. A vision test might reveal that the clerk needs reading glasses. In this case, the organization would regard the individual as less culpable than if he or she didn't suffer from an impairment.

If investigators have ruled out both intent and incapacity, the inquiry goes on to consider the question of compliance (the "Compliance Test"). Performance issues often reflect failures to follow policies, processes, or protocols. However, investigators must consider whether employees had access to the policies and whether those policies were comprehensible and in routine use. If the answer to those questions is yes, then in the absence of mitigating circumstances investigators might find the individual culpable for the policy violation. Let's say a medical technician administered an expired vaccine to a child in a clinic and admitted that he didn't check the date before administering. The policy for checking vaccines (for right med, right dose, expiration data, and so on) was clear and in routine use by other medical technicians. In this case, the technician would bear culpability.

If investigators have discounted all the other tests, the inquiry should consider whether other similarly trained and experienced individuals would have made the same choice (the "Substitution Test"). Leaders should refrain from applying broad generalities such as "no radiologists do positive patient identification when consulting with physicians," but rather evaluate how a peer in this specific context, acting reasonably and in a mature manner, might have responded to the situation. The substitution test also evaluates whether training, experience, or supervision may have played a factor in decision-making.

Work through the tree separately for each individual involved

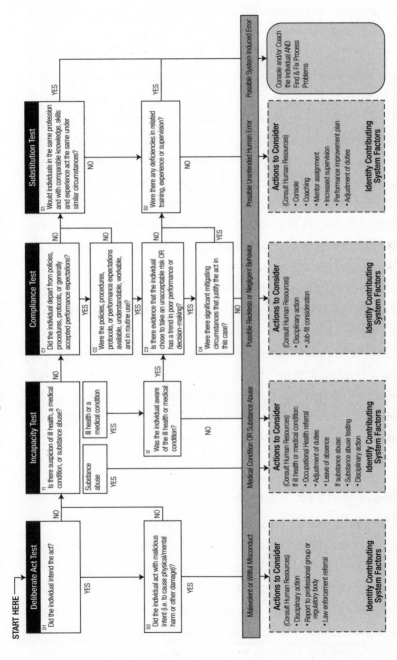

*Adapted from James Reason's *Decision Tree for Determining the Culpability of Unsafe Acts* and the *Incident Decision Tree* of the National Patient Safety Agency (United Kingdom National Health Service)

Figure 7.1 Performance Management Decision Guide

In implementing a just culture algorithm, organizations should consider customizing it to reflect local terminology and to reference the organization's specific actions, policies, and procedures. The organization might also wish to develop a version of the algorithm formatted as a documentation tool in order to create a written record on performance. When Virginia Commonwealth University Health System (VCUHS) wanted to implement a Performance Management Decision Tree for their organization, leaders reviewed examples from other industries and healthcare organizations. They found that none of those examples represented a good "fit" for VCUHS because they weren't specific enough to VCUHS's culture, language, and policies (for instance, they didn't refer VCUHS managers to the organization's existing human resources policies related to progressive discipline). Applying the principles of rapid cycle improvement, the VCUHS Just Culture Steering Group developed a number of versions of the algorithm, tested those versions with real-life examples of events from their organization as well as with frontline managers, and then incorporated the feedback into a final "VCUHS-centric" version.[12] Where the algorithm indicated that disciplinary action might be appropriate, a reference to the specific VCUHS policy guiding disciplinary action was inserted.

Requirement #3: Promotion

Once the steering committee has finalized the organization's policies and associated tools, and those items have been formally approved, the next step is to communicate the policy and materials to the organization. Organizations can incorporate messages about just culture into posters, newsletter articles, intranet sites, management talking points, and town hall sessions. While communication alone may not change behavior, it helps to demonstrate leaders' commitment and to validate the policy statements.

Additionally, messaging should emphasize the individual's role in a just culture: to openly identify, report, and discuss errors, and to offer peer checking and coaching (Chapter 5). In some high reliability industries such as aviation, organizations waive disciplinary action if the individual involved in the event or performance issue has fulfilled his or her role by filing self-reports and participating in the cause solving and action planning processes (unless evidence exists of negligence or intentional wrongdoing).[13]

Organizations should also formally educate leaders on just culture principles and tools, while also offering this training to new leaders (both outside hires and internal promotions). Training in just culture includes a review of the principles and policies as well as scenario-based learning; attendees should have a chance to practice applying the organization's Performance Management Decision Guide. Organizations can develop scenarios from actual cases that the organization has experienced (with identities hidden), or from other sources. The box presents a sample outline for the educational program as well as two case study examples.

Sample Outline and Case Studies for Just Culture Training

Educational Session Outline

I. Definition and history of just culture
II. Compelling case for just culture as a part of safety and reliability transformation
III. Our organization's just culture policies and procedures (including the Performance Management Decision Guide)
IV. Practice application of the Performance Management Decision Guide with case studies

(usually a small group activity followed by large group discussion and debrief)

V. Leadership responsibilities and expectations for just culture (next steps)

Sample Case Studies

The Master Key

Michael is the lead security officer for the evening shift at All-Saints Hospital. He has worked there for the last five years and was promoted to his role two years ago. Michael has no disciplinary incidents in his file, and all of his performance evaluations have been excellent to date. He is well liked by the staff and his coworkers. As the evening lead, Michael is responsible for overseeing the other security officers and carries the master key that unlocks all of the doors in the building.

On the evening in question, Michael had just returned from a week's leave because his wife had given birth to twins. Things had been difficult at home because the twins were not sleeping well, but his wife's mother was arriving to help soon, and Michael felt like he needed to get back to work. One of his coworkers had mentioned to Michael that he could request family medical leave, but Michael was concerned that it would reflect poorly on his record if he asked for that leave.

Michael met with his supervisor (the day shift security manager) at the beginning of his shift. He mentioned to his supervisor that he was very sleep deprived but would do his best to stay awake during the shift. The manager slapped him on the back and said he was sure Michael could "man up!"

Around 11:00 p.m., Michael was struggling to stay awake, so he went to the cafeteria for some coffee. An employee from Finance approached him and told him she had been working late on a project and had locked herself out of her office. Michael went to the Finance department with the employee and was in the process of unlocking her door with the master key when he received a stat call to the emergency department to deal with an aggressive patient. Michael rushed off to the ED, leaving his coffee behind and the master key still in the lock.

Michael helped the emergency department staff deal with the patient. Afterward, he realized that he had no longer had the master key. He hurried back to the Finance department, but the employee had left and the key was missing. Michael obtained the employee's telephone number from the house supervisor. When he called, the employee said that she didn't have the key.

There were no reported thefts or missing items, but as a precaution the hospital decided to rekey all of the locks at considerable expense.

Wrong Breast Milk

In two separate incidents over the past nine months, staff at All-Saints' Family Centered Care fed the wrong breast milk to infants. Neither event resulted in a negative medical outcome, but patients suffered considerable emotional consequences. Following the first event, the organization instituted a policy requiring the mother to write her name and date of birth on the bottle of expressed milk. Before feeding milk to the baby, the nurse and the mom had to check the signature and date of birth. After the second incident, the hospital realized that the breast milk refrigerators were a "mess" and spent thousands of dollars on new refrigerators with individual bins for each patient. Risk management had suggested that the unit begin bar-coding and scanning breast milk. Staff rejected that recommendation as too time-consuming for something that wasn't "high risk."

Angela is a nurse on FCC and has worked there for the past seven years. Supervisors have always evaluated her as an excellent worker, and she is well liked by patients and colleagues. She serves as her unit's representative on the Shared Governance Practice Council. On the day in question, Angela is busy helping several new moms assigned to her care. One of her patients asks Angela to retrieve a bottle of expressed milk. Going to the refrigerator, Angela finds that there is no milk in the patient's bin. The fridge is a mess, as usual, because staff and patients generally don't use the bins as required. Angela grabs a bottle that she believes belongs to the patient and drops it off to the mom. Before leaving the room, she reminds the patient to check the signature, even though the patient has already started feeding her baby. Rotating the bottle, the patient realizes that her signature and date of birth don't appear on the bottle. As in the prior cases, the baby suffered no harm, but both sets of parents found the event extremely upsetting.

While introductory training is important, a one-time education session won't ensure that leaders consistently behave in support of the just culture. In addition to the oversight processes discussed in the next section, organizations might consider offering periodic refresher trainings or reminders. During management team meetings, for instance, leaders might review articles or publications related to just culture or discuss additional case studies.

Requirement #4: Oversight and Learning Systems

If policies, procedures, and messaging constitute important foundational activities, frontline staff and physicians will ultimately judge the culture's "fairness" according to how the organization treats individuals when a safety or performance management issue arises. Organizations should establish processes ensuring that leaders consistently apply the Performance Management Decision Guide (PMDG). The human resources department or the applicable peer review committee might review and approve PMDG decisions, particularly when those decisions involve any level of progressive discipline. Alternatively, the organization might decide to form a just culture review committee with representatives from senior leadership, managers, and even employees on hand to review performance decisions.[14]

Organizations should also monitor leading, implementation (real-time), and outcome (lagging) metrics to assure that they are supporting their just culture properly. Leading measures might include culture of safety survey results and pulse checks (limited, less formal surveys with staff and physicians to gauge just culture implementation). Surveys might pose questions like: "Do you feel that our organization is making positive progress toward establishing a just culture?" and "Are you aware of any examples of where you have seen just culture practiced at our organization?" Real-time metrics include the percent of current and new leaders who have completed just culture education and the number or percent of safety success stories related to peer checking and peer coaching (indicating that individuals are taking responsibility for just culture). Lagging metrics include the percent and number of disciplinary actions undertaken *without* applying the PDMG and/

or oversight by human resources (these numbers should be zero), overall event reporting (an indicator of individuals taking responsibility for just culture), and the percent or number of events that staff report themselves.

In implementing a just culture, organizations must keep individual performance management decisions strictly confidential. At the same time, organizations should include as much information about just culture as possible when sharing safety stories. Suppose a technician at a behavioral health group home administered medication meant for a patient named Alec Williams to another patient named Alex Williams. Upon investigation, the organization discovered that medications delivered to the group home from a contract pharmacy were only labeled with the patient's name and not the date of birth, as required by the organization's positive patient identification policy. The organization didn't regard punishment for the technician as appropriate because of this systemic issue. The organization might communicate about this event as follows:

Safety Event Communication

Recently, a patient in one of our group homes received medication that was meant for another patient. The patients had the same last name and very similar first names. During the investigation, we learned that medications for the group home (which were prepared by a contract pharmacy) were only labeled with patients' names and not their dates of birth. This created a high-risk situation for patients and a difficult situation for staff, as they lacked the information required to identify patients safely. Since this event, we have found a new contract pharmacy to prepare the medications for the group homes with labels containing the patients' full names *and* dates of birth. Because the technician self-reported this error, we learned about a potential deadly system problem. If you become aware of situations that you believe may pose a risk to patient or worker safety, please report them to your manager or supervisor as soon as possible. Reporting potential threats helps us all to have a safe day!

Learning from Our Mistakes

In 1997, Dr. Lucian L. Leape, MD, chair of the Lucian Leape Institute at the National Patient Safety Foundation, testified on safety before the US Congress, remarking that the greatest obstacle we face in healthcare is that "we punish people for making mistakes."[15] As we've seen, such punishment impedes frontline employees from reporting safety lapses, and that in turn prevents organizations from moving proactively to fix systemic issues. Just cultures can dramatically improve safety for patients and healthcare workers, just as they have for airline passengers and crew. To move closer to zero harm, healthcare organizations must become far more adept than they currently are at building trust and helping their workforces feel safe and comfortable. Just cultures enlist everyone, management and employees, in a common cause: making the organization *better*. Henry Ford had it right: "The only real mistake is the one from which we learn nothing."[16] Let's stop making these real mistakes, and instead treat every mistake as a chance to improve our systems for providing care.

IN SUM

- Just cultures are nonpunitive cultures of shared accountability in which organizations bear responsibility for their own systems and for treating team members fairly, and team members bear responsibility for speaking out when something is wrong with the system.
- Just cultures don't do away with culpability, but rather levy it in thoughtful, structured ways.
- Healthcare organizations have often had trouble implementing just cultures effectively.
- To succeed in implementing just cultures, organizations require a safety management system for just culture, including commitment from senior leadership, clear guidance for culpability determination and management, integration into current performance management and peer review programs, education for leaders, consistent application, and metrics to monitor progress.

CHAPTER

8

Measurement and Control Loops

Cheri Throop, RN, and Martin Wright

To become safer, organizations must carefully measure their performance. This chapter presents a balanced scorecard that organizations can use to measure patient safety and reliability. We also discuss "control loops," management systems that monitor performance, identify deviations, resolve problems, and make changes to systems to improve performance.

IN HEALTHCARE, DETERMINING what to measure can quickly become an overwhelming task. Organizations track a dizzying array of processes, from financial performance to patient outcomes to costs. Legal and regulatory standards require and shape such measurement, as do incentive-based payment systems, market-driven and stakeholder expectations, strategic goals, financial stewardship, and commitments to improvement initiatives related to safety, quality, experience, engagement, and efficiency.

When it comes to safety in particular, it's essential that organizations measure intelligently and efficiently, avoiding chaos and deploying "metrics that matter." How else will leaders understand current levels of performance, and whether the efforts they're making to achieve specific safety outcomes are bearing fruit? How else will they receive early warnings when the organization has veered off-course and might miss its improvement goals?

This chapter surveys the measurement practices organizations should use in journeying to zero preventable harm. Most healthcare organizations already deploy a measurement system built around key performance indicators (KPIs), displaying these measures on a dashboard that is real-time, virtual, and easily visible. Organizations typically align KPIs with their strategic pillars (for instance, the Kaplan and Norton "balanced scorecard" approach),[1] incorporating data on a full range of perspectives (discussed below). Such measurement systems provide an exceptional foundation for continuously monitoring safety and reliability performance.[2] But within those systems, not all measurement is created equal.

As we argue, organizations should deploy metrics that are linked to their strategic goals; that provide meaningful, actionable information; that are comprehensive; that encourage the right behaviors among the workforce; and that are easy for people to understand. In particular, organizations should measure three dimensions of safety and reliability performance: prevention, detection, and correction.[3] Given that safety and reliability initiatives ultimately seek to prevent harm-related failures from occurring, organizations should deploy metrics that allow them to understand how likely problems are to occur, establish accountability for addressing problems as they arise, and understand our actions' ultimate consequences.

Understanding Safety-Related Metrics

Let's first consider the basic types of metrics typically employed at high reliability organizations. To measure performance comprehensively, such organizations tend to use a three-pronged model designed to predict the probability of performance, reinforce what is expected or course-correct before it is too late, and examine how effective an organization is at preventing, detecting, and correcting harm and suffering. Three types of indicators correspond to these various purposes: *leading indicators*, which capture what organizations believe they can achieve; *real-time indicators*, which describe how organizations actually perform; and *lagging indicators*, which convey the consequences of our behavioral performance.

Leading indicators exist to measure how a healthcare organization likely will perform and should be considered early warning system signals. Leading indicators are metrics that provide early signals of changes in activities known to correlate with particular events or outcomes. They reflect movement to or from the edge of an organization's desired performance expectations.

The changes or flat results of serial safety culture or workforce engagement surveys, for example, can predict a potential upward or downward trend in the number of preventable harm events. Known links exist between safety performance and workforce engagement; employees who are more invested personally in workplace safety feel that their organizations are committed, too.[4] Organizations also know that leaders who communicate effectively leave workers feeling more supported and perceiving a more positive safety climate. In general, safety produces engagement, and vice versa.[5]

To further gauge how an organization's safety and reliability culture will perform going forward, leaders might also consider financial metrics, such as rates of employee vacancy and overtime, turnover rates among senior and operations leaders and medical staff, and the operating margin. Leaders might look at customer experience metrics such as the patient's willingness to return for care or recommend the organization. And leaders might consider other internal workforce metrics such as the perceptions leaders, medical staff, and employees have of the safety culture; work unit resilience; and overall organizational alignment. Finally, organizations might track employees' perceptions of the organization's overall transparency and the attention it pays to professional skills and development. Leaders can obtain all these measurements using a combination of patient experience survey tools, safety culture survey tools, engagement survey tools, and similar instruments.

Aside from using metrics to predict future safety performance, leaders can use a second class of measurements—real-time indicators—to hold people accountable for taking action in the present. These metrics measure the reliability of processes and activities and are generated at roughly the same time as the conditions they monitor. In particular, leaders and managers perform rounding observations, audits, or other monitoring, and on this basis can track group and individual performance in relation to clearly defined expectations. Leaders can then use these real-time metrics to address urgent performance issues that might arise before they become entrenched as habits.

Real-time indicators evolve over time as the organization's safety and reliability culture matures, and as people move from becoming aware of desirable behaviors, to actually performing them, to doing so habitually. Typical measures include the number of instances in which caregivers failed to comply with care bundles; the percentage of safety problems that were resolved; the feedback that patients and their families provide during rounds; social media activity related to the organization; in-person observations as to whether workers, leaders, and medical staff are complying with expectations; and the extent to which workers, leaders, and medical staff are aware of behavior expectations. To make the most of real-time indicators, leaders must commit to making rounds, observing, coaching, and monitoring staff performance.

They must also adopt desired behaviors into their own daily work habits, practicing the leadership skills described in Chapter 4 as well as the high reliability principles described in Chapter 3.

From a clinical perspective, real-time indicators of patient physiological well-being are well researched and considered industry standards of practice. Examples include the Pediatric Early Warning System (PEWS)[6] and the later Modified Early Warning System (MEWS),[7] illness-ranked scoring systems that trigger an urgent response when the patient's condition warrants closer monitoring or immediate action.[8] Organizations continue to study how much these scoring tools enhance patients' outcomes. Initiatives related to measurement of the actual scores, assessment of the patient's present condition, and timeliness in determining the best course of action are examples of preventable harm early warning system indicators. These early warning systems suggest how organizations might anticipate and prepare in real time so as to prevent safety failures and reduce harm.

Organizations can use a third kind of measurement, lagging indicators, to understand the consequences of behavioral performance and gauge the impact of tactical improvements and strategic changes. Lagging indicators are *outcomes measures* that reflect an organization's effectiveness at preventing, detecting, and correcting problems that can lead to harm or suffering. Such measures include the percentage change in workers' compensations claims, perceptions of the quality of care and service provided by the organization, perceptions of how much the organization cares about employee safety, and the number of "safety success stories" shared by employees over time.

Another important example of a lagging indicator is the measurement of preventable patient harm. In 2006, Healthcare Performance Improvement (HPI) developed the Safety Event Classification (SEC©) as a way of classifying the severity of harm events that result when caregivers deviate from generally accepted performance standards (GAPS),[9] and the Serious Safety Event Rate (SSER©) as a volume-adjusted measure of the Serious Safety Events. The SEC system (Figure 8.1) evaluates patient and worker events as either a Serious Safety Event (SSE©), a Precursor Safety Event (PSE), a Near Miss Event (NME), or an event that doesn't compromise safety (service failure–related events are classified using an identical algorithmic structure). A small group of trained clinicians evaluates each significant or serious event using facts available from the initial cause analysis process (see Chapter 9). If care was appropriate (i.e., caregivers didn't deviate from generally accepted performance standards), the event is deemed to be "not a safety event."

As a single, global measure of harm, SEC allows every organization to see the "big picture" and to avoid the confusion that occurs when a few harm types show improvement and others reveal a decline. SEC also allows every organization to become part of a learning community in which we benchmark for best

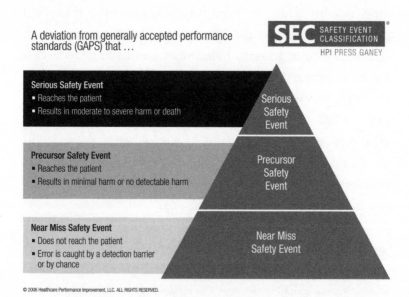

A deviation from generally accepted performance standards (GAPS) that ...

SEC SAFETY EVENT CLASSIFICATION ®
HPI PRESS GANEY

Serious Safety Event
- Reaches the patient
- Results in moderate to severe harm or death

Serious Safety Event

Precursor Safety Event
- Reaches the patient
- Results in minimal harm or no detectable harm

Precursor Safety Event

Near Miss Safety Event
- Does not reach the patient
- Error is caught by a detection barrier or by chance

Near Miss Safety Event

© 2006 Healthcare Performance Improvement, LLC. ALL RIGHTS RESERVED.

Figure 8.1 The Safety Event Classification (SEC) System

practice and gauge our relative progress toward zero patient harm. Virtually all of the HPI client community's 1,200 hospitals use the SEC system and the resulting SSER.

Organizations calculate the SSER on a monthly basis as the number of Serious Safety Events (SSEs) that occurred over a 12-month period per 10,000 Adjusted Patient Days,[10] a commonly monitored financial metric. The 12-month average methodology normalizes infrequent data points, presenting a clearer picture of overall trends in the number of events. This methodology encourages robust rather than short-term improvements in the prevention of Serious Safety Events. To achieve a "zero" SSER, the healthcare organization must boast 12 straight months of SSE-free operations.

The SSER can give us a quick sense of the impact that embracing safety science and high reliability can have on safety. Nationwide Children's Hospital implemented its Zero Hero patient safety program in the fall of 2009. The results, made public online,[11] reveal a sustained reduction not only in the SSER (currently at 82 percent), but also in other key lagging indicators such as surgical-site infections and medication errors.[12]

The SSER also provides a consistent methodology for measuring an organization's effectiveness in preventing, detecting, and correcting safety lapses. Safety experts consider it a reliable measure of *internal* improvement, rather than a means of comparing an organization with others. The declaration of Serious Safety Events (SSE) depends on consistency in event detection, urgency of event reporting, and the internal inter-rater SEC application capabilities. As an organization strengthens its culture of reporting and becomes increasingly aware of the behavioral and system vulnerabilities that contribute to harm events, SSER will initially rise. In Figure 8.2, note the 80 percent reduction in patient events that organizations can theoretically achieve, as described earlier in this book. Note, too, the increase in harm that often occurs as complacency takes hold and team members fall back on poor practice habits.

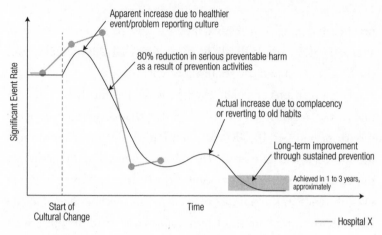

Figure 8.2 Safety Events over Time for a Typical Hospital Undertaking an Improvement Effort

Organizations can measure psychological and emotional harm and suffering as lagging indicators, reflecting the perceptions of patients or workers who have experienced a safety event and its aftereffects. The trauma and suffering that individuals experience is their unique reality, and organizations shouldn't rely on clinicians' blanket perceptions of it, as those might prove biased. Consider a scenario in which the ambulatory surgical cases on a given day have been exposed to potentially infectious material due to improperly sterilized surgical instruments. Once members of the care team discover this lapse, they inform the 35 exposed patients, provide them with free laboratory testing (which initially yields negative results), and give them prophylactic antibiotic therapy. Of the 35 patients, 5 confide that they have experienced significant emotional harm due to their fear of the unknown ("Will I develop an infection?"), while the other 30 patients have not expressed undue concern. Is the point of view of these 30 more important than that of the 5 emotionally harmed patients? Not at all. Each patient's experience is unique given his or her perception of harm and suffering, and caregivers should respect it as such.

One way organizations have begun to measure psychological and emotional harm experienced by workers is by assessing their resilience levels, or their ability to "bounce back" in the face of adversity. Deirdre Mylod, PhD, executive director at the Press Ganey Institute for Innovation, has developed a framework that helps organizations separate sources of stress and reward in the care environment into two categories: those inherent to the work of healthcare and those exacerbated by outside forces. In her *Harvard Business Review* article titled "One Way to Prevent Clinician Burnout," Mylod states: "The goal of clinicians and their organizations is to mitigate suffering *inherent* to patients' conditions and to prevent suffering caused by the dysfunction of the *external* delivery system."[13] Measurement in this area now allows leaders to assess employees' ability to connect to the meaning in work (an employee's "level of activation") and their ability to disconnect from work when they want to (an employee's "level of decompression"). By understanding these two components of resilience, organizations can assess how much harm the stressfulness of the work environment is causing, and whether it's prompting the emotional exhaustion and depersonalization that causes burnout.

Charting Progress

To ensure operational safety and reliability, smart organizations don't rely on external signals of poor performance such as lowered bond ratings, newspaper articles, lawsuits, or grievances. Rather, they monitor leading, real-time, and lagging indicator metrics continuously, correcting procedures and processes as required. Taken together, these metrics make up an early warning system that captures key trends. If real-time indicators are stagnant or declining while others are improving, the organization's safety improvement efforts might generally remain on track, although local performance remains uneven. A well-developed culture will help turn around weak performance in a few months, but in the meantime, the organization should take localized, temporary actions to change people's behavior. If leading indicators are the problem, then the organization can expect to see real-time and lagging indicators stagnate or fall in the near future. The organization should prepare for these negative changes and take strategic action to correct underlying systemic issues. If lagging indicators are stagnant or declining while real-time and lagging indicators are improving, then the organization should maintain its present activities—it is only a matter of time before the lagging indicators improve.[14]

The only way to know if your organization is continuing to move in a positive direction is by monitoring the key measures that allow executive and management level leaders to chart organizational performance. Your measurement strategy will evolve over time, but be sure to start with measures that are appropriate for your phase in the safety and reliability transformation journey, and that are readily accessible and/or easy to obtain. Consider combining these internal and external measures into an organization-wide inventory, with the expectation that units and department will frequently report their numbers. Table 8.1 depicts an example of a metrics inventory, aligned with an organization's strategic pillars, that encompasses relevant leading, real-time, and lagging safety and reliability indicators.

As you achieve internally defined performance targets, add to the current group of indicators, or select a second group. Set a timetable for measurement that aligns with your implementation strategies, making sure to include at least one leading, real-time, and lagging indicator for each of your measurement domains or pillars. To further anticipate and predict safety problems, organizations can deploy existing, adaptive, and emerging technologies.

Table 8.1   A Sample Metrics Inventory

Organization Pillars	Leading Indicators	Real-Time Indicators	Lagging Indicators
Financial Perspective	• Employee vacancy rate & overtime • Senior leaders, operational leaders, and medical staff turnover rates • Operating margin	• Number of care bundle non-compliance cases (****) • Problem resolution rate: Percentage of identified problems that are resolved • Action Aging: Number of days corrective actions extend beyond the due date	• Percentage change in reserves/losses • Value-based incentives payment percentage • Percentage change in Serious Safety Event Rate (SSER) • Annual TCIR (Total Case Incident Rate) compared to prior year • Annual average DART (Days Away Restricted & Transferred) compared to prior year
Customer Perspective(*)	Patient willingness to • Return for care • Recommend	• Patient/family experience-specific feedback during daily rounding • Social media activity associated with the organization	• HCAHPS value-based reporting measure results • CMS Hospital Compare quality ratings • Leapfrog Hospital Quality Score
Internal Perspective	Leader, medical staff, and employee perceptions of: • The safety culture (**) (***) • Overall engagement (***) • Work unit resilience (***) • Overall organizational alignment (***)	Observed compliance with behavior/performance expectations Worker Leader Medical staff Call Offs for staff	• Days since last (patient) Serious Safety Event (SSE) • Days since last (employee) Serious Safety Event (eSSE) • Days since last HAI • Days since last fall • Late starts • Perceptions of quality of care and service provided by the organization (**) • Perceptions of how well the organization treats the employee with respect (**) • Perceptions of how much the organization cares about employee safety (**)
Learning & Growth Perspective	Employee perception of organization's: • Overall transparency (***) • Attention to professional skills and development needs (***)	Knowledge & application awareness of behavior/ performance expectations Worker Leader Medical Staff	• Incident report volume trends • Safety Success Story sharing volume trends

(*) Defined as the patient receiving care or services/measured using patient experience survey tool or instrument
(**) Measured using a safety culture survey tool or other relevant instrument
(***) Measured using a safety culture or engagement survey tool or another relevant instrument
(****) Impact on value-based or other incentive-driven payment systems

Electronic shared data management systems (eSMS) help analyze external events that other organizations might have experienced due to causal factors that you now see emerging within your own organization. Using event type and causal factor trends, and remaining mindful of the lessons other organizations have learned, leaders can preemptively adjust their own improvement efforts. Participation in an eSMS also provides readily available indicator benchmarks that can influence improvement efforts.

Safety culture, workforce engagement, and medical staff engagement metrics serve organizations particularly well as a harm-related early warning system. As we've seen, safety culture and engagement track closely as indicators, so best practice is to measure both together as a single, psychometrically validated instrument (survey) and to conduct a continual cycle of improvement for both.

High reliability organizations also align key workforce engagement indicators with the work of safety and reliability. From our Press Ganey experience in measuring and improving engagement survey data,[15] we have identified several key metrics that leaders could and should align in order to gain deeper insights into safety and engagement. These include the "Tier Score," a marker that indicates how well members of a work team perform together; the "Action Planning Readiness Score," which tracks the team's trust in the leader's ability to drive change and his or her ability to communicate; the "Engagement Indicator Score," which measures pride in and loyalty to the organization as well as a team member's willingness to provide the extra, discretionary effort that contributes to safety; the "error prevention and reporting," "pride and reputation," and "resources and teamwork" measures, critical for both workforce engagement and patient and workforce safety; and finally, resilience data, which can help us understand the team's ability to bounce back from adversity. The last of these also includes patient experience measures of loyalty (likelihood of recommending and overall rating) to fully understand team performance.[16]

Utilizing integrated, cross-domain analytics provides more specific information about the performance of a given unit. For example, if engagement, safety culture, and resilience are low, the work unit likely has poor patient experience outcomes. Leaders can also use these data as an early warning system to identify where harm to a patient or workers may occur. If a work unit has low engagement, safety culture, and resilience outcomes, the risk of a serious safety event is high. Consider the organizational dashboard you have designed, and monitor it as another powerful early warning system for detecting harm. What are the leading and real-time indicators telling you about behavior, processes, and systems performance?

Accountability and Control Loops

In addition to the right metrics, the organization's accountability system figures critically in any organization's journey to zero harm. Organizations must measure how they build and reinforce accountability, assessing which controls have worked and which haven't. Control loops—management systems that monitor performance, identify deviations, resolve system problems, and adjust systems to improve performance—serve organizations well, helping them set performance boundaries and accountability according to the organization's goals.[17]

One type of control loop in particular, the "closed loop stepwise" model (Figure 8.3), helps us understand "what good looks like" as well as the continuous cycle for improvement. This model yields eight key steps that an organization might take to improve:

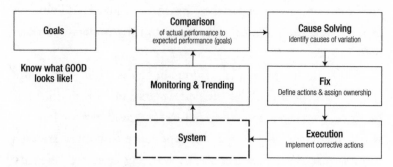

Figure 8.3 Control Loop Model

Source: Adapted from the Generalized Feedback System management tool developed in Chapter 2 of Paul F. Wilson, Gaylord F. Anderson, and Larry D. Dell, *Root Cause Analysis: A Tool for Total Quality Management* (Wisconsin: ASQC Quality Press, 1993).

Step 1: Goals

First, leaders define the organization's safety and reliability transformation performance expectations as its overarching goals. Organizations can take a number of steps to commit publicly to zero harm, including declaring zero as the goal, communicating safety events transparency, and "putting a face" on safety, reminding everyone that every safety event affects a person, not a number.[18] Organizations can build transparency and trust by keeping the goals and subsequent measures of patient and worker harm, suffering, and vulnerability visible across the organization.

Step 2: Comparison

Compare your actual performance to expected performance. Consider developing two scorecards or dashboards, a first that senior executives can use on a quarterly or semiannual basis to gauge the organization's general direction, and a second that operational leaders can use to gain advance warning of where to intervene in order to prevent further degradation. Develop a mechanism for communicating relevant performance results to the front line, using executive leader forums, quarterly town hall meetings, regular rounding on staff, and similar venues.

Step 3: Cause Solving

Initiate a process called *cause solving* to identify the specific causes behind performance variation. Cause solving unfolds incrementally. First, review incidents and stakeholder feedback to define relevant problems. Next, determine the behavior, process, and systemic factors that may negatively affect performance, and establish potential solutions.[19] Keep the measures dashboard in front of leaders, assuring that they understand both how the measures relate to specific causes and actions the organization might need to take to improve safety practices and reliability performance.

Step 4: Fix

Explicitly define each of the corrective actions, assigning to each a specific leader who will "own" the action, a due date for the action's completion, and reporting accountability. Operational leaders should bear primary responsibility for identifying and prioritizing problems to be resolved, and for ultimately fixing their underlying causes. Leaders should ask frontline personnel to help them develop workable solutions that don't add additional performance burden. This not only helps improve safety outcomes, but can also increase workforce engagement, since team members are more inclined to support solutions that they had a hand in devising.

Step 5: Execution

Prioritize and implement the owner-assigned corrective actions, bearing in mind the reasons why action plans tend to fail. Leaders might agree to take action only to back out later, failing to understand why the action is worth the effort given competing priorities. Solve this problem by choosing the most cost-effective solution at the outset, by involving employees early in the process, and by approaching them tactfully. Action plans also often fail because nobody takes responsibility for implementing them. As mentioned, it's so important to assign responsible parties to the action plan by name, clearly specifying the respective deadlines for completion of the action items.[20]

Step 6: System

Adopt the corrective actions as part of your organization's daily operating system. Operational leaders should remain alert to how the system is responding to the change management process. Can the system continue to support the improvements? Do vulnerabilities or barriers still exist that can hamper expected performance? Is the organization prepared to deploy additional resources to support the push toward sustained performance?

Step 7: Monitoring and Trending

Establish performance monitoring requirements (for instance, rounding or observational audits with immediate feedback), and specify leading and real-time indicators associated with the relevant lagging indicator targeted for improvement.

Step 8: Comparison

Repeat the initial comparison step (Step 2) to examine the current-to-desired performance. Subsequently repeating the closed loop process (Steps 3–7) creates a continuous improvement management system that is clearly focused on the organization's committed goals to zero harm.

Measuring *and* Monitoring Our Way to Zero

As a well-known aphorism has it, not everything we can measure matters to organizations, and not everything that matters lends itself to easy measurement. This insight applies to the zero harm journey, but with the right approach, we can use data to drive our improvement efforts. One health system partnered with Press Ganey to develop a "Critical Metrics Map" that aligned data sets at individual care sites and work unit levels. Leaders shared this tool with human resources and nursing leaders, asking CHROs and CNOs from each site to review the integrated data and revise and prioritize interventions based on several key performance indicators. If a work unit showed poor resilience, for instance, leaders stopped all other cultural interventions and built resilience. If the data revealed high resilience but limited trust in leadership and its ability to drive change, leaders created a plan to focus on leadership skill development. By strategically triaging interventions based on the performance outcomes identified by carefully chosen and integrated analytics, this organization saw tremendous improvements in its overall resilience, safety culture, and engagement scores.

How is your organization using safety-related metrics? Are your safety initiatives thwarted by the chaos created by too many, poorly chosen metrics? As high reliability organizations can attest, analyzing leading and real-time indicators allows organizations to detect, contain, and correct problems before harms materialize. But of course, organizations must also monitor performance by aligning the appropriate metrics and establishing a process for understanding and addressing the early warning signals. If organizations remain fuzzy on how they are performing against critical measures of success, they will likely fail to sustain improvement gains. For them, zero harm for patients and workers will loom, sadly, as a distant and unobtainable goal.

IN SUM

- When journeying to zero harm, it's essential that organizations measure intelligently and efficiently, avoiding chaos and deploying "metrics that matter."
- Organizations should attend to three kinds of metrics: leading indicators, real-time indicators, and lagging indicators.
- Rather than relying on external signals of poor performance, high reliability organizations monitor leading, real-time, and lagging indicator metrics continuously, using them as an early warning system, and correcting procedures and processes accordingly.
- Control loops—management systems that monitor performance, identify deviations, resolve system problems, and make changes to systems to improve performance—help organizations maintain performance boundaries and accountability.

9 | Learning Systems

Tami Strong, RN, MSN-HCQ

> *To progress toward zero patient harm and zero workforce injury, organizations must improve their ability to learn from mistakes. Merging two topics that healthcare leaders normally consider separately, safety culture and process improvement, this chapter reviews the major components of learning systems, including root cause analysis and daily leader practices such as learning boards.*

DIANNE, THE SYSTEM director for quality and safety at a large healthcare organization, was watching her high school daughter's tennis match when she received a call from Jacqueline, the organization's risk manager. "Dianne," she said, her voice somber, "if you're not sitting down, you might want to. We've had an incident on our family birthing unit. A baby has died. We think it was likely preventable and due to a delay of care. We have initiated the crisis intervention team for our staff; please come back to the hospital."

Dianne left the tennis match and rushed back. At the family birthing unit, she found the care team in shock, and a flurry of executives, unit leaders, and quality team members already on the scene. As she discovered, the night nurse had earlier observed a "slight change" in an unborn baby's heart rate while reviewing a fetal monitoring strip. The nurse had a "gut feeling" that things weren't right, but she didn't view the change as significant enough to justify calling Dr. Jones, the on-call physician. A couple of hours later, further changes in the baby's heart rate prompted her to make an urgent call, but unfortunately Dr. Jones didn't answer nor did he return the call. So, the nurse called the hospital's house supervisor, a nurse, and asked her to please continue to try to contact Dr. Jones. "This baby is not doing well," she said, "it's urgent!" After many unsuccessful attempts to reach Dr. Jones, the doctor finally called the supervisor, telling her that he was on vacation out of state, and that a different physician, Dr. Smith, was covering for him. The supervisor quickly called Dr. Smith but learned that he was "double booked" for on-call and working at another hospital 60 minutes away.

The supervisor then called each of the hospital's obstetrics physicians—she knew that the mother needed an immediate C-section for what was likely an umbilical cord wrapped around the baby's neck. State law required that hospital obstetrics departments maintain an ability to conduct emergency C-sections within a half-hour of a decision to operate, as that reduced the risk that a baby would suffer brain damage from oxygen deficiency. Eventually, the supervisor got one of the OB doctors, Dr. Murphy, on the line. Dr. Murphy rushed over to the hospital and delivered a baby girl, but it was too late. Despite frenzied attempts to resuscitate her, she died.

Attempting to get the situation under control, the hospital's CEO now initiated a formal cause analysis, quickly delegating the process to the organization's "safety team of experts." Over the next few weeks, this group—which included Dianne, the risk manager, and two clinical educators—reviewed the hospital's investigation policy. The investigation policy served the team as a guide, helping assure that it properly completed its investigation, analysis, and development of corrective actions. Applying a cause solving template (see Chapter 7), the team considered if the baby's death stemmed from potentially criminal conduct, a personal failure, or a system process failure. Concluding that the death likely owed to both systemic and personal failures, the team interviewed caregivers, reviewed the patient's chart, and used a performance improvement tool called a process map to reconstruct the incident (the team documented the steps required in the care of the unborn infant, comparing how long each step took with how long it should have taken).

On the basis of this work, the team concluded that three primary failures had led to the baby's death: nurse competency, physician behavior, and the lack of an adequate structure that would allow caregivers to obtain help from senior administrators in case of emergency. As the team found, the nurse should have contacted the physician when she first noted the slight heart rate decline while reviewing the fetal monitoring strip. Dr. Jones, meanwhile, hadn't notified the hospital of his on-call arrangements with another physician. Dr. Jones had a long history of ignoring the medical staff policy regarding the 30-minute C-section standard, and for going "rogue" in how he approached coverage. Other OB physicians didn't regard him as a team player—a fact known to senior leadership. Finally, the team faulted the hospital for failing to contact another provider after it couldn't reach the on-call physician. At no point during the event had caregivers notified hospital administration.

With this analysis in place, the investigatory team went on to create a detailed action plan for the organization. It recommended that the organization develop a hospital-wide chain of command policy that would allow caregivers to "escalate" safety concerns up the chain of command if necessary, and that the hospital also implement a process for triggering help from medical and administrative staff to head off safety concerns in real time. The team also recommended that the organization educate the family birthing unit (FBU) staff on the new policy and require all team members to formally acknowledge that they had been trained. To address the competency issues, the team advised the hospital to put the main nurse on probation pending further investigation for not recognizing early signs of fetal distress. It also advised the hospital to conduct formal interviews and hearings with Dr. Jones, and to warn him that another situation like this would lead to his termination.

The organization accepted these recommendations and within a few months had carried them out. As far as Dianne could tell, this particular problem had been solved, with an action plan that was thoughtful, comprehensive, and appropriate. Sadly, though, she was wrong. Approximately six months after the baby's death, Jacqueline stood at Dianne's office door, tears streaming down her face. "We had another incident in the FBU," she said. "Another baby has died."

Improving How Organizations Learn

Healthcare organizations today often fail to learn from safety incidents when they occur, and as this story suggests, the consequences can prove devastating. In this case, not only did two babies die from preventable harm, their families were devastated and forever changed. The nurse caring for the first baby, an 18-year veteran, also felt so traumatized that she left the profession and became suicidal. The physician involved was eventually forced to abandon the practice of medicine, while the organization came under intense regulatory and public scrutiny.

How can organizations aspiring to zero harm ensure that they do learn from mistakes and make the necessary safety adjustments? The answer is to set up special mechanisms for learning, what safety experts call "learning systems." Such systems allow organizations to monitor performance so that they can improve care delivery and respond quickly to safety lapses. In Chapter 2, we listed 10 discrete elements that make up effective learning systems (Table 9.1). This list boils down to mechanisms for measuring or monitoring for risk of harm, understanding systemic causes, implementing safety assessment programs that audit operations for safety, and sharing lessons learned within the industry and beyond.

Table 9.1   10 Components of Effective Learning Systems

✓ Harm measures

✓ Injury measures

✓ Culture measures

✓ Climate measures

✓ Engagement measures

✓ Cause analysis

✓ Common cause analysis

✓ Self-assessment

✓ Independent assessment

✓ Operating experience

As our work in healthcare and with high reliability organizations (HROs) in other industries shows, organizations must adopt all 10 elements on our list in order to have any hopes of eventually achieving zero harm. Yet even organizations that do incorporate all 10 sometimes flounder, for two reasons.

First, they lack an underlying philosophy of how to properly view and address causes of harm, and thus can't fully parse the systemic causes of harm as well as the interaction between those causes and the behavior of individuals.[1] In their handling of cause analysis,* organizations must communicate to the workforce that people aren't to blame for safety events—systems are. They must also stay focused on identifying the real, systemic causes as well as corresponding solutions.

Second, most organizations aren't set up to support optimal learning. Efforts to support safety, reliability, and process improvements often become siloed, leading to uneven and inefficient progress. Likewise, organizations delegate safety learning and improvement to experts, failing to engage teams to capture day-to-day errors in the process.

Thanks to these two significant weaknesses, organizations wind up making potentially horrible mistakes—and then, like Dianne's hospital, making them all over again.

Getting Cause Analysis Right

Let's take a closer look at the first of these organizational shortcomings. Lacking a clear philosophy related to cause analysis, organizations tend to miss the important step of understanding what the individual caregiver was experiencing while committing the error in question, and they also fail to consider all possible causes of an event, including organizational culture.[2] By contrast, high reliability organizations adopt five underlying principles in conducting cause analyses:

- Organizations can't regard individuals as the only barrier preventing harm events. Everyone makes mistakes, even highly skilled professionals.

---

* An investigative approach that seeks to identify the systemic causes that led to an individual incident of harm or injury, actions that might address each cause, and a plan to implement those actions.

- Risky care activities are "predictable, manageable, and preventable."
- Individual behavior is strongly influenced, for better or for worse, by the organization's culture.
- High-risk behaviors result in human error or actions that trigger events. Conversely, an organization can optimize human performance if it encourages, teaches, and reinforces appropriate behaviors as suggested in Chapter 5.
- Organizations can prevent harm events by understanding near misses and applying lessons gleaned from cause analyses of past significant events gained through rigorous cause analysis.

High reliability organizations also adopt a specific methodology to conduct cause analysis, what is known as a *technology-based RCA (root cause analysis)*. Used in industries such as aerospace, aeronautics, manufacturing, and nuclear power, technology-based RCA prompts investigators to examine a predefined system of causal factors, ensuring that they'll consider all possible causes of a harm event. HPI's cause analysis methodology is a technology-based RCA approach, one that many healthcare organizations have adopted so as to become highly reliable. To identify the human error that precipitated a harm event, our methodology considers the harm incident in light of 20 possible *individual failure mechanisms* (ways people make mistakes) organized into five categories (knowledge and skills, attention, information processing, cognition, and motivation). We then go on to identify the systemic failures that caused the human error, considering 26 possible mechanisms also organized into five families (structure, culture, process, policy and procedure, and technology and environment). Testing each of these mechanisms against the facts in the case, we determine which ones functioned as root causes. Typically, this method allows us to identify two or three root causes.[3]

As noted earlier in this book, analysis of our database of 4,868 safety lapses from 120 healthcare sites indicates that organizations might have prevented 73 percent of these lapses by using a cultural intervention to reduce overall patient harm.[4] We've also found that healthcare organizations do reduce errors and improve quality by deploying technology-based RCA. Leaders at these organizations tell us that the methodology just "feels" different, since it allows them to look much more carefully and respectfully at how human beings experienced a harm event. As we saw earlier in this book, a systemic approach to cause analysis incorporates interview strategies to capture the nuances and complexity of human experience. By failing to understand those nuances, organizations can't detect vital systemic problems that might have contributed to the error. What was supposed to be an analysis of systemic factors turns out to become a pathway for blaming the caregiver while keeping the flawed system essentially unchanged.

Dianne's organization's cause analysis is a case in point. Perceiving caregivers' competency as the ultimate cause of the repeated harm events, investigators recommended disciplining the caregivers involved and focusing on policy development and education as solutions. What investigators didn't do was ask the primary nurse involved and her teammates how *they* had experienced the harm event. If the organization had established a five-point philosophy and adopted a technology-based RCA method, the safety team would have probed their subjective experiences and identified *culture* as an influencing cause of the individuals' behavior.[5]

Learning that the nurse had misinterpreted a fetal strip and that the on-call doctor hadn't notified the hospital that another physician would shoulder his responsibilities, the safety team had questioned the nurse bluntly about her training and competency and whether she had followed the correct procedures. Had she received training on fetal monitoring? Had she ever found herself in a similar situation? Did she know about the stat C-section policies? Such aggressive questioning, which likely prompted a defensive response from the nurse, allowed the team to identify systemic problems or contributing factors, but not true root causes.

If the team had embraced the five principles, it would have pursued questioning built around trust and shared understanding. "Please tell us what your experience was during the care of this patient," they might have asked. The nurse would have been more inclined to discuss a range of factors that influenced her mistake, including her deeper thoughts, fears, and concerns. Dianne and the team would have learned that she felt nervous about speaking up to the on-call doctor when the baby's heart rate was only slightly low. After all, she had seen people in positions of power repeatedly decline to listen to others when they brought up safety-related concerns.

In recent months, this nurse and others had spoken up about the on-call process and the policy for escalating safety concerns. They had specifically noted that the existing policy wasn't specific enough to address conditions in the FBU unit, and they predicted that patients could suffer serious harm as a result. They had also identified a range of other safety issues—that the hospital's nurse and physician staffing didn't conform with leading practices and quality standards, that new nurses and others weren't competent, and that critical equipment was not available or functioning as intended. Nobody had listened to these concerns, much less acted on them—not the chief nursing officer, union leaders, medical staff, chief executive officer, or even Dianne. If the safety team had embraced a philosophy of considering *culture* as a root cause, it would have made recommendations to improve the culture, and specifically, to create conditions that allowed frontline employees to feel comfortable speaking up (see Chapters 4 through 7). Instead, Dianne's organization missed an opportunity to learn from the cause analysis.

By contrast, consider how a team at MedStar Healthcare, a large healthcare system located along the East Coast, responded to a serious harm incident. A diabetic patient told the nurse caring for her, Annie, that she wasn't feeling well and thought her blood sugar was high. "I know my body," this patient said. Checking the patient's blood sugar, Annie did indeed find that the glucometer machine read high. The visual display read: "Out of Reportable Range: Critical Value; Repeat; Lab draw for >600." Nurse Annie twice treated this patient for high blood sugar based on the repeat message.[6]

Within minutes, Annie's patient became unresponsive, requiring a rapid response and transfer to the intensive care unit (ICU) with severe hypoglycemia (low blood sugar). The care team continued to treat the patient for high blood sugar after the glucometer came back repeatedly with the same message. During an initial investigation, Annie's nurse manager blamed Annie for reading the glucometer wrong, recommending that the hospital suspend her for further investigation. Soon after this incident, however, it happened again—another patient cared for by a nurse became hypoglycemic after the glucometer had reported excessively *high* blood sugar.

The MedStar team became suspicious that a design issue with the glucometer machine might have contributed to both harm incidents. Safety experts performed an analysis, this time asking Annie to share details about her experience during the harm incident and assessing the actual glucometer machine. They treated her as a respected colleague, not a potential perpetrator. The experts concluded that these incidents hadn't simply occurred as a result of nurse incompetence. Rather, an important cultural problem had caused the incidents—the failure of a number of people to question why the patient wasn't responding as one would anticipate. Also, poorly designed equipment had played a role, as the glucometer's visual display was confusing staff by communicating two messages at once. The most prominent message—"Out of Reportable Range"—implied a high blood sugar reading. But close inspection of the display revealed a second message, one that communicated the actual finding of a critically low blood sugar reading.

To prevent further instances of harm, the group investigating the harm events shared its revised conclusions with clinical units that were using the same glucometer. Meanwhile, Annie received apologies from the leaders and was restored to her job. With this resolution, Annie felt vindicated and could confidently return to her professional career.[7]

Both Dianne's organization and Annie's saw two patients harmed within a short period. In both cases, initial investigation pointed to the nurse's competency as the likely cause of the event. Unlike Dianne's organization, however, Annie's was transitioning from the traditional approach of viewing and addressing causation to a more highly reliable, system-oriented approach.[8] As a result, her organization would be in a far better position to remedy the human failures involved and to grasp the systemic failures. Instead of just addressing policies and staff competency, leaders could take steps to build the universal skills described in Chapter 5, thereby prevent human errors from triggering or reaching the patient.

A second technique, *common cause analysis*, also on our list of 10 components of a learning system, would also benefit many healthcare organizations, including Dianne's, that seek to understand situations in which multiple failures have occurred. In such an analysis, the organization aggregates instances of patient harm or injury into a single dataset, which it uses to identify common causes of harm. The bigger the dataset, the more effective the learning. Deploying this strategy, Dianne's organization could have helped the team in question recognize the lack of a reliability culture as a broad, systemic cause, one that affects many units and departments, not just the FBU. The organization could then take action to fix systemic causes, preventing harm from occurring across the system.

In 2014, when the large nonprofit health system Providence Health started on a system-wide journey to high reliability, it began with a study that included a common cause analysis. As this analysis revealed, 71 percent of Providence's safety lapses owed to cultural factors. In response, leaders at Providence created a high reliability set of universal skills for all employees, and a separate set for leaders, under the moniker "Caring Reliably Behaviors, Tools, and Tones" (see Chapters 4–6 for descriptions of these skills). As of May 2018, Providence has reduced serious safety event rates by 48 percent across its 35 hospitals. A recent safety climate survey filled out by 65,028 showed a 5 percent improvement. Employees are finding it easier to learn because they can report concerns without blame and are encouraged to learn from mistakes. Common cause analysis provided a robust set of data, and Providence used it to develop an effective strategy to reduce harm.[9]

Organizational Tweaks That Enhance Learning

Beyond improving how they view and address systemic causes of harm, organizations implementing the 10-point learning system outlined in this book must also implement a high reliability organizational structure in order for those learning systems to function well. As our work with organizations in healthcare, manufacturing, nuclear power, and aviation shows, a combination of three strategies proves effective here.

First, organizations should align the roles of safety team members with those of members of the process improvement team, focusing everyone on patient safety and workforce harm as the top priority. In many organizations that struggle with their learning systems, these two teams tend to become siloed, competing for resources and making it harder for the organization to uncover systemic causes of harm. Doug Cropper, president and CEO for Genesis Health System, grew concerned when the organization cut its rate of serious harm by 40 percent, only to see it climb back up again.[10] An external assessment revealed that the safety and process teams were competing for resources and working at cross-purposes. Under Doug's leadership, Genesis aligned the two teams around a focus on zero harm. In 2017, Genesis proudly achieved that goal.[11]

Organizations should also invest in widespread training of leaders around high reliability principles, safety science, process improvement methodology, and cause analysis. Typically, organizations forgo that training and instead delegate safety improvement to a "team of experts." This tends to weaken the ability of people throughout the organization to spot systemic causes of human error, delaying the pace of learning and improvement. The organization spends more time, money, and energy implementing changes that don't prevent harm. High reliability organizations expect *all* leaders to become well versed in all elements of the zero harm approach, leading safety initiatives as a part of their operational responsibilities.

Finally, leaders should engage with frontline staff, teaching them problem-solving and thinking skills using local learning systems. If staff understands how to improve processes, they'll be able to provide leaders with a better understanding of the daily problems and errors that exist throughout the organization, as well as how to solve them. As one organization recently told us, it couldn't act to reduce patient falls until a team of experts had time to prioritize it among many other "projects." This organization would have moved much quicker if leaders and frontline employees were working together on a continuous basis to make operations safer.

Moving Toward Zero—and Sustaining the Gains

As we at Press Ganey have seen firsthand, organizations that make these three adjustments improve safety. Kim Hollon, president and chief executive officer of Signature Healthcare in Brockton, Massachusetts, told us that his organization had done substantial work on its work processes, striving to transform itself into a "lean" organization. But during his long career, Hollon had never heard organizational change experts talking about safety culture "as a complementary strategy necessary to get to zero harm." As a result, like many healthcare leaders, Hollon and his team didn't understand all that the organization could gain by also deploying high reliability principles and safety culture. After reading an article on high reliability organizing, Hollon concluded that "we would not get to zero defects from process alone, and no process can be error proofed to the point that it works 100 percent of the time. I realized we needed to do something directly about our culture of safety as an additional component to our process improvement work."[12]

Over a four-year period, Hollon and his leadership team adopted a high reliability safety culture with the same intensity they had formerly applied to lean. They implemented mandatory training of all leaders and employees in safety science and high reliability as well as ongoing leader training in both safety and process improvement. Signature also aligned its safety, process improvement, and communications/marketing teams behind this new effort, allocating sufficient funds to support the integration. Instead of holding their usual daily lean management huddles, Hollon and his team now began each huddle by reporting on safety related metrics: the number of days since the last patient harm event, the number of days since the last workforce injury, and the number of "great catches" or near misses. This new format sent a signal to everyone: safety was now the top priority.

To further enhance the organization's ability to learn, Hollon and his team made efforts to engage frontline employees in identifying daily problems. Initially, employees seemed reluctant to contribute, a reaction Hollon found puzzling. Eventually, Hollon and his team realized that managers were influencing frontline staff by putting forward their own concerns and claiming that staff had advanced them. To overcome this barrier, Hollon and other leaders went directly to the care teams and asked what motivated them. The response: clear, attainable goals. So, Hollon adopted key performance measures including harm, workforce, engagement, patient experience, and cultural measures.

When teams still continued to struggle, Hollon and other leaders rolled out two "countermeasures." As he related, "We set a safety/quality goal of setting two safety/quality standards, and performing them at 100 percent for a 90-day period. We wanted the manager to learn that setting a goal that high required much more staff engagement around the clock, much more transparency and focus; and that if they got staff buy-in, the amount of observation, problem recognition, and suggestions would grow as the staff got closer to the goal and did not want to reset the clock back to zero days." Hollon learned that measuring the number of days since the last failure helped teams because it gave them a sense of accomplishment as the number of days increased. Further, adding a list capturing the "point of recognition" (POR) for each failure (in other words, the point at which a team member identified the failure and caught it) enhanced accountability, allowing the organization to credit the team for identifying and fixing the failure. In essence, Hollon and other leaders needed to teach teams how to set meaningful goals. Now that they were doing that, teams could move forward toward zero harm and injury.

Thanks to these efforts to better align the organization behind safety learning, Signature saw an 88 percent reduction in serious harm events over a two-year period. Further, the organization was able to sustain zero harm for a full 365 days. Since then, Signature has maintained a serious safety event rate (SSER) reduction of 80 percent and reduced its workforce reportable injury frequency rate (RIFR) by 75 percent. The organization's Hospital Consumer Assessment of Healthcare Providers and Systems (HCAHPS) communication with nurses' domain score improved 4 percent between 2013 and 2018. Safety Culture assessment scores between 2013 and 2017 also improved in 7 of 12 dimensions. The organization notched a 20 percent improvement in its ability to respond to errors in a nonpunitive way, reaching the eighty-fifth percentile nationally. Signature also experienced a 16 percent improvement in communication openness, putting them at the ninetieth percentile. The organization's ability to design a high reliability organizational structure mobilizing the three strategies outlined here has turned it into a learning powerhouse.

Comparing Signature's approach to learning with that of Dianne's organization, we find a stark difference. Dianne's organization relied on a team of "experts" to conduct cause analysis and to act as a repository of safety science and performance improvement methodology. Doing so led to delays in event analysis, improvements, and shared learning. Dianne's organization also failed to mobilize frontline teams in the learning. As a result, Diane and her colleagues lacked a process for capturing ideas for operational improvements advanced by employees. By contrast, Signature Healthcare's operational structure made provisions for such "local learning systems." The organization also boosted its ability to learn by using the universal skills described in Chapters 5 and 6, incorporating them into the process by which frontline teams assessed and solved safety problems.

Another organization that utilized the three strategies presented in this chapter to build a high reliability organizational structure is Utah-based Intermountain Healthcare. Led by president and CEO Dr. Marc Harrison, Intermountain has adopted a comprehensive and integrated local learning huddle board as well as an organizational structure that helps staff escalate safety concerns up the chain of command. Leaders across Intermountain engage staff for approximately 15 minutes at the beginning of each shift to focus on the entire patient experience, including safety, quality, efficiency, and patient engagement. The purpose is to help employees become more sensitive to operations and more aware of situations as they arise. Using huddle boards, unit and departmental leaders and their teams review safety issues that arose over the preceding 24 hours, putting strategies in place to mitigate these issues, and they anticipate concerns that might arise over the upcoming 24 hours. Issues requiring more attention are escalated as needed up the chain of command using a *tiered huddle* (a system of huddles that draws on information from frontline caregivers and incorporates it into huddles among leaders, up to and including the executive team). Intermountain maintains six tiers of sequentially timed huddles, each of which takes place before 10:30 a.m. each morning.

With guidelines for holding these huddles in hand, each leader at Intermountain goes on to review the number of days that have passed since the last serious safety event and workforce injury, and discusses a universal skill of the month on which the team is working. Leaders ask staff to share a safety story (a "good catch") related to the use of the universal skill and invite others to share similar stories. The team reviews how many patients are expected that day, and the impact of that flow for safety. The team then reviews quality of care metrics, produces safety ideas to be placed on an "idea board," and reviews safety items the team is working on, such as reducing patient falls and improving performance in the handling of pressure ulcers. Finally, the leader thanks the team, celebrates successes, and reviews patient engagement metrics, such as measures of staff responsiveness and nurse communication.

As a result of the tiered huddle process, leaders up to and including Intermountain's CEO can obtain data and learn of any issues that arise within 24 hours. All leaders can resolve issues in a timely way and share lessons learned. Intermountain has also integrated local learning into their huddle structure using a visual display (i.e., a learning board) to facilitate daily reviews for situational awareness. The boards capture the learnings and ideas from the 10 elements of learning systems.

These efforts have led to rapid improvements in patient safety, capacity management, and safety alert communications. After only three months, for instance, staff concerns received at the executive suite declined 25 percent from a year earlier, while patient access at the organization's medical group clinics dramatically improved (the number of appointments available rose by over 30 percent). Intermountain has also become much better at spreading best practices across the organization.[13]

Signature Healthcare, Intermountain Healthcare, MedStar, Providence St. Joseph, and Genesis Health System have all committed to a high reliability journey aimed at improving both safety and overall outcomes. These organizations aren't just pursuing the 10 elements of a learning system—they're backing them with high reliability tools and practices built into the organization.

Critically, these organizations are also using both internal and external safety assessments to evaluate their safety management system, including the effectiveness of their learning system. These reviews help organizations understand how they compare with other high reliability organizations, allowing them to identify weaknesses and develop action plans for addressing them. Are leaders and employees developing the right skills? Have they done so only to see their habits lag? Has a just culture taken root? Are the board, executive leadership, and medical personnel engaged? Are organizational learning systems adequate? Frequent self-assessments by leaders querying employees, managers, and caregivers provide the organization with real-time feedback it can use to improve. Independent assessments by outside experts provide the organization with an additional, objective points of view.

The high reliability organizations described in this chapter have all adopted these assessments into their learning system. They have turned their high reliability organizing into "the way we do our work," not just another short-lived program or initiative. As a result, they're getting close to zero, and even attaining it. We can only hope that organizations like Dianne's that are already on zero harm journeys but failing to make much headway will take note. If they implement learning systems in the right way, they, too, can prevent individual instance of harm from turning into recurring tragedies.

IN SUM

- Although learning systems are a critical component of a safety management system, organizations that adopt all 10 elements can still struggle to get to zero.
- In assessing the causes of human error, organizations should embrace a five-point philosophy and adopt a technology-based RCA approach to consider all systemic causes and identify the true root cause(s).
- Organizations should also make sure they have the right structures in place to support learning. In particular, they should align safety and process improvement teams, train leaders, and engage leaders and frontline teams in local learning.
- Some organizations on the journey to zero harm and workforce injury have worked to sustain and strengthen their safety management systems, including their learning systems.

Emily Halu, RN, MSN, and Joseph Cabral

Healthcare experiences much higher rates of worker
injury than other industries, including manufacturing,
construction, rail transportation, and nuclear power. This
chapter makes a business case for reducing workplace
injuries and describes a safety management system for
improving workforce safety in healthcare.

GAIL SANDIDGE, A nurse with 20 years of experience, was just beginning her shift at Good Shepherd
Ambulatory Surgical Center in Longview, Texas. An
expert at caring for preoperative patients, Gail loved
her job and was considered a "protector by nature."[1]
Little did she know that this shift would be her last.
Without warning, a patient's family member entered
the surgical center with violence in his eyes and a
knife in his hand. He rushed at staff, stabbing anyone
he could. Gail stood in his way, trying to protect her
colleagues and patients. The family member stabbed
her, and she later died of her wounds.

Three years earlier, at Crozer-Chester Medical
Center near Philadelphia, veteran nurse Tove Schuster
was also harmed on the job. During her night shift,
Tove heard a coworker yell for help to assist a patient

who had fallen to the floor. Along with other coworkers, Tove helped to lift the 300-pound patient from the floor back to the bed, with Tove bearing the weight of one leg. Although the hospital had equipment that allowed for the safe lifting of patients, Tove's team wasn't using it. As Tove strained under the weight, she heard a "pop" in her back and knew something bad had happened. Thus began a lengthy story of injury and pain, leading to the end of Tove's nursing career.[2]

Stories like Gail's and Tove's are all too common. Although healthcare organizations have improved worker safety in recent years,[3] far too many workers are still getting hurt. The total case incident rate (TCIR)—defined by the Occupational Safety and Health Administration (OSHA) as the number of injuries and illnesses sustained on the job per annum by approximately 100 full-time workers—for US hospitals has declined from 9.1 in 2000 to 5.9 in 2016. But compare that to nuclear power, where the TCIR in 2016 was only 0.3, some *20 times lower* than at US hospitals. In construction, the rate was 3.2, nearly half that of healthcare, and in manufacturing it was 3.6.[4] Similar results obtain for another key OSHA metric, the number of Days Away, Restricted or Transferred (DART), defined as the illnesses and injuries that result in lost work days (due to time off, restriction, or transfer of duties) per 100 full-time workers. All told, 228,200 healthcare workers were injured in hospitals alone in 2016— 91,100 of which were injured to the point of having to spend days away, restricted, or transferred.[5] The sad truth is that you are probably safer working on a construction crew that is building an acute care hospital than caring for patients inside it once it is built.

Healthcare thought leaders have tried to raise awareness of this issue for some time, with only limited success. In this chapter, we'll first examine the business case for reducing injuries, demonstrating the financial impact reducing workforce injuries has had in other industries. From there, we'll describe a safety management system for improving workforce safety in healthcare, one that we regard as a blueprint for the industry. We *know* how to make healthcare settings far safer for workers than they are today. We just have to muster the will to make it happen. Let's do it—for the sake of our workers as well as the success of our organizations.

The Business Case for Workforce Safety

Available data overwhelmingly suggests that ensuring safety for healthcare workers is not merely the right thing to do—it also makes good business sense. The financial costs of injuries to workers are enormous—both for the workers themselves and for our organizations. To calculate cumulative organizational costs, we must consider a range of more specific costs, including workers' compensation costs, turnover costs, the costs of overtime to replace workers who are injured, and productivity losses. The most recent cumulative data dates from 2011, where healthcare worker injuries cost the healthcare industry some $13.1 billion.[6]

Conversely, safe environments allow for much higher organizational performance across a range of metrics. As Press Ganey related in its 2016 Nursing Special Report, nurse workplace safety was "significantly associated with performance on nurse, patient, patient experience and pay-for-performance outcomes."[7] The safest organizations for nurses (those ranked in the top quartile) saw roughly half the rate of "RN perceived missed care" (required patient care that is significantly delayed or not completed), a "27% higher rate of job enjoyment," a "22 percent higher score for quality," and "3% higher average Likelihood to Recommend scores."[8] Because safety allows nurses to enjoy their jobs more, it supports higher engagement levels—itself an economic imperative for healthcare organizations. Indeed, organizations with a high rate of engaged workers report 22 percent higher productivity than those with lower rates and are more successful overall.[9] On the other hand, unsafe working conditions create physical and emotional stress for workers, leading to burnout and its attendant costs. Remove this source of stress, and you can dramatically reduce burnout in healthcare workers.[10]

As frightening as they are, formal OSHA safety metrics don't capture all of the emotional harm healthcare workers experience. Workers routinely suffer verbal threats from patients, family members, and coworkers. A young patient who disagrees with a physician's treatment plan might shout, "When I get out of here, you better watch your back!" A 90-year-old woman suffering from dementia might shout, "I'm going to punch you!" Such threats can raise stress levels and impair work performance, leading to decreased productivity and morale and increased turnover. Worse, the threats sometimes prove real. According to data from the US Bureau of Labor Statistics, healthcare workers are more than *four times* as likely to experience assaults at work that result in injuries requiring time off than any other private sector employees in the United States.[11] In addition, patient harm can cause worker suffering—even the toughest workers experience intense guilt and sadness when they inadvertently harm patients during preventable safety incidents (the so-called "second victim phenomenon").[12] Workers can also feel traumatized by their organizations' poor *response* to patient harm. If a healthcare organization hasn't adopted and promoted a fair and just culture (Chapter 7), it might treat workers unfairly following a harm event.[13] Workers become alienated from their organizations and disengaged from their jobs.

Intangible as it is, emotional harm is quite significant for workers and the organization. Crissy B., a young nurse in southern California, was known as a hardworking, energetic, and extremely thoughtful worker. One day, while caring for a heroin addict in a methadone treatment program, she unintentionally

stuck herself with a used needle. Crissy was now at risk for con-
tracting disease from the exposure, and so was her infant son,
whom she was breastfeeding at the time. Crissy had to wean him
immediately, earlier than she had planned, so that he wouldn't be
at risk—an extremely traumatic decision. Crissy's follow-up surveillance lasted three years, at which time she was told she hadn't
contracted anything and was cleared from further testing and
worry. As Crissy relates, this experience caused her great emotional and psychological harm, impacting her ability to care for
her son and causing her to doubt her job and career.[14]

Healthcare *Can* Do Better

Confronted with stories like Crissy's, a safety skeptic might throw
up his or her hands and conclude that our organizations can't do
much—a relatively high level of workplace injury is inevitable in
healthcare. After all, this skeptic might reason, treating patients is
extremely complex, and the environment is "high pressure," making accidents inherently more likely. Healthcare workers encounter
any number of hazards in the course of treating patients, including radiation, airborne bacteria, and dirty needles. Meanwhile,
a "perfect storm" exists in care environments for violence against
providers. One of us, Emily Halu, summarized it in a blog posting: "Caretakers see patients and their families at their most
difficult moments, working in buildings that are unsecured and
open to the public. Some patients might have physical symptoms
that make them more prone to sudden movements, aggressive
actions, or lack of awareness of their current physical limitations.
Add to that the pain, fear, and uncertainty that often accompany
healthcare visits or procedures; any number of personal, emotional, logistical, and financial problems that patients and families
may face; and an open-door policy that allows the public to enter

freely, and it's not surprising that emotions can run high and routine interactions can escalate into dangerous confrontations."[15]

Given all this risk, it seems, we might just have to accept worker injury rates that are higher than we'd like. In fact, healthcare workers often treat injuries as routine and unavoidable—just "part of the job." It's no accident so many nurses are injured attempting to "catch" a patient from falling, and that so many technicians are injured in the process of chasing after a behavioral patient attempting to leave the facility. Many clinicians and nonclinicians alike will willingly put themselves at risk in order to help a patient and fulfill their professional duty to "do no harm."

As laudable as such dedication is, high levels of worker harm in healthcare aren't inevitable, nor are they acceptable. Other industries are also just as complex and high risk, and they've managed to reduce harm to their workers to a far greater extent. As Figures 10.1 and 10.2 show, the construction and manufacturing industries both saw much steeper declines in safety issues between 2000 and 2016 than healthcare did, ultimately making these industries safer for workers than healthcare. In these industries, workers face serious and frequent risks of falling from great heights, receiving electric shocks, and losing body parts to heavy, fast-moving machinery.

So, why hasn't healthcare made more impressive safety gains to date? The progress made so far has largely reflected implementation of safer practices for handling patients. The nursing profession was founded on the notion that nurses had to be fit enough to physically move, reposition, and transport patients (a 1906 nursing textbook advised nurses that: "It is very good for strength to know that someone needs you to be strong").[16,] But as experience has shown, it's not safe for nurses to physically move patients. Sprains and strains are the leading cause of DART cases, as well as of workers' compensation claims (count and dollars).[17] As of 2018, 11 states passed legislation governing

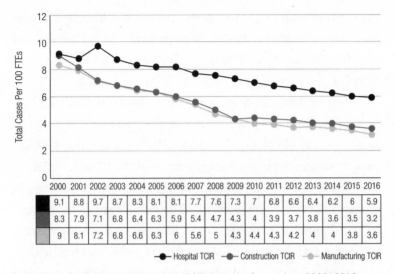

Figure 10.1 Total Case Incidence Rate (TCIR) Industry Comparison 2000–2016

Source: "Injuries, Illnesses, and Fatalities," Bureau of Labor Statistics ("Table 1—Incidence rates—detailed industry level—2016 [XLSX]") accessed July 17, 2019, https://www.bls.gov/iif/oshsum.htm.

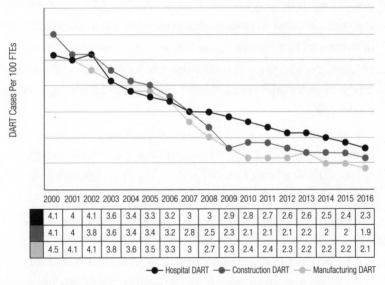

Figure 10.2 Days Away, Restricted or Transferred (DART) Industry Comparison 2000–2016

Source: "Injuries, Illnesses, and Fatalities," Bureau of Labor Statistics ("Table 1—Incidence rates—detailed industry level—2016 [XLSX]") accessed July 17, 2019, https://www.bls.gov/iif/oshsum.htm.

the safety of workers around safety patient handling and mobility.[18] These laws mandate that employers adopt a prevention plan for musculoskeletal injuries related to patient handling and mobility.

Most healthcare organizations have implemented tactics to prevent workplace injuries, including the purchase of lift equipment, annual skills fairs, and detailed policies about safety equipment usage. However, organizations have failed to reinforce the need to use this equipment among the workforce, or to build accountability among workers for using safety equipment and protecting themselves via other means. More generally, as we've seen, organizations have floundered on safety by either making lackluster efforts or focusing narrowly on tactics without trying to build a broader safety or high reliability culture. Many organizations have a hard time gaining momentum around worker safety because corporate leadership doesn't take direct responsibility, instead leaving it to the occupational health department to "own" safety. While departments like human resources, workers' compensation, security, and even local police often contribute to worker safety, they rarely come together as a cohesive team to address the issues our workforce faces.

By contrast, industries like construction, manufacturing, and nuclear power have made a range of improvements—structural, technological, environmental, and most important, cultural—in order to boost worker safety. In the nuclear power industry, for instance, measures taken by organizations have included:

- Sharing injury data transparently, not just among leaders (especially senior leaders) but also frontline team members.
- Establishing clear expectations, with governance documents that outline corporate directives, policies, safety procedures, and standards.

- Providing significant safety training to all workers. Key safety-related training sessions include dynamic learning activities (identifying risks in the environment through walk-arounds and direct observation), as well as simulators to ensure safe work practices including fall simulators that train staff how to walk in icy conditions.
- Strengthening their injury-reporting processes and policies, requiring mandatory reporting of all injuries.
- Training operational leaders and expecting them to investigate all worker injuries, involving workers in the process.
- Requiring operational leaders to become actively involved in managing injuries once they occur, helping team members navigate their injury and accommodate potential work restrictions.
- Undergoing broad cultural transformations whereby everyone owns safety. Walk into any nuclear power plant, and you'll find that all workers, including leaders, carry safety handbooks so that they can refer quickly to standards and expectations that apply in specific situations.

Among these measures, cultural transformation has been the most consequential. To be sure, culture didn't change overnight in other high reliability industries. Training people to put safety first has been—and remains—a challenge. Yet nuclear power plants understand the value of safety-first decision-making, even in the face of serious financial pressures. Stories abound of plants that made significant short-term financial sacrifices to ensure that workers were as safe as humanly possible.

At one US plant, contract electricians were rebuilding a massive pump during a planned refueling outage—a period of time when the plant is offline and not producing electricity. Nuclear power plants typically conduct refueling outages every 18 or 24 months depending on the type of reactor, using the time to perform major work on vital equipment such as turbine generators, pumps, motors, piping, and so on. This work is an enormous effort, generally requiring more than 1,000 supplementary contract workers to perform. As a result, supervisors do everything they can to get teams to work efficiently, restore reactivity, and produce power. Lost revenue typically exceeds more than $1 million per day of outage.

At this plant, workers had disconnected electrical power prior to beginning work on the pump, but they hadn't performed an essential OSHA safety requirement—called lockout/tagout—as required. The lockout/tagout standard for controlling hazardous energy requires workers to disconnect and physically lock specific power sources, affixing a tag to indicate that workers can't use equipment attached to the power source until the tag is removed. Workers in this case believed the team didn't need to perform the lockout/tagout procedure, since they were in the vicinity of the power source that had been switched off and could control access to it. However, other workers in the area required power from the source and reconnected it, resulting in a safety event that could have proven fatal.

Thankfully, work immediately stopped, safety was restored, and nobody was injured. Still, a human performance review board was convened, as is standard practice after failure events. Leaders don't convene these boards so as to blame individuals, but to understand the human error that occurred as well as systemic factors that might have contributed. In this case, the board interviewed workers and learned that they didn't fully understand the fundamentals of the lockout/tagout process. Interviewing leaders responsible for the program, the board determined that they, too, didn't fully understand the standard's essential elements. The utility temporarily discontinued all work requiring lockout/tagout until they could formally interview all personnel trained on this requirement. Three days later, once employees had received the necessary training, work resumed. The safety-related stoppage added three extra days to the outage, representing $3 million in lost revenue. The plant sustained the loss, valuing safety over production. As leaders know, the consistent performance of lockout/tagouts could one day save workers' lives.[19]

Sadly, healthcare organizations simply haven't made this kind of commitment to worker safety. In boardroom meetings, healthcare leaders are more apt to discuss the financial impacts of decisions rather than their safety consequences. Healthcare boards certainly want to make a positive impact, but they have traditionally seen their goal as overseeing the organization's financial status, not its safety status.[20] As a result, healthcare leaders usually don't put safety first in their decision-making. This must change. Healthcare organizations must understand the value of adopting patient and worker safety as a top priority so that they can ultimately reach zero harm for patients and workers. And they must adopt a comprehensive workforce safety management system (WSMS) to guide their efforts at reducing working injuries.

Building Workforce Safety Management Systems in Healthcare

Moving an organization closer to zero injuries for workers requires that leaders deploy the right mix of tactics and cultural changes. St. Vincent's Medical Center in Bridgeport, Connecticut, significantly reduced worker injury by taking a system-wide approach, "that [addressed] policies and procedures; resource allocation (staffing, equipment, capital expenditures); organizational structures (committees, departments, lines of authority); risk and hazard assessment; adverse-event surveillance systems and analysis; and performance measure data collection, analysis, and use."[21]

The WSMS (Table 10.1) helps to outline the right mix of elements, offering a "recipe" that any healthcare organization can use.

Table 10.1   Workforce Safety Management System (WSMS)

Commitment	Culture	Safety Promotion	Local Learning
Safety Statement	Reliability Skills	Hazard-Specific Prevention	Injury Measures (OSHA's TCIR & DART)
Zero Harm Goal	Relationship Skills (collegiality)	Visual Media (artifacts; posters)	Safety Action Teams: 1. Slips, trips, falls 2. Repetitive motion 3. Workforce violence 4. Blood/body fluid exposure (including needlesticks) 5. Safe patient handling
Just Culture	HRO Leader Skills	Safety Coaches	Cause Analysis (RCA & ACA)
			Common Cause Analysis (aggregate)
			Local Learning Systems

The elements of this WSMS reflect our knowledge and experience from high reliability industries, and they align with accepted thinking on the establishment of strong safety organizations.[22] In order to transform behavior and organizational expectations, we must start with an organizational commitment and policies that align with that commitment. From there, workers and leaders must understand the behaviors and actions that support the commitment. An alignment of actions with values and beliefs creates the safety culture, so leaders must constantly articulate safety-related messages and continue to improve safety through local learning.

As a review of Table 10.1 reveals, workforce safety management systems are similar to the patient safety management systems described in Chapter 2. This is hardly a coincidence: by laying the foundation for patient safety, a high reliability organization can achieve consistent performance in other areas, too. As one safety expert has noted, "health care organizations that are most successful in reducing worker safety and health risks focus their primary efforts on developing an organization-wide culture of safety that addresses all safety issues,"[23] regardless of individuals' status or role.

In implementing a WSMS, organizations should first perform a broad analysis of present conditions. Leaders can choose an element of the WSMS under one of the four categories (commitment, culture, safety promotion, or local learning) and ask themselves: "What, if anything, are we doing in this area?" If you're already strong in certain elements (your organization has a strong safety statement in place, for instance, or it has well-developed programs in place to build relationships skills), then adjust your overall strategic plan for workforce safety accordingly, ensuring that you continue to strengthen and reinforce those elements. If you have yet to deploy any initiatives in a given element, or have only partially deployed them, make strategic and tactical plans for implementation. Let's take a closer look at a WSMS's key elements.

Safety Statement and Zero Injury Goal

In 1987, Paul O'Neill became the CEO of aluminum manufacturer Alcoa. From his first day on the job, O'Neill shared his vision of making Alcoa America's safest company. It was only by focusing on the workers and their safety, he declared, that Alcoa could truly succeed. This hypothesis was confirmed: over time, safer workers led to more engaged workers, which resulted in a more profitable organization. During O'Neill's 13-year tenure as CEO, Alcoa's DART plummeted from 1.86 to 0.2 (and by 2012 had declined even further to 0.125). Alcoa saw its profits rise to its highest levels ever just a year after O'Neill took over.[24]

O'Neill serves as a model that many healthcare leaders should emulate. Like all strong patient safety management systems, a WSMS begins with commitment from senior leadership as well as the rest of the organization. Just as healthcare organizations began to realize during the early 2000s that responsibility for patient safety didn't just lie with the patient safety department, so the industry is now realizing that responsibility for workforce safety doesn't just lie with the occupational nurse. While the occupational nurse might play an essential role as a subject matter expert and influencer, organizational leadership and the workforce itself "owns" workplace safety. Senior and operational leaders must commit to zero worker harm, and they must communicate this commitment by promulgating a clear and visible safety statement on behalf of the organization, and by establishing and sustaining a just culture (Chapter 7). Leadership's commitment to reducing workforce injury is fundamental to the journey to zero worker harm.

Leaders also have to convey their commitment to frontline staff by leaving their offices, getting out into the departments, identifying hazards, reinforcing safe work practices, and explaining why zero harm for patients and team members matters. A leader who strolls down the hall and notices a facility's engineer standing on a ladder with no spotter has to stop, ask the engineer to come down, explain how important it is that the engineer work safely, explain why spotters are necessary, and confirm that the engineer doesn't resume work until he obtains a spotter. Likewise, a leader who visits an inpatient unit and sees a nursing aide pushing a Hoyer lift down the hall to safely lift a patient should smile and flash a thumbs-up in order to reinforce this safety behavior.

Sisters of Charity of Leavenworth Health Systems (SCL Health), a 10-hospital health system in Colorado, Kansas, and

Montana, exemplifies organizational and particularly executive level commitment to zero harm for patients and team members. SCL Health committed publicly to safety, adopting the following as a core value: "SAFETY—We deliver care that seeks to eliminate all harm for patients and Associates."[25] Executives not only firmly believed in this commitment—they consistently communicated it. At SCL Health, you'll see leaders at daily huddles discussing the importance of workforce safety. You'll see executives rounding and influencing workers to work safely. You'll see managers and executives visiting hospital departments to meet with workers who experience injuries, exploring how and why the injury occurred. As a result of such sustained effort, SCL Health saw a 58 percent reduction in TCIR between 2014 and 2016, in addition to significant reduction in patient harm.

Just Culture

The just culture outlined in Chapter 7 "balances the need to learn from our mistakes with the need to take disciplinary action."[26] Without a fair and just culture, workers won't feel safe to report hazards or injuries for fear of repercussion. If an organization mishandles worker injuries, say by firing a worker for becoming injured due to a perception that "he should have known better" or "he wasn't following the policy," workers will never come to understand their own vulnerabilities and the measures they should take to protect themselves. Punishing workers for actions that the system helped induce creates a downward spiral, ultimately resulting in an unsafe work environment.

Reliability, Relationship, and Leadership Skills

Beyond a just culture, culture generally influences behaviors that lead to workforce injuries. The safety culture that supports workforce safety is similar to that which supports patient safety. Both start with the organization's CEO, and both ultimately become everyone's responsibility. Healthcare leaders' shared values and beliefs have always centered on keeping our workers safe, but we have to assure that our *actions* align.

In particular, leaders must champion the specific skills or behaviors that foster safety. Universal skills, including the reliability skills reviewed in Chapter 5, are just that: universal, applicable among everyone in the organization and at all times. Similarly, teams must practice the relationship skills from Chapter 6 at all times in order to sustain a high reliability organization. The same universal and team-based skills deployed to care for patients reliably also ensure that workers are consistently safe. In fact, you can use these same skills—like the STAR method, Validate and Verify, and phonetic and numeric clarification—throughout your life to stay safe, whether you're communicating with a phone operator, remembering to pick up cupcakes for a birthday party, or waiting at an airport gate for your plane to board.

Likewise, the same HRO leadership skills described in Chapter 4 apply. Leaders need to perform three kinds of behaviors well. First, as we've seen, they must live the core value of zero workforce injury, speaking up about workforce hazards and injuries, telling stories about workforce hazards and injuries, thanking workers for adhering to safety protocols, and putting workforce safety first in decision-making. Second, they must help the organization avoid safety events by holding daily safety huddles. Finally, leaders should build accountability by performing rounds and providing five-to-one feedback to workers on safety issues. During rounding, leaders might emphasize the use and management of safe lifting equipment and personal protective equipment (PPE), how to recognize hazards while caring for patients, and how to calm aggressive patients, to name a few.

Worker Safety Items to Report On During the Daily Safety Huddle

- The number of days since the last worker injury
- Details of worker onboarding slated to take place
- Patients with notable behavioral issues that have been admitted
- Areas or shifts with overworked clinical staff (for instance, staff working back-to-back shifts)
- Any unfamiliar or extremely stressful situations that might occur over the next 24 hours
- Any trends in workforce injuries
- Any anticipated issues related to workforce compliance with mandatory requirements
- Any recent trends in communicable diseases reported within the community that require precautions on workers' part

Hazard-Specific Prevention

After your organization has committed to workforce safety and a culture of safety, the workforce safety management system calls our attention to other, seemingly more tactical elements. Hazard-specific prevention, for instance, entails identifying, assessing, and mitigating workplace risks that contribute to worker injuries. Some risks are physical in nature (for example, worker slips, trips, falls, and needlesticks), and thus properly mitigated through engineering controls. As OSHA has explained: "Engineering controls redesign the work process to eliminate hazards entirely or reduce them to a minimum. Strategies include eliminating the process, process step, equipment, or substance that is creating the hazard; substituting a less hazardous process, equipment, or substance;

or using physical barriers (such as enclosures or guards) or ventilation to reduce employee exposure to the hazard."[27] To identify physical hazards in the healthcare environment, leaders must perform regular rounds and solicit frontline input through focus groups.

Aside from physical risks, resource or job function–related issues like understaffing or a cumbersome structure for responding to urgent situations can present hazards. Healthcare organizations can mitigate these risks by implementing strict administrative controls. OSHA has advised, "Administrative and work practice controls are appropriate when engineering controls are not feasible or not completely protective. These controls affect the way staff perform jobs or tasks."[28] Examples of administrative controls include supportive policies on staffing, code alerts for aggressive or violent patients or visitors, tracking patients with known histories of violence, and maintaining an injury reporting system that is easily accessible and not overly time-consuming. OSHA's 2016 guidelines describe specific engineering and administrative controls for preventing workplace violence.[29]

Beth Israel Deaconess Medical Center (BIDMC) in Boston, Massachusetts, is making great strides in using administrative controls to reduce violence against caregivers. The hospital has created an electronic medical-record alert for patients with previous violent behavior in order to warn workers. BIDMC also created a standard protocol for responding to patients who attempt to leave the facility, giving workers more clarity about when they might safely intervene. When someone threatens a BIDMC worker, a threat assessment team responds, reassuring the worker that the organization is supporting them, so that the threat won't materialize. Through these types of administrative controls, in addition to engineered controls, hospitals can reduce workplace violence to zero.[30]

Visual Media and Safety Coaches

Given the many hazards healthcare workers face, organizations must make training a key element of all hazard prevention. Such training covers techniques for deescalating emotionally intense situations, self-defense methods, safe patient handling programs, and practices for using safety equipment (needle safety, panic button usage, personal protective equipment application, and so on). For maximum impact, this training should include simulations and hands-on experiences. As an effective and engaging way to train safe patient handling, Northwell Health, a 23-hospital and 665-outpatient facility health system in New York[31] held the "safe patient handling Olympics." During this event, hospital workers gathered in teams and had to properly lift and transport one another and were judged by leaders and peers. Teams even won medals![32]

Organizations should remember that healthcare workers require frequent reminders in order for messages to "stick." As we've seen, an effective way to keep workers focused on workforce safety messages is to use artifacts like posters, screen savers, promotional materials, signage, and so on. Healthcare organizations that focus on reducing workforce injuries display the message loud and clear so that workers are reminded every day how important their safety is. One particularly effective campaign, from Wy'East Medical Corporation, used the portrait of a nurse dressed in the uniform of different "dangerous" jobs (construction, football, firefighting) to highlight nursing's true dangers. In one poster, a young female nurse appears with an older, hefty male slung over her shoulders. The caption states, "Sure. You can lift him. But should you?" The image occasions a chuckle while reminding workers not to manually lift patients, and to use safe patient handling equipment instead.

Organizations can also reinforce workforce safety messages by deploying peer-to-peer coaching. They should appoint safety coaches to interact daily with their peers about safety issues, choosing individuals who are influential, well-respected, and strong role models. Coaches should provide positive feedback to team members when they perform actions and behaviors that promote workforce safety, and negative or corrective feedback about risky or unsafe behaviors. To prepare safety coaches, the organization should train them on how to recognize and address safe and unsafe conditions and to provide feedback in the moment. The mere presence of safety coaches makes the organization's commitment to workforce safety palpable for workers. Safety coaches provide peer-to-peer accountability for *both* workforce and patient safety, helping colleagues hone their universal skills as well as all other patient and workforce safety related behaviors and actions.

Injury Measures and Other Local Learning Elements

Earlier in the chapter, we introduced OSHA's key workforce safety metrics, Total Case Incidence Rate (TCIR) and Days Away, Restricted and Transferred (DART). To reduce workforce injuries, organizations must collect these metrics consistently, not merely once a quarter, and share them with leaders and frontline personnel. At all times, a hospital CEO should know how many workers in his or her organization have suffered harm. Injury metrics raise awareness and allow organizations to measure progress toward zero injuries. Share metrics daily at safety huddles (sitewide and department-specific) and display them on a visual board. Many organizations find it helpful to use "days since last worker injury" as a daily metric instead of using TCIR or DART. That's fine, so long as they also use TCIR and DART on organizational scorecards.

As essential as injury measures are, they don't allow us to spot specific opportunities for improving operations. Organizations can do so by forming safety action teams around the following five injury categories: slips, trips, and falls; repetitive motion injuries; workforce violence; blood and bodily fluid exposures; and patient handling. Members of these teams should address the policies, processes, protocols, and technological and environmental issues that contribute to the specific injury. In 2016, San Diego–based Sharp HealthCare established action teams in these five areas as part of a structural model for improving safety. Meeting on a monthly basis, these teams ensured that all policies were up to date, assessed equipment that could prevent injuries, and created promotional materials related to their specific injury type. In addition to these teams, Sharp hired two injury prevention specialists to guide leaders in performing cause analysis on injury events as they happened. At Sharp, after an injury occurs, a specialist interviews the worker involved, seeking to understand the scenario and contributing factors. Then, in conjunction with the operational managers, the specialist develops an action plan to remediate the contributing factors. Accountability for following through with the action plan lies with the operational leader. The collaboration between the five action teams, injury specialists, and operational leaders allowed Sharp HealthCare to reduce workforce injuries by 16 percent in just the first year.[33]

While healthcare has created systems for performing root cause analyses after patient injuries, organizations rarely have systems like the one at Sharp for worker injuries. Ideally, the process of assessing an injury's causes should become part of the larger workforce injury and illness management (WIM) process. When an injury first occurs, the operational leader should be notified and then respond to the worker, who should receive immediate medical attention as necessary. The injury should be logged into the formal reporting structure (usually electronic reporting), and the operational leader should investigate causes of injury, developing an action plan to remediate these causes. The operational leader should then help the injured worker manage the injury and make plans for him or her to return to work. Also, the operational leader should update senior leadership on the injured worker's status as well as that of the action plan, sharing the lessons the organization has learned as a result of the safety incident. Although injury specialists can participate in this process, as at Sharp HealthCare, operational leaders must take the lead, interviewing the worker and managing the care and organizational response.

The individual cause analyses that occur during the WIM process help the organization learn and improve to prevent harm, but another activity—the common cause analysis discussed in Chapter 9—provides a deeper understanding of the causes of worker injuries. By reviewing the contributing factors of all workforce injuries on an annual or semiannual basis, organizations can understand the "common causes" of worker injuries and devote resources to addressing them. Organizations can perform a common cause analysis by "coding" each event, applying a standard coding dictionary for the type of injury, type of behavior that led to the injury, the injured person's profession, and the process or activity the person was engaging in at the time of injury, among other key elements. Such coding can help reveal untapped opportunities for improving worker safety.

Learning opportunities also present themselves every day— *before* they cause an injury. Identifying issues proactively means engaging frontline workers in local learning—having them identify and resolve issues that might pose a risk. Organizations can deploy the concepts of local learning and cause solving described in Chapter 9 to their workforce safety improvement efforts. The learning board offers a particularly helpful visual representation of workforce related issues. Whenever a team member presents a concern related to worker safety, supervisors should add it to the learning board next to any other patient- or process-related issues.

Progress *Can* Happen

The injuries and illnesses that healthcare workers face are alarming, and for moral as well as economic reasons, leaders and their organizations must act. Let's save nurses like Gail Sandidge, who died trying to save others during a stabbing. Let's prevent injuries like the one that ended Tove Schuster's career as a floor nurse. Leading-edge organizations are already doing so. WellStar, a five-hospital healthcare system in the southeastern United States, experienced a whopping 84 percent decline in worker injuries and a 50 percent decline in workers' compensation costs thanks to its high reliability organizing in patient and worker safety. This safer environment also led to improved worker satisfaction at WellStar.[34]

Primary Children's Hospital, a freestanding facility in Salt Lake City, Utah, within Intermountain Healthcare, began its zero harm journey in 2012. In 2015, with their reliability chassis built and their safety culture established, administration recognized the need to also focus on worker safety. Since then, Primary Children's environment of care committee has sought to better define worker injuries based on types, trends, volume, frequencies, and locations. The safety coordinator performed a job hazards analysis in each hospital department, focusing on the top three departments with the greatest worker injury rate over a three-year period. The team shared its data with leadership in each department, encouraging directors to develop the staff's awareness by demonstrating how to use zero harm error prevention techniques (universal skills) and posting injuries on huddle boards. Thanks to these efforts, the hospital has become significantly safer for staff, reducing DART injuries by 39 percent between 2015 and 2017.[35] Administrators are still working on safety, continuing the organization's path to zero harm.

Your organization can take this journey, too. Make worker safety a more prominent role in your organization than it has had to date. Enable employees to go home after each shift in the same physical state in which they arrived. Improving workforce safety won't take an outrageous or inexplicable effort at your organization, but it will require focus. By applying the fundamental HRO principles of the safety management system, in addition to the specific workforce-related elements described in this chapter, you can protect your workers, enabling your hospitals and other care facilities to become healing, nurturing places—for *everyone*.

IN SUM

- Although organizations have improved worker safety in recent years, far too many workers are still getting hurt.
- The financial costs of injuries to workers are enormous—both for the workers themselves and for our organizations.
- High levels of worker harm in healthcare aren't inevitable, nor are they acceptable. Other industries are also just as complex and high risk as healthcare, and they have managed to reduce harm to their workers to a far greater extent.
- Moving an organization closer to zero injuries for workers requires that leaders deploy the right mix of tactics and cultural changes as part of their worker safety management systems.

High Reliability Organizing and the Patient Experience

Deirdre Mylod, PhD, Stacie Pallotta, MPH,
and Thomas H. Lee, MD, MSc

> *If high reliability organizing can boost safety, healthcare organizations can also deploy it to improve how they serve patients. This chapter explores the early application of reliability principles to the care experience. It then goes on to explore how reliability might serve organizations as the pathway to better patient experience.*

CAN HIGH RELIABILITY organizing help organizations enhance the experiences they provide patients? The answer is a resounding yes. In moving toward zero harm, our client organizations have seen significant gains in other areas by expanding the notion of harm to include suboptimal patient experiences. These gains are so profound that we believe all organizations should reconceptualize efforts to improve patient experience, defining them as attempts to reduce patient suffering by implementing high reliability principles.

In using the term *suffering*, we seek to acknowledge how patients actually experience healthcare. The very word *patient* originates in the Latin root *patior*, meaning "one who suffers" or "I am suffering."[1] Indeed, most patients don't expect to leave hospitals and other healthcare settings delighted by their care, as they might feel delighted by the service they receive at a fine restaurant. Rather, they simply wish to minimize suffering. They seek the peace of mind that comes with knowing that they are receiving the best possible care, given their medical circumstances. They expect caregivers to address their clinical needs and either return them to health or slow its decline. They expect that the care they receive will be safe and free from any harm that could worsen their condition. Finally, they hope to encounter a compassionate environment that supports their healing, rather than one in which inefficiencies or lack of coordination compound suffering.

Redefining improved patient experience as the reduction of suffering is also important because it keeps patients' goals foremost in employees' minds. Organizations often ask staff to improve patient experience without educating them fully about the goal. Employees perceive service-related tactics as tangential to clinical care—something "extra" they must do for the sake of pushing a number higher. Not surprising, their enthusiasm wanes. But when organizations adopt reduced patient suffering as the goal, employees appreciate the link between these improvement tactics and the provision of safe, high-quality, and compassionate care. Improving patient experience becomes an inspiring strategy, and caregivers reconnect with their original purpose in entering the medical profession: to heal patients. Perceiving that changes how they work can improve care and reduce suffering, caregivers commit themselves more fully to that effort. Improvement initiatives become far more successful and sustainable.

The Birth and Evolution of Patient Experience

To better understand the connection between reliability principles and the reduction of suffering, let's review the history of patient experience as a concept in healthcare. Organizational efforts to measure experience first arose out of 1980s-era patient advocacy work that emphasized understanding, categorizing, and responding to patient complaints. Healthcare leaders assumed that organizations delivered high-quality care, even if they found it difficult to measure quality in a rigorous way, and they interpreted patient complaints as aberrations in this otherwise "good" care. To address those aberrations, they deployed so-called "service recovery techniques," formulas employees could use to respond to patient complaints. These formulas included rote apologies, communication of concerns to managers, and freebies like parking passes or small gift cards that employees could use to "make it right."

The healthcare industry began to understand patient experience more deeply thanks to Dr. Irwin Press, a medical anthropologist at the University of Notre Dame. Studying interactions between premodern, shamanistic cultures and Western medicine, Press hypothesized that US healthcare would feel foreign and confusing to people who blame their illnesses on spirits or curses rather than, say, germ theory. Press's work eventually led him to conclude that Western healthcare felt foreign and confusing to nearly *everyone*, not simply people with premodern worldviews. If you think about it, entering healthcare as a patient does feel like entering a foreign country. People experience an erosion in their personal autonomy, authority, and sense of identity. They must navigate a host of new social mores while attempting to puzzle their way through confusing healthcare processes and procedures. Dr. Press noted that while other elements of quality measurement were gaining traction, healthcare organizations were failing almost entirely to listen to and empathize with the patient's plight.

Building on this research, Press partnered with Dr. Rodney Ganey, a Notre Dame sociologist and methods expert, to develop the first validated instruments aimed at measuring patients' view of the care they received. These tools asked patients to evaluate each major step or process within their healthcare journey as well as the key clinician or staff groups with whom they interacted. Healthcare organizations began to voluntarily use these tools to measure their performance and improvement efforts, and to compare themselves with other organizations that valued patient perspectives. The tools reported on issues that patients had identified as being critical, such as information, compassion, privacy, choice, and care coordination. Perceiving the tools as measuring "satisfaction," organizations focused on improvement so as to reduce risk (early research had linked overall composite patient satisfaction to reduced malpractice risk).[2] This approach largely conformed to existing efforts to address complaints via service recovery.

As national benchmarking became available, competition among organizations arose, prompting them to embrace proactive improvement initiatives. Still, leaders continued to perceive care as predominantly high quality and already meeting patient needs in a compassionate way. Patients were "lucky" to access care, many leaders felt, regardless of how patients might have perceived the healthcare experience. Still, the practice of comparing patient satisfaction scores against external benchmarks led leaders to regard patients for the first time as consumers. To mark themselves as unique in the minds of patients, organizations began offering amenities that would hopefully meet patients' increasing expectations, such as on-demand room service, nicely renovated birthing suites, and concierge-like services.

Organizations tended to conceive of such improvement efforts as "service initiatives" focused on providing "delightful" patient experiences. As organizations innovated their service, however, they often overlooked serious defects in care and processes. An organization might teach its staff to apologize for long waits and offer a gift card to patients who complained, but it would do little if anything to remedy underlying problems with patient flow and throughput. Clinical personnel didn't oppose efforts to improve service per se, but they viewed them as unrelated to their definition of quality. As a result, they didn't commit fully to improving patient satisfaction.

The healthcare industry began to link patient evaluations with the overall quality of care thanks to the publication of *To Err Is Human*,[3] the Institute of Medicine's landmark 2000 report on patient safety, as well as its 2003 successor *Crossing the Quality Chasm*.[4] These reports clarified that US healthcare organizations didn't consistently deliver high-quality care—in fact, care was often unsafe and unresponsive to patients' needs. The reports recommended that healthcare respond better to patient needs; that leaders design the system to accommodate individuals' preferences while also meeting needs common to all patients; that organizations better support patient autonomy and shared decision-making; and that clinicians learn to communicate better with patients. Collectively, such recommendations contained the first inklings of "patient experience" as a foundational concept, broadening the definition of high-quality care to include incorporating the patient's viewpoint.

Over the next decade, the federal government explicitly advanced the notion of patient experience, incorporating patient experience measures into quality initiatives. Researchers with the Centers for Medicare and Medicaid Services (CMS) and the Agency for Healthcare Research and Quality (AHRQ) developed standardized, public domain instruments to measure patient perceptions of care, including the Hospital Consumer Assessment of Healthcare Providers and Systems (HCAHPS), a survey instrument administered to randomly selected patients after their discharge from the hospital. With HCAHPS in place, organizations could now use patient experience measures as part of both public reporting and payment initiatives. The National Quality Forum approved the HCAHPS survey in 2005, while CMS adopted it in 2006. Two years later, voluntary public reporting of HCAHPS results began. Federal payment models incented organizations to use this instrument by linking hospitals' annual payment update to participation in public reporting initiatives ("pay for reporting") via the Reporting Hospital Quality Data for Acute Payment Update (RHQDAPU) program.

By 2007, nearly 93 percent of US hospitals were collecting and reporting patient experience scores.[5] The 2010 Affordable Care Act went on to tie a small portion of Medicare reimbursement to a hospital's level of performance and improvement on HCAHPS measures, effectively shifting the healthcare model to "pay for performance" or value-based purchasing. Other healthcare settings have seen a similar pattern: experts have created and validated CAHPS-style surveys for these settings and made them available for voluntary use, with subsequent payment initiatives eventually creating financial incentives for reporting and improvement.

Prior to these regulatory efforts (i.e., during the 1980s and 1990s), Press Ganey had developed and validated survey instruments for more than 20 patient populations, including emergency room patients, those who had visited a doctor's office, those who had received laboratory or x-ray testing, those who had received a home care visit, and those who had undergone chemotherapy or radiation for a cancer diagnosis. With each instrument, Press Ganey incorporated input from both patients and caregivers, taking into account the care process and the nature of patient interactions with caregivers. Likewise, the CAHPS program has expanded beyond HCAHPS for hospital stays to include instruments designed to measure home health (HH-CAHPS), emergency care (ED-CAHPS), in-center hemodialysis (ICH-CAHPS), and office visits with a provider (Clinician & Group CAHPS or CG-CAHPS).

If the IOM reports had helped dispel the notion that care was already "good enough," value-based purchasing and public transparency boosted the industry's motivation to close that gap. Transparency—the availability of publicly reported data for individual patient experience measures—also changed the scope of work, since organizations could no longer limit their thinking to the global summary perceptions that patients reported (e.g., their overall rating of the facility, or their stated "likelihood to recommend" the facility). Now that members of the public, competing hospital system executives, and hospital board members could all access hospital data on specific issues such as how well doctors listened, how well nurses explained care, or whether patients felt adequately prepared for their discharge, leaders felt compelled to remedy subpar performance in those areas. And as these leaders increasingly realized, improvement efforts had to move beyond enhancing the hospital's "brand" to include thoughtful process redesigns supported by feedback, change management, and sustainability.

During the late 2000s, organizations began speaking of "patient experience" instead of "patient satisfaction"—a subtle but important shift. As the new language suggested, healthcare organizations had to do more than meet or exceed consumers' expectations (in other words, "satisfying" them). Rather, they had to meet their needs reliably, efficiently, and safely. If the concept of "patient satisfaction" conveyed individuals' emotional assessment of the care they received, "patient experience" returned healthcare to the purpose of its earliest measurement tools: to address *everything* that directly or indirectly affects patients across the continuum of care, including the relief of their suffering, physical discomfort, and anxiety. Gauging "patient experience" required using tools to measure a wide range of experiential elements, including nuances of the communication patients experienced, the ease of healthcare processes and transitions, the extent to which organizations taught patients how to care for themselves at home, clinical processes, and the compassion that staff showed for patients. Healthcare hasn't fully internalized this more complex view of measurement; regulatory programs today still categorize patient experience as measures reflecting only patient perception of care. As we see it, that needs to change. The definition of experience should encompass all outcomes related to safety, quality, and compassion.

The Sources of Patient Suffering

As healthcare organizations sought to identify and reduce suffering in order to improve, they confronted a basic question: What were the primary sources of patient suffering?[6] To the extent the medical profession has addressed suffering, it has tended to emphasize the inherent or unavoidable suffering associated with diseases themselves. Illness creates both physical and psychological suffering for patients in the form of symptoms, limitations, and disability as well as fears about one's future outcome and prognosis. Inherent suffering also arises thanks to the treatment of illness. Even "perfect" medical care can cause discomfort and side effects, and patients can feel uncertain and anxious about the care process. In addition to inherent suffering, patients can also suffer thanks to dysfunctions in the way organizations and individuals deliver care. Such "avoidable" suffering can occur when patients wait longer than they need to, receive conflicting information that erodes trust, are treated insensitively or without compassion, or in extreme cases, when they experience harm.

Understanding and categorizing the types of patient suffering leads us to varying approaches for addressing it. To mitigate and reduce inherent suffering, organizations must focus on delivering high-quality care in a compassionate and supportive way. To mitigate or reduce avoidable suffering, organizations must focus on *prevention*. It turns out that the mantra "First, do no harm" means much more than simply preventing falls or infections—it means avoiding the creation of suffering of all kinds.

If that sounds daunting, the history of high reliability science offers reason for hope. In industries like nuclear power and aviation as well as healthcare, organizations have dramatically reduced instances of harm because courageous individuals decided that their industry could do so, and indeed, because they defined harm in the first place as preventable. At one time, organizations perceived hospital acquired pneumonia as an unfortunate but unavoidable consequence of care. Only when a few inspired, forward-thinking leaders took a stand and reframed hospital acquired conditions as "preventable" did protocols emerge to track and successfully prevent them. Today, we need such leaders to look anew at the industry, calling out the many elements of dysfunction that we currently expect patients to endure, including delays in obtaining appointments, excessive waits in the emergency room for inpatient beds, poor communication among staff, and inefficient or broken processes. It is both radical and necessary to assert that individuals and organizations have not the slightest right to worsen suffering for patients.

In recent years, formerly discrete definitions of quality have begun to converge, irrespective of whether we're considering an operational process, a clinical protocol, a safe practice, or the delivery of compassionate care. For example, organizations have long looked to nurse hourly rounding as a process for improving how they organize and deliver care, but more recently they've helped staff members see that such rounding improves efficiency and patient safety as well. Removing artificial barriers between formerly siloed areas or functions, organizations have sought to build engaged workforces (clinicians *and* nonclinicians) that focus on delivering care properly and reliably. Research demonstrates

that patient experience indeed contributes to quality in general—
that better experiences and better outcomes go hand in hand. For
example, HCAHPS star ratings correlate inversely with risk-
adjusted mortality and readmission rates,[7] and hospitals with
higher performance on HCAHPS see lower surgical mortality,
failure to rescue, and minor complication rates.[8]

Some organizations still struggle to incorporate patient experience into reliability processes, subscribing to the misguided
notion that good patient experience is simply about being "nice."
In reality, patients experience care as a result of manifold processes and behaviors, not simply "niceness." Organizations can
shape, refine, and optimize their processes and behaviors to render the care they provide more reliable and safer. In due course,
they improve patient experience. Patients might not know whether
staff followed the perfect clinical protocol or if they implemented
all required safety checks, but they are the only ones who can discern if the organization has met their own needs.

The same principles and strategies used to prevent harm and
ensure safety also help organizations identify the root causes
of poor patient experience, address those causes, and promote
compassionate behaviors to meet patient needs. For example,
organizations can apply common cause analysis (Chapter 9),
which they might already use to improve safety, to identify common and root causes of service failures. By taking the opportunity
to identify these causes, organizations position themselves well to
offer preventative solutions rather than struggling to address problems once they occur.

Organizations have sometimes shrunk from using reliability
processes to improve patient experience because of the perceived
"slipperiness" of patient experiences. Patients experience care
through their own subjective lenses. Younger patients may expect
greater transparency of information and speedier communication
with providers, while older and sicker patients may need more

time to process health education information. How can an organization address these different needs using standardized protocols? It's true that patients might harbor different expectations, biases, and preferences, but evidence-based practices such as nurse hourly rounding, bedside shift report, and the use of whiteboards in patient rooms can enhance care across the board. Organizations can also segment patient experience data into cohorts with similar needs, deploying reliability science techniques to address root causes within any cohort. In this way, organizations can both standardize *and* customize care delivery, achieving optimal outcomes.

Although care has become more complex in recent years, performance on patient experience outcome measures continues to rise, creating an ever more competitive market. The level of performance that would have placed an organization in the fiftieth percentile in 2013 would have only placed it in the thirtieth percentile in 2017.[9] In this context, organizations must take concerted and strategic action—disparate or disconnected initiatives will only overburden staff and undermine success. Organizations that incorporate patient experience efforts within, rather than in addition to, high reliability practices will see the best results.

Measuring Patient Experience

How might organizations best track their progress in avoiding suffering? Patient experience measures don't explicitly ask patients to report suffering directly, nor do they capture the extent to which individuals or the organization reduced or increased it during the care process. What these measures do reveal is how well the care met the patient's needs, with unmet needs assumed to yield suffering.

Press Ganey designed each of its validated patient experience tools through a rigorous process that included focus groups with patients and quality improvement leaders, multiple field tests of survey versions, and formal psychometric analysis.[10] During focus groups, moderators prompted patients to describe the patient journey from beginning to end, to describe the staff members they encountered, and to identify the attributes of care that enhanced or detracted from the care process. Psychometric analysis then honed the sets of questions to the most critical core measures that would capture the patient experience within the setting in question. Although designed specifically for each patient population, these tools incorporated needs that patients consistently expressed across care settings (see Figure 11.1).

Figure 11.1 Patient Needs Measured Through Patient Experience Surveys

We can organize the task of responding to patient needs by grouping these needs according to the actions required to address them most completely. One framework, the Compassionate Connected Care™ model,[11] does precisely this, identifying four key elements of optimal care: clinical excellence, operational efficiency, caring behaviors, and culture. If patient surveys reveal deficits in pain management or patient education, organizations should review clinical care. If patients find wait times or the physical environment subpar, organizations should address the relevant operational processes. When patients report a lack of empathy, courtesy, or responsiveness in their care, organizations must modify the caring behaviors staff use during patient interactions. And when patients perceive a lack of teamwork or feel uncertain about their own safety, the organization might need to work on its broader culture.

Although categories of needs might remain consistent across patient populations, specific survey questions will vary according to the care context. Within the inpatient setting, measures related to the need for information include items such as how well the nurses and doctors kept patients informed, and whether they did so in a manner patients could understand. Within the emergency department setting, organizations might inquire whether patients received information about their treatment and next steps. In the physician office setting, organizations might ask whether clinicians did enough to describe and explain the patient's status, condition, and treatment needs as well as follow-up care. These nuances match the care setting while addressing the more universal need that patients have to learn about and understand the care process.

With these preliminaries in place, we might wonder how well the industry is doing in meeting patient needs. Figure 11.2 depicts industry-wide performance on HCAHPS measures based on national data from more than 200,000 patients who received care in January 2018. For brevity's sake, we used only the HCAHPS inpatient measure set, omitting key drivers of patient experience from the Press Ganey tools such as teamwork, shared decision-making, privacy, emotional support, and service recovery. Organizations publicly report HCAHPS measures using a "top-box score"—the proportion of respondents that chose the best possible response option for that measure ("Always" on a "Never to Always" scale,

"Definitely Yes" on a "Definitely No to Definitely Yes" scale, or overall ratings of 9 or 10 on a 1-to-10 scale). Organizations can use this short set of HCAHPS measures tied to public reporting and value-based purchasing to begin to identify general patterns in care and opportunities for improvement.

Compassionate Connected Care	Patient Need	HCAHPS Item	0% 10% 20% 30% 40% 50% 60% 70% 80% 90% 100%
Global	Recommend Rating	Recommend hospital	26%
		Rate hospital 0-10	27%
Clinical Excellence	Pain	How often staff talk about pain	34%
		Staff talk about pain treatment	37%
	Discharge Prep	Staff talk about help when you left	15%
		Info re symptoms/prob to look for	10%
		Understood purpose of taking meds	39%
		Good understanding managing health	47%
Caring Behaviors	Courtesy	How often staff talk about pain	13%
		Staff talk about pain treatment	13%
	Inform	Nurses expl in way you understand	24%
		Doctors expl in way you understand	24%
		Tell you what new medicine was for	23%
		Staff describe medicine side effect	52%
	Personalize	Nurses listen carefully to you	23%
		Doctors listen carefully to you	21%
	Responsiveness	Call button help soon as wanted it	38%
		Help toileting soon as you wanted it	33%
	Choice	Hospital staff took pref into account	53%
Operational Efficiency	Environment	Cleanliness of hospital environment	29%
		Quietness of hospital environment	44%

Figure 11.2 National Proportion of Non–Top Box Scores for HCAHPS Measures, Based on 208,826 Inpatient Survey Responses in January 2018

As these data show, optimal care—care that earns a "top box" or best possible response (right side of bar)—is common but hardly universal. The frequency of top box responses varies by measure and category of need. Considering the same data in a less positive light, non–top box responses (left side of bar) indicating suboptimal care occur across all measures and account for between 10 and 53 percent of responses. Clearly, ample room for improvement exists.

Patients bestow the fewest non–top box responses—indicating more reliable care that meets patient needs—for issues such as the courtesy and respect shown by doctors and nurses (13 percent), elements of discharge preparation including whether staff provided information about symptoms to monitor (10 percent), and the effectiveness of staff efforts to describe the help patients might need following discharge (15 percent). Patients rated nurses and doctors less favorably for their willingness to listen (23 percent and 22 percent, respectively) and their ability to explain care to patients understandably (24 percent). All other measures have non–top box responses of at least 25 percent, indicating that one in every four patients reported a suboptimal experience with these elements of care.

Perhaps most troubling from a safety perspective are the non–top box responses for call button assistance (38 percent) and cleanliness (29 percent), given that call button response is correlated with the incidence of patient falls,[12] and patient evaluation of cleanliness with infection rates.[13] The sum total of these experiences is sobering: A full 27 percent of patients wouldn't give their hospital care an overall top box rating of 9 or 10, and 26 percent of patients wouldn't "definitely recommend" their hospital to a friend or family member who needed care.

When reporting patient experience at the board and executive team level, organizations tend to use global evaluations—such as overall hospital ratings from 0 to 10 and patients' self-reported "likelihood to recommend" the hospital—as key performance indicators (KPIs). Each of these measures provides a summary rating from the patient's point of view. The hospital's overall rating on a 0-to-10 scale is included within value-based purchasing (VBP) calculations, the process by which CMS calculates hospitals' reimbursements; it represents patients' aggregate view of care within that inpatient stay. The likelihood of recommendation measure reflects the organization's larger brand as well as an element of patient trust. If patients would recommend care with a provider or location, they would trust that care not only for themselves, but for a friend or family member. Trust implies that patients believe they would emerge from care in the healthiest possible state given their own personal set of circumstances.

Tracking trust as a so-called "outcome measure" allows providers to prioritize elements of care that most influence patients' experiences and, ultimately, their peace of mind. Survey data from more than 1 million patients indicates that perceptions of teamwork most determine whether a patient would completely trust the care they received at a hospital. Specifically, patient responses to the Press Ganey survey item "Staff worked together to care for you" most differentiates top box and non–top box responses on the HCAHPS "likelihood to recommend" measure. Of patients indicating an optimal or top box experience of staff working together, 88.9 percent would definitely recommend the hospital. Among patients indicating anything less than optimal teamwork from staff, just 41.7 percent would "definitely recommend" the hospital.[14] Just as safety and high reliability organizing hinges on teamwork, so patients' ability to trust the quality of their care hinges on their *experience* of teamwork.

Reliability of Process and the Patient Experience

By articulating key issues that affect how much patients trust the care they receive, and by identifying areas where care practices fall short, we can generate actions and behaviors to better meet all patients' needs. To change behaviors throughout an organization, we can apply the same techniques of high reliability and safety science described elsewhere in this book. Of course, patient experience efforts will also benefit if leaders select evidence-based practices, designing them to confer cascading benefits on multiple elements of care. It would be inefficient for organizations to rely on separate actions to optimize each area of patient experience, such as teamwork, information, respect, empathy, pain control, response to the call button, and so on. Rather, organizations should use integrated practices such as nurse hourly rounding as a framework for optimized care. With that structure in place, organizations can design the rounding process to support multiple facets of care within the same practice.

We now have evidence showing how important effective hourly rounding can be for a wide array of patient experiences. As early research found, the practice of nurse hourly rounding reduced call button use and incidence of falls[15] and led to improved patient evaluations of care.[16] A 2013 study by researchers at The Institute for Innovation revealed the influence of rounding practices on each of the questions patients respond to for the HCAHPS survey. Researchers collected data at 108 organizations, including patient responses to HCAHPS questions as well as to the question, "Did a staff member visit you hourly during your stay (Yes/No)"? Figure 11.3 shows the differences in top box scores on HCAHPS measures for patients who said yes versus those who said no to the

Compassionate Connected Care	Patient Need	HCAHPS Item	Difference in Top Box	
Global	Recommend Rating	Recommend the hospital	29.1%	
		Rate hospital 0-10	26.7%	
Clinical Excellence	Pain	Pain controlled	22.5%	
	Discharge Prep	Staff talk about help when you left	10.4%	
		Info re symptoms/prob to look for	16.1%	
		Understood purpose of taking meds	20.6%	
		Good understanding managing health	23.8%	
Caring Behaviors	Courtesy	Nurses treat with courtesy/respect	21.0%	
		Doctors treat with courtesy/respect	13.3%	
	Inform	Nurses expl in way you understand	24.5%	
		Doctors expl in way you understand	17.8%	
		Tell you what new medicine was for	22.9%	
		Staff describe medicine side effect	29.2%	
	Personalize	Nurses listen carefully to you	27.0%	
		Doctors listen carefully to you	17.5%	
	Responsiveness	Call button help soon as wanted it	27.5%	
		Help toileting soon as you wanted it	25.5%	
	Empathy	Staff do everything to help pain	24.9%	
	Choice	Hosp staff took pref into account	24.1%	

Figure 11.3 Impact of Hourly Rounding on Clinical Excellence and Caring Behaviors, Based on 120,164 Inpatient Survey Responses from 108 Organizations

rounding question. Top box scores are higher for every measure when rounding takes place, with top box improvements of 10 percent to nearly 30 percent depending on the measure.

Given how beneficial nurse hourly rounding is, one might expect to find this practice everywhere. However, the same study indicated that hourly rounding had occurred for only 76.7 percent of patients. Here again, organizations have ample room for improvement. Applying high reliability principles and practices, they can make nurse hourly rounding universal and ensure the practice's sustainability over time.

One organization that did, the Adventist Health System ("Adventist"), embarked on a multiyear journey that incorporated hourly rounding into standard work.[17] Adventist provided staff with standardized training and role-playing, and established goals for adopting hourly rounding. Adapting their ongoing surveys, Adventist queried patients as to whether hourly rounding had occurred, and used the data to convince staff of the rounding process's impact on patient experience evaluations. Adventist aimed for 90 percent or more of patients to report an experience of hourly rounding during their inpatient care. Adventist also implemented nurse leader rounding and executive rounding on staff, bolstering the focus on patients by incorporating patient stories as part of each summit and meeting. The work delivered impressive results. Between 2009 and 2016, Adventist's top box scores for "Overall Rating of the Hospital" spiked from 57 percent of patient responses to over 80 percent.

Properly conceived and implemented, standardized approaches such as hourly rounding can enhance multiple dimensions of quality at once. A healthcare system in New York reviewed its current rounding practices, seeking to improve both efficiency and patient outcomes. The organization identified more than 10 active programs or styles of rounding with varying goals. In place of these rounding practices, the organization adopted a single, standardized rounding program based on the principles of high reliability, training all employees in the program. Although work is ongoing, efficiency and patient outcomes have so far both improved.

Organizations can identify root causes for service failures—whether complaints, concerns, or grievances—just as healthcare providers do for safety. Similarly, organizations can commit to eradicating so-called "never events," agreeing that there are some experiences that patients just shouldn't have to encounter, just as there are some safety lapses that organizations should never allow to happen. Service failures might not put lives in jeopardy, but they do diminish the trust patients and their families place in their care, and organizations should take a commensurately hard line. Of course, that begs the question: What tactics can organizations deploy to improve the patient experience in addition to quality and safety?

As Table 11.1 suggests, a range of standardized and evidence-based tactics are available, varying according to the care environment. Medical practices might deploy communications and guidelines to ensure that patients understand their diagnoses and self-care instructions, and team-related skills to prevent patients from worrying that their care might fall through the cracks during handoffs. In emergency departments, waiting area rounds, huddles, and communication tools might help reduce patients' uncertainty about their care and next steps. And in inpatient settings, organizations can turn to hourly rounding, nurse manager rounding, whiteboards, and bedside shift reports, among others, to reduce problems like delays in the provision of medication or in nurses' responses to call lights, or to clarify communication between team members and patients. All of these techniques are well known to help organizations get closer to zero harm, with documented improvements in patient experience.

Table 11.1 Examples of Specific Tactics
for Improving the Care Experience

Inpatient	Emergency Department	Medical Practice
Hourly patient rounding	Waiting area rounds	Communication guidelines (sit, don't interrupt)
Nurse manager rounding	Behaviors and language to demonstrate concern and urgency	Technology guidelines (introduce the EHR as a tool for the discussion—positioning of screen for co-viewing)
Whiteboards	Huddles	Promotion of team—actual process and verbal acknowledgment
Post-discharge phone calls	Service recovery program	
No-pass zones		
Bedside shift report		
Patient and family advisory boards		

More Collaboration, Less Suffering

As we've argued, we need less suffering in healthcare, and that means more organizations that incorporate patient experience under the umbrella of high reliability. When organizations apply high reliability principles to their standard tactics and behavioral training, they can dramatically improve the care experience, just as they can safety. As a first step, organizations should become more transparent about goals, initiatives, activities, and performance across these domains, so that leaders might begin to identify areas of redundancy and areas of alignment. From there, adopt a set of shared metrics and goals—either a balanced scorecard that includes key measures of safety, quality, experience of care, and engagement, or a set of organizational goals that can only be achieved by a cross-functional team. Such metrics drive collaborative performance while also reinforcing a set of shared principles.

Organizations like Pennsylvania Hospital can attest to the power of using high reliability to improve patient experience.[18] In 2012, prompted by struggling patient experience scores, the hospital's nursing leadership began to study why their patient evaluations of care didn't match nurses' perception of their own work. Though the organization used a relationship-based care model and engagement surveys indicated that nurses felt they were providing individualized and inclusive care, patient evaluations for nurse communication consistently fell below the fiftieth percentile. Rather than seeking a "quick fix" solution, chief nursing officer Mary Del Guidice asked nurses themselves to redesign standard work to support the relationship-based care model, as well as patient experience and so-called "nursing sensitive metrics" (e.g., falls, pressure ulcers, and central line–associated bloodstream infections).

During an all-nurse retreat, participants defined goals for their nursing practice with the acronym HEART— "Holistic," "Evidence-based practice and research," "Advocates," "Resourcefulness," and "Teamwork." HEART allowed the nurses to tie all performance improvement efforts back to their own professional goals and desired outcomes. Building on established literature, they chose to implement bedside shift reports, conceiving of it as a bundle that would address safety, nurse communication, and patient goal setting. They used a Plan-Do-Study-Act (PDSA) model to deploy the bundle across units, training teams on the bundle in small groups.

One component of the bundle in particular enabled nurses to connect with each patient's personal circumstances. Within the shift-report protocol, nurses asked patients to share their biggest concern that day, which nurses then documented on the patient whiteboard. This step conveyed to patients that the team cared about them as individuals, and it gave nurses a moment to pause and acknowledge the patient's needs. Throughout the rest of the day, the note on the whiteboard would prompt staff to remain cognizant of the patient's concern and to address it. As a result of the culture-building and bundle process, nurse communication scores have jumped to above the eightieth percentile rank nationally—while nurse engagement has risen as well.

At so many healthcare organizations, the persistence of silos hinders efforts to improve patient experience and sustain the gains over time. Leaders might share a commitment to reducing suffering, but their efforts get bogged down in competition and inefficiency. By adopting a common vision and shared metrics, organizations can follow institutions like Pennsylvania Hospital and foster shared responsibility for safety and the reduction of suffering. Instead of an obscure initiative led by courageous leaders acting alone, patient experience can become what it should be: a strategic priority, one that galvanizes the entire organization to improve.

IN SUM

- Organizations should reconceptualize efforts to improve patient experience, defining them as attempts to reduce patient suffering.
- When organizations apply high reliability principles to their standard tactics and behavioral training, they can dramatically improve the care experience, just as they can safety.
- To improve patient experience, organizations must address two classes of suffering: inherent and avoidable. Efforts should focus on mitigating or reducing the impact of inherent suffering, and on preventing avoidable suffering.
- A range of evidence-based tactics can help organizations reduce suffering. These tactics vary according to the care environment.

Epilogue: High Reliability Organizing's Full Promise

James Merlino, MD

THIS BOOK HAS presented a number of stories in which individual caregivers inadvertently compromised safety. Although each episode was traumatic for the patients involved, it was also unforgettable and perhaps even haunting for the caregivers as well. I know how these caregivers feel. In 1997, while working as a surgical intern, I received a call to manage a patient who was experiencing severe delirium, a common occurrence in elderly surgical patients. I wrote an order for a strong sedative, 10 mg of the benzodiazepine Ativan. The medication controlled the patient's delirium, but the dose I prescribed was significantly higher than required, and the patient remained unconscious for over 48 hours. Most doctors didn't disclose details of medical treatments back then. In this case, the care team told the family that the patient had a bad "reaction" to the medication, but that everything would be all right. For the entire time this patient was sedated, I was terrified, believing that she was going to die (which she almost did). Afterward, I was petrified that something I had done had almost killed a patient. When I apologized to my attending surgeon, he simply said: "Don't do it again."

It wasn't until some two decades later that I truly grasped the significance of what had happened. This episode was not a near miss—it was a direct hit, a serious safety event. A cascade of cultural failures had allowed me, a naive and inexperienced new intern, to nearly kill a patient. I made a mistake, to be sure, but nursing didn't question the order, pharmacy didn't stop it, my attending didn't use it as a learning opportunity for me or anyone else, and the organization didn't perform a root cause analysis to understand what had taken place and prevent it from ever happening again. Because nobody had died, no discussion ensued—it was just another seemingly "harmless" error swept under the rug. My organization had also failed to recognize the emotional toll the episode took on me, the caregiver. I came away paranoid about injuring future patients (which was probably a good thing), but my confidence as a doctor was also deeply shaken.

We in healthcare must intensify our work to improve safety by applying high reliability principles. It's the only way we'll reduce the risk we pose every day both to patients and to employees. This book has provided a cohesive, tested methodology for doing that, one derived from work with over 1,200 hospitals. But while safety must remain our primary focus, Chapter 11 made the case that high reliability and safety science might allow us to achieve another, related objective simultaneous: dramatically improving the experiences patients have in healthcare settings.

So, is that what high reliability organizing is all about—safety and superior patient experiences? Actually, no. What if we could apply the same high reliability principles we've used to improve safety to transform the organization generally? What if we could improve not only safety and patient experience, but quality as well, simply by committing ourselves to the journey of zero harm and staying the course?

The Oxford dictionary defines transformation as "a marked change in form, nature, or appearance."[1] Transforming the way we in healthcare do business might seem easy, but alas, it's not. One difficulty organizations have is that they only focus on one of the three big "verticals"—safety, quality, and patient experience— at a time, shifting between them as time passes. This year, the organization might work on safety. A year or two later, it might make a big quality push. A year or two after that, attention might shift to patient experience. Meanwhile, gains in previous areas of focus are lost or fail to advance further. Prior to 2017, Mount Sinai Health System in New York City pursued safety and quality on the one hand and patient experience on the other as strategically distinct verticals. The result: the organization made progress in safety but lagged in patient experience. If healthcare organizations could combine these verticals into a single, common strategy built around high reliability organizing, as Mount Sinai subsequently did, we would not only improve safety, quality, and experience all at once, but impact our workforce engagement and efficiency as well.

Healthcare providers intuitively understand the three key dimensions of care, but we tend not to recognize their interconnectedness and embed that recognition in a holistic, transformational change strategy. Let's pause for a moment to consider why that is—and how we might better connect the dots among safety, quality, and patient experience. It comes down to the way organizations are led and structured. Board stewardship is critical to transformation, and organizations seeking a comprehensive strategy need board members who are better informed about critical issues such as safety and quality. Our industry must train board members, giving them a basic understanding of healthcare safety, quality, and experience, as well as key metrics for each area (balanced scorecards will help board members keep up with their organization's progress in transforming itself). A well-developed and informed board will more likely adopt a cohesive strategy to improve all aspects of care at once, direct leadership and frontline caregivers to prioritize this strategy, and sustain the strategy through any significant leadership transitions.

In addition to stronger, more focused boards, organizations need executive leadership to drive the totality of patient care. In several of this book's chapters, authors explored leaders' pivotal role, suggesting how to mobilize them to build highly reliable organizations. Multidimensional, enterprise-level transformation requires that very same leadership focus. If executives aren't talking about transformation and managing it as part of their own KPIs, their subordinates won't perceive it as a genuine organizational priority. As Gerry Lupacchino, chief experience officer at Hartford Healthcare, states: "Moving the broader leadership team from passive participation to active accountability increases engagement and commitment throughout the organization."[2]

Executive leadership poses a special challenge in larger systems, since here executive leadership teams of discrete business units are expected to align their separate KPIs with common enterprise goals. Failure to "cascade" the work of transformation beyond the enterprise leadership team will hamper the entire system's ability to execute. San Francisco–based Dignity Health solved this problem by adopting an enterprise strategy for patient experience. Every leader in the organization understands that improving the experience is a critical issue. Their KPIs are aligned to the work, and every business unit has access to the enterprise playbook.

As authors in this book have further pointed out, organizations tend to execute in fragmented ways, dividing operations into key areas or "silos" that include safety, quality, patient experience, clinical delivery, human resources, and nursing (Figure 12.1). Not only do these silos compete for limited resources; they also have their own leaders managing safety, quality, and experience. An organization might have a system-wide leader for quality, a nursing leader for quality, and a physician leader of the medical staff also responsible for quality. Each of these leaders might pursue quality goals for his or her respective area, failing to integrate his or her work with the overall enterprise strategy. These individual leaders might or might not report to a single individual, such as a chief medical officer, which further impedes the coordination of efforts. Even when a unified reporting structure does exist, strategy and tactics might still align poorly.

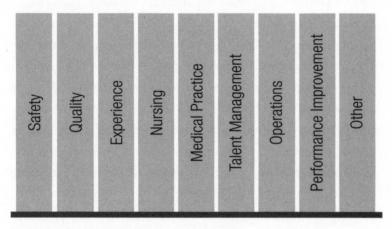

Figure 12.1 Typical Silos in Healthcare Organizations

Healthcare organizations need to streamline how they think and function. Holistically improving patient care requires tight coordination and integration of a number of critical operational areas such as hospital operations, performance improvement, medical staff management, and human resources management. Better performance and alignment of these verticals also requires the use of common goals to ensure that all leaders are serving the enterprise's strategy.

Intermountain Healthcare overcame silos by appointing a single leader, Shannon Phillips, MD, as its chief experience officer, moving all operational verticals for safety, quality, and experience under her leadership. Now a single enterprise strategy drives this varied work, and her close partnerships with human resources and performance improvement allows her to ensure that all of the resources necessary for success are aligned. Functional leaders for safety, quality, and experience still exist, but they work under the direction of a single, overall leader.

Strong silos also exist within individual initiatives and tactics. Many hospitals will embrace a single solution supporting a strategy in one department, and an aligned solution supporting a different strategy in another department. Likewise, many organizations deploy separate surveys for culture of safety, employee engagement, and NDNQI data, with different departments executing on the respective surveys. Today, we at Press Ganey might deploy a single, unified survey to capture data from all three domains. Such a survey would yield an integrated view of performance, reducing duplicate work and survey fatigue. The left side of Figure 12.2 points to additional examples of inefficient organizing, all of which prevent healthcare organizations from extracting as much value as they otherwise might.

Some organizations have modified their internal structures to become more strategic (the middle portion of Figure 12.2), aligning complementary solutions and positioning the resulting verticals to partner with other strategic areas. New York–based Northwell Health System has tightly bound together strong verticals for patient experience and workforce strategy. Chief experience officer Sven Gierlinger exercises either complete influence or operational control over every aspect of patient experience, from measurement of the experience to the type and quality of food patients receive. His close partnership with leaders from human resources ensures that culture development strategies align with the organization's patient experience strategy. Healthcare organizations should take lessons from this playbook, and they should go even further, as Intermountain Healthcare has done, and adopt an "enterprise transformation approach" (right side of Figure 12.2) that connects all the critical elements driving effective and efficient patient care in a single, unified entity.

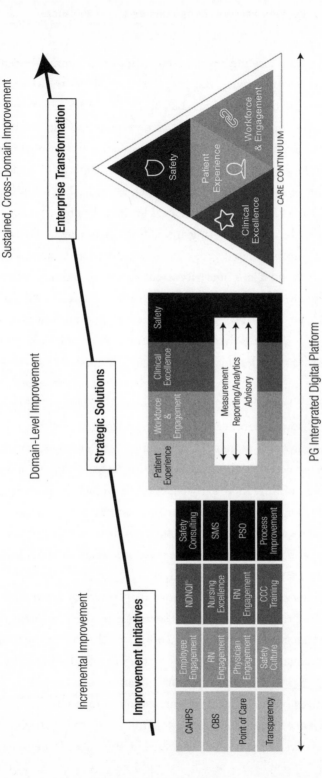

Figure 12.2 Advancing Healthcare Toward Transformational Solutions

At many organizations, competing or disruptive initiatives can ultimately prevent holistic, enterprise-level transformation from taking hold. Individual business units decide to take matters into their own hands and ignore an enterprise approach—an especially vexing problem for large health systems that have attempted to standardize and integrate work streams. Enterprise leadership may adopt a specific best practice such as leadership rounding for the entire organization, but a local leader may not appreciate the value of the work, favoring instead his or her own tactics. The result: uncoordinated programming across the system, diluted resources, and a lack of clarity about strategies and their effects.

Lyn Ketelsen, RN, chief experience officer at Nashville, Tennessee–based HCA, overcame competing initiatives by creating a series of playbooks for specific best practices. Senior leadership provides the enterprise mandate, and she provides the training materials and coaching to ensure success at the local business unit. Local leaders may supplement their work on improving care delivery with other best practices, so long as they also execute on the enterprise strategy. One specific tactic embraced by HCA, also referenced by other chapters in this book, is purposeful nurse hourly rounding. In an early paper on the topic, Ketelsen demonstrated that rounding improves not just patient experience, but also safety, quality, and nurse efficiency as well.[3] This high-value tactic has become an "enterprise nonnegotiable" for HCA because of its impact on overall care delivery.

Many initiatives might prove disruptive for organizations, including the upgrading of an electronic medical record system, the completion of a merger or acquisition, the implementation of a cost reduction program, or the pursuit of a leadership reorganization. Some will argue that organizations must complete such initiatives before tackling initiatives to improve safety or patient experience. But delaying important initiatives—particularly those related to safety—isn't the right approach. If we integrate our strategies carefully, we can treat disruptive changes as hidden opportunities to strengthen or accelerate our work on improving our overall delivery of care.

Paul Sternberg, MD, chief medical officer and chief patient experience officer at Vanderbilt University Medical Center, knew that installing a new electronic medical record system (EMR) would unsettle the organization, potentially reversing progress the health system had made on patient experience. "We went into this eyes-wide-open," Dr. Sternberg said, "and prepared our leaders and our organization."[4] Vanderbilt had studied data from other organizations to better understand the potential impacts, and it used this information to educate people on what would happen and how to respond. While the organization did see experience metrics decline during the EMR's implementation, the advance preparation allowed the organization to recover quickly. The patient experience strategy continued apace.

To help leaders better integrate and accelerate the work of safety, quality, experience, engagement, and efficiency, we at Press Ganey sought out common operational and strategic principles that hold valid throughout and across healthcare organizations. Based on our experience working with a large number of organizations, and summarizing a number of ideas advanced throughout this book relative to improving safety, we believe that organizations can best transform themselves by adopting the following six core organizing principles—three strategic, three operationally focused (Figure 12.3). Let's examine each of these in turn.

Principle 1: Commit to a Goal of Zero Harm

As we've seen, safety and our commitment to zero harm must be our top strategic priority. If you take away nothing from this book, recognize that America's healthcare system still has a safety problem, despite previous work performed over the past two decades.

Strategic	Operational
Commit to a goal of Zero Harm	Drive change using data and transparency
Put patients at the center of the planning, delivery, and assessment of care	Transform culture and leadership
Recognize, define, and understand the critical interdependency of safety, quality and patient-centricity as the three primary elements of the patient experience	Focus on accountability and execution

Figure 12.3 Six Principles for Transforming Healthcare Organizations

The statistics and case studies presented in this book leave little doubt: healthcare harms patients; we must do more to stop it, and we *can* do more. We will only reduce serious safety events, and improve organizations' overall performance, if every US healthcare system commits to zero harm as a sacred core value.

Principle 2: Become Patient-Centric

If we adopt zero harm as our top strategic priority and patient safety as a core value, then patient centricity must be our "true north." As we saw in Chapter 11, most patients don't verbalize their needs explicitly, beyond their desire for caregivers to address a specific medical condition they might have. They don't tell us, "I don't want to wait longer than two weeks for this procedure," or "I want my physician to spend 15 minutes explaining my condition and treatments to me." We in healthcare are left to assume we know what matters to patients, and sometimes our assumptions prove inaccurate.

An organization's first step to operationalize patient centricity is thus measuring the voice of every patient to ensure that we capture what matters most to them. Many leaders believe that patient centricity starts with making people happy or trying to satisfy them. As we saw in Chapter 11, patient and family needs are much more complicated than that. Take, for instance, our perceptions of patients' desires regarding the emergency department. Healthcare leaders typically believe that long wait times impact patient experience most significantly in these settings. Actually, other factors—like providing empathy and keeping patients informed—matter more. A study of 1.2 million emergency department patient encounters found a baseline ED CAHPS likelihood to recommend rating of 65 percent.[5] If emergency department personnel improved their concern for patient worries (i.e., demonstrated empathy), likelihood to recommend ratings improved to 91.4 percent. If staff kept patients better informed, the rating improved further—to 97.0 percent. Across all wait times up to eight hours, providing empathy and keeping people informed consistently yielded a 98 percent likelihood to recommend rating.

Beyond understanding patients' needs, implementing a patient-centric strategy requires us to prioritize elements that we know are important but that patients might not always understand, including safety and quality. One survey queried 2,884 patients about their perceptions of feeling safe in a hospital. Only 5.2 percent stated that they would feel very unsafe, while 74.9 percent of patients said that they would feel pretty or very safe, without any evidence to support that belief.[6] Patients don't specifically ask for safe, high-quality care—they *assume* that they will receive it, and we as leaders must deliver it.

Operationalizing patient centricity requires that leaders consistently behave in ways that put patients at the center of planning and care delivery. At all times, we must remain mindful of how our operations impact our focus on the patient. For every new initiative and project, we should ask the question: "How will this work impact patients?" Patient centricity must become a *mindset* that all leaders adopt, spread, and execute upon. Of course, doing so benefits the organization as well as patients.

Taking patients as our "north star" is the right thing to do, but it is also a solid business decision. Every business must remain fixated on its customers if it is to survive. We in healthcare don't usually like to conceive of patients as customers, but we must. The Internet and social media are empowering patients, allowing them access to more data than ever before. Armed with these data, patients are flexing their muscles, choosing organizations that promise to treat them better. As recent data demonstrate, 90 percent of patients will research a provider online even after receiving a referral from their primary care physician or specialist.[7]

Some leaders believe that organizations should prioritize patient centricity above all else, since orienting ourselves around the patient will by definition entail committing to safe care and zero harm. Patient centricity does require us to commit holistically to doing right by patients, including providing safe care. But given harm's overwhelming prevalence in healthcare, we feel that we must recognize harm prevention as the single greatest priority for intervention. First address the harm, then the patient experience.

Principle 3: Recognize the Interdependency of Safety, Quality, and Patient Centricity

One study analyzing all publicly reported safety, quality, and experience data from upwards of 4,100 hospitals reporting to the Centers for Medicaid and Medicare found that organizations in the top quartile of HCAHPS performance had seen significantly improved safety and quality performance, including decreased hospital acquired infections, reduced readmission rates, and shortened length of stays. Drawing on Press Ganey's employee engagement database, currently the industry's largest with over 1.6 million caregivers and 80,000 physicians, we find that results like these connect with engagement. When organizations rank in the top quartile of engagement, all three sets of metrics—publicly reported safety, quality, and experience—are also significantly improved. Clearly, patient experience isn't about happiness or satisfaction—it relates to safety and quality. Consequently, strategies and tactics that improve safety, quality, and experience individually will likely enhance all three. We should thus expand our definition of patient experience to include safety and quality as well.

These first three principles in our framework for organizational transformation relate to strategy. Turning to operations, we believe that the following three additional principles also allow organizations to strengthen safety, quality, and experience all at once:

Principle 4: Adopt Good Data and Analytics

As we saw in Chapter 8, an effective strategy for safety entails measuring and monitoring the *right* metrics, so that we don't bury ourselves in enormous amounts of meaningless data. A similar point holds true for enterprise transformation. We can't improve without monitoring performance. Our challenge is to develop an effective data strategy that supports our work, recognizing that collecting data in of itself isn't a strategy. In building a transformation initiative, select a few metrics for each key operational area and create a balanced scorecard that you apply consistently from the boardroom to frontline managers. A balanced scorecard contains the key metrics that the board and senior leadership have determined are important to steer the organization well. Every leader should have access to data and bear responsibility for monitoring performance in his or her respective area.

Cross-domain analytics provides a strong, data-centered basis for connecting safety, quality, experience, and engagement, allowing us to track how all of these critical metrics interact to drive overall organizational performance. For instance, our ability to overlay engagement metrics for particular business units on other operational metrics like safety and experience helps provide a more holistic view of a unit's performance, so that we can better focus our improvement efforts and resources.

Principle 5: Transform Culture and Leadership

As we've seen throughout this book, the path to zero harm hinges on culture and leadership—an insight that applies to the other key verticals of quality and patient experience. Shaping culture seems slippery and difficult, but it need not be. Previous chapters have presented tools and techniques that organizations can use to build strong safety cultures. Leaders can deploy these same tools and techniques to influence quality and patient experience. More broadly, organizations must render their human resources (HR) management more strategic. HR has long performed foundational tasks like hiring, paying, and promoting staff on a transactional basis. Strategic talent management serves these functions while also recognizing how employees impact the organization's culture and strategic agenda. As HR becomes more strategic, culture becomes a top priority. HR not only endeavors to hire the right people, but to provide comprehensive onboarding around mission, values, vision, and other critical employee competencies, such as their responsibility for safety, quality, and experience. Strategic HR also invests heavily in workforce training and development, enabling the organization to link employee behavior to the mission, vision, and values.

At a more advanced level, strategic HR management provides personal and professional development opportunities for leaders and managers, training them how to execute for safety and experience, how to pursue goals using metrics and a balanced scorecard, how to better manage the workforce's performance, and how to empower employees using emotional intelligence and communications skills. Healthcare organizations must also take care to measure the health of their cultures through engagement surveys, which afford a window into employee perceptions. Segmenting engagement data by leadership units, we can guide strategies to better reward and develop our managers and leaders.

By focusing on culture and leadership, we can better care for our people and attack workforce cancers like bullying and burnout, which put patients as well as employees at risk. Bullying and burnout have reached epic proportions in the United States, and wherever they spread, they degrade an organization's culture. We must measure burnout and address the factors that cause it and invest in programming to build workforce resiliency. More organizations are investing in employee wellness programs and hiring chief wellness officers to bear responsibility for employee experience. Bullying or incivility is nearly impossible to measure and harder to stop, since it tends to happen covertly. Leaders at all levels must understand it, talk about it, and ensure that the organization follows up on all reported incidents. A strategic approach to culture also improves workforce safety by layering in the concepts described in Chapter 10.

Finally, strategic talent management must include organizational succession planning. If a new chief quality officer assumes overall responsibility for safety, quality, and experience, bringing new ideas and perspectives to bear, momentum behind current programming might flag. At every level, change and departmental turnover can lead to staff burnout, uncertainty, and loss of productivity as senior leaders struggle to understand any new strategic direction and worry about their future employment status. Board involvement in succession planning can help here. During significant leadership transitions, the organization should clarify the board's enduring commitment to culture and talent investment, as well as to the three elements of safety, quality, and experience. Any profound deviation from this strategic orientation should be clearly off limits.

In addition to cultural development, building a robust and comprehensive performance improvement capability will ensure that leaders driving an integrated strategy have the tools and improvement system they need in order to succeed. Many healthcare systems have adopted improvement frameworks like Lean or Six Sigma, and others have enhanced that capability by assembling dedicated teams of individuals with expertise in these areas to serve the enterprise. These teams tackle important initiatives like reducing readmissions, decreasing falls or medication errors, and other tactical problems the enterprise may face.

Although performance improvement capability can impact many initiatives on an individual basis, true transformation happens when we teach managers and leaders, as well as frontline staff, the basic improvement skill sets required to address all problems across the continuum of care. Charles Hagood, PhD, one of our consulting partners and an expert in Lean process improvement systems, calls this "creating an army of problem solvers." As he notes, "Although it's essential to have internal consulting and coaching expertise in your organization, not everyone needs to be a so called expert in Lean, Six Sigma, or process improvement. But what we want to do is give everyone an understanding of the methodology and a problem-solving skill set so that they can identify problems, determine the root cause, develop the new and improved future state, and test the improvement using basic scientific principles."[8] Hagood also advises that organizations adopt a daily management system to support the "army of problems solvers," as without it that army's improvement activities will prove difficult if not impossible to sustain.

A number of organizations have trained, coached, and developed an army of problem solvers and achieved outstanding longer-term results. Sharp HealthCare trained 99 percent of its workforce and volunteers in improvement skills, an effort that led to a 48 percent decrease in serious safety events and a

92 percent improvement in days between employee injuries.[9] Baptist Memorial Health System has seen improvements in safety events of over 90 percent, improvements in patient satisfaction of over 50 percent, and improvements in denials of over 40 percent since creating armies of problem solvers.[10]

Principle 6: Focus on Accountability and Execution

To succeed in transforming our organizations holistically across multiple dimensions, we must do a better job of holding people accountable for doing the work. That means teaching effective management and leadership skills as part of the talent management strategy discussed above. Organizations must also implement strong operating models that inform leaders and managers how to set goals that support an enterprise strategy, how to use metrics to monitor performance, and how to intervene as necessary with people and processes so as to ensure successful execution.

Getting Started

I hope this framework helps you begin to realize the full promise of safety science, high reliability, and zero harm. Our approach isn't just about improving safety. It's about transforming the entire enterprise—for the sake of patients, caregivers, and organizations themselves. If the principles presented in this chapter sound abstract and difficult to operationalize, rest assured—they're not. To get started, take the following four easy steps:

1. **Adopt the zero harm/transformational mindset.** If you're a senior leader, begin to set organizational objectives for the work. If you're a middle manager, make headway by discussing the interconnectivity

of safety, quality, and patient experience with your colleagues. Challenge them to tell you why an integrated strategy doesn't make sense. As you'll find, they won't be able to! Before long, your colleagues will intuitively "get" how to connect the dots.

2. **Converge leadership.** If you're a senior leader, enlist others behind the transformation effort, including quality, safety, and experience leaders as well as leaders from nursing, the medical staff, and human resources. With organizational objectives in place, challenge everyone to codesign how to integrate this effort. If you work in the middle of the organization, gather your colleagues together and ask them to integrate their improvement efforts with yours. Be vulnerable and demonstrate goodwill by offering to give up something of yours for the sake of better integration.

3. **Assess existing efforts.** Create an inventory of all projects in your organization or team that touch safety, quality, experience, and engagement. Flag both duplicative and complementary initiatives, asking how you might alter individual tactics to apply to all of your verticals. For instance, if your organization or team regularly conducts safety huddles, can you add two additional focus points to drive experience and employee engagement as well?

4. **Apply high reliability principles.** Think about how you might deploy the concepts of high reliability described in this book across safety, quality, and experience. As you'll find, universal skills and learning systems apply to all areas of healthcare operations.

As a caregiver who has experienced gaps in safety firsthand, and as one who yearns to see our organizations deliver more of what patients need, want, and deserve, I urge you: Think boldly and expansively. Take issue with the status quo. Push back against common refrains like "this is the way we've always done things," or "it can't work here," or "we're already doing this." Challenge yourself and your people to approach their daily work with new eyes, and to identify and fix problems proactively.

Each of this book's chapter authors understands the challenge and complexity of transformation, and each is keenly aware that improvement doesn't unfold neatly according to a single playbook, however well-articulated it might be. Yet each of us has also lived on the other side of healthcare—we are all healthcare consumers, patients, and family members of patients. Our experiences embolden us to push harder and behave as respectful stewards of the organizations with whom we work. We all feel obliged to deliver on the holistic promise of safe, high-quality, patient-centered care. And we hope you'll join us in making this promise a reality.

Notes

Introduction

1. Christina Dempsey, *The Antidote to Suffering: How Compassionate Connected Care Can Improve Safety, Quality, and Experience* (New York: McGraw Hill Education, 2018).
2. Linda T. Kohn, Janet Corrigan, and Molla S. Donaldson, *To Err Is Human: Building a Safer Health System* (Washington, DC: National Academy Press, 2000), 31.
3. Martin A. Makary and Michael Daniel, "Medical Error—the Third Leading Cause of Death in the US," *British Medical Journal* (2016): 5.
4. John T. James, "A New, Evidence-Based Estimate of Patient Harms Associated with Hospital Care," *Journal of Patient Safety* 9, no. 3 (2013): 122.
5. Within the healthcare industry, administrators and clinicians tend to use the words *harm* when speaking about patient safety and *injury* when speaking of adverse workforce safety events. In common usage, the two words function as synonyms, so I and other authors in this book will use the words interchangeably.
6. "Injuries, Illnesses, and Fatalities," *Bureau of Labor Statistics*, "Table 1—Incidence rates—detailed industry level—2016 (XLSX)," accessed July 17, 2019, https://www.bls.gov/iif/oshsum.htm.
7. Sang D. Choi and Kathryn Brings, "Work-Related Musculoskeletal Risks Associated with Nurses and Nursing Assistants Handling Overweight and Obese Patients: A Literature Review," *Work* 53, no. 2 (2016): 439–440.
8. Christina Dempsey, *The Antidote to Suffering* (New York: McGraw Hill Education, 2018).
9. Donald Kennerly et al., "Journey to No Preventable Risk: The Baylor Health Care System Patient Safety Experience," *American Journal of Medical Quality* 26, no. 1 (2011): 44.
10. Diana Mahoney, "Leading to Zero: Advocate Health Care's Plan to Eliminate Harm Starts at the Top," *Industry Edge* (2016): 1–3.

11. Douglas P. Cropper et al., "Implementation of a Patient Safety Program at a Tertiary Health System: A Longitudinal Analysis of Interventions and Serious Safety Events," *Journal of Healthcare Risk Management* 37, no. 4 (2018): 6.

12. Although we do need more studies to document such savings at the level of individual healthcare delivery systems.

13. Thomas H. Lee, *An Epidemic of Empathy in Healthcare* (New York: McGraw Hill Education, 2016); James Merlino, *Service Fanatics* (New York: McGraw Hill Education, 2015).

14. The 73 percent is based on the latest data from HPI*Compare*, an aggregated dataset of harm data in the HPI client community, from calendar years 2014–2016, comprising 4,868 acts leading to serious preventable harm.

Chapter 1

1. NORC at the University of Chicago and IHI/NPSF Lucian Leape Institute, *Americans' Experiences with Medical Errors and Views on Patient Safety* (Cambridge, MA: Institute for Healthcare Improvement and NORC at the University of Chicago, 2017), iv, 9 *et passim*.

2. NORC and IHI/NPSF, *Americans' Experiences*, 2.

3. Michelle A. Dressner, "Hospital Workers: an Assessment of Occupational Injuries and Illnesses," *Bureau of Labor Statistics*, June 2017: 6.

4. Martin L. Gross, "Dirt, Infection, Error and Negligence: The Hidden Death Threats in Our Hospitals," *Look*, March 22, 1966: 27–30.

5. Lucian L. Leape, "Error in Medicine," *Journal of the American Medical Association* (JAMA) 272, no. 23 (1994): 1851.

6. Lucian L. Leape et al., "The Nature of Adverse Events in Hospitalized Patients: Results of the Harvard Medical Practice Study II," *New England Journal of Medicine* 324, no. 6 (1991): 377–384, doi: 10.1056/NEJM199102073240605.

7. Leape, "Error in Medicine," 1857.

8. For background on this story I relied on Lawrence K. Altman, "Big Doses of Chemotherapy Drug Killed Patient, Hurt 2d," *New York Times*, March 24, 1995, https://www.nytimes.com/1995/03/24/us/big-doses-of-chemotherapy-drug-killed-patient-hurt-2d.html; and Charles Kenney, *The Best Practice: How the New Quality Movement Is Transforming Medicine* (New York: Public Affairs, 2008).

9. Christine Gorman, "The Disturbing Case of the Cure That Killed the Patient," *Time*, April 3, 1995.

10. Kenney, *The Best Practice*, 68.

11. Quoted in Kenney, *The Best Practice*, 81, 83.

12. For more on this topic, please see "Crossing the Quality Chasm: The IOM Health Care Quality Initiative," *National Academies of Sciences, Engineering,*

and Medicine, accessed July 9, 2018, http://www.nationalacademies.org /hmd/Global/News%20Announcements/Crossing-the-Quality-Chasm -The-IOM-Health-Care-Quality-Initiative.aspx.

13. Kenney, *The Best Practice*, 85.

14. Institute of Medicine's Committee on Quality of Health Care in America, *Crossing the Quality Chasm: A New Health System for the 21st Century* (Washington, DC: National Academy Press, 2001).

15. Erika Niedowski, "How Medical Errors Took a Little Girl's Life," *Baltimore Sun*, December 14, 2003, http://www.baltimoresun.com/bal-te .sorrel14dec14-story.html#.

16. Karen Nitkin and Lisa Broadhead, "No Room for Error," *Johns Hopkins Medicine*, January/February 2016, https://www.hopkinsmedicine.org /news/articles/no-room-for-error.

17. C. Joseph McCannon et al., "Saving 100 000 Lives in US Hospitals," *British Medical Journal* 332, no. 3 (2006), https://doi.org/10.1136/bmj.332 .7553.1328.

18. Andrew Clarkwest et al., "Project Evaluation Activity in Support of Partnership for Patients: Task 2 Evaluation Progress Report," *Center for Medicare and Medicaid Innovation*, 2014: 1.

19. Clarkwest et al., "Project Evaluation Activity," 1.

20. Mark R. Chassin and Jerod M. Loeb, "High-Reliability Health Care: Getting There from Here," *Milbank Quarterly*, 91, no. 3 (2013): 459–490.

21. Chassin and Loeb, "High-Reliability Health Care," 485.

22. Please see the Children's Hospitals' Solutions for Patient Safety Network (SPS Network), *Agency for Healthcare Research and Quality*, accessed July 11, 2018, https://www.ahrq.gov/workingforquality/priorities-in-action/sps -network.html#note10; Children's Hospitals' Solutions for Patient Safety, *SPS Network: 2017 Year in Review*, http://www.solutionsforpatientsafety .org/wp-content/uploads/2017-Year-in-Review.pdf.

23. John T. James, "A New, Evidence-Based Estimate of Patient Harms Associated with Hospital Care," *Journal of Patient Safety* 9, no. 3 (2013): 122.

24. Martin A. Makary and Michael Daniel, "Medical Error—the Third Leading Cause of Death in the US," *British Medical Journal*, May 3, 2016, doi: 10.1136/bmj.i2139.

25. "Saving Lives and Saving Money: Hospital-Acquired Conditions Update: Final Data from National Efforts to Make Care Safer, 2010–2014," *Agency for Healthcare Research Quality*, December 2016, last reviewed January 2018, https://www.ahrq.gov/professionals/quality-patient-safety/pfp/2014 -final.html; see also the updated report: "AHRQ National Scorecard on Hospital-Acquired Conditions Updated Baseline Rates and Preliminary Results 2014–2016," *Agency for Healthcare Research Quality*, June 2018, https://www.ahrq.gov/sites/default/files/wysiwyg/professionals/quality -patient-safety/pfp/natlhacratereport-rebaselining2014-2016_0.pdf.

26. Kerry Johnson and Craig Clapper, "Hospital Impact: 8 Cultural Barriers That Impede Efforts to Reduce Medical Errors," *Fierce Healthcare*, February 8, 2017, https://www.fiercehealthcare.com/hospitals/hospital -impact-8-cultural-barriers-to-achieving-high-reliability-healthcare.

27. "Free from Harm: Accelerating Patient Safety Improvement Fifteen Years After *To Err Is Human*" *National Patient Safety Foundation*, 2015, accessed July 11, 2018, http://www.ihi.org/resources/Pages/Publications /Free-from-Harm-Accelerating-Patient-Safety-Improvement.aspx. See also, "National Center for Health Statistics," *Centers for Disease Control and Prevention*, accessed July 11, 2018, https://www.cdc.gov/nchs/fastats/.

28. *A Strategic Blueprint for Transformational Change*, Press Ganey, 2018: 2 *et passim*, available at http://healthcare.pressganey.com/2018-Strategic -Insights?s=White_Paper-BI.

29. "Free from Harm: Accelerating Patient Safety."

Chapter 2

1. Matthew Weinstock, "Can Your Nurses Stop a Surgeon?" *Patient Safety*, September 2007.

2. Dr. Rishi Sikka (Advocate's vice president of clinical transformation), interview with author, July 9, 2018.

3. Dr. Lee Sacks (chief medical officer of Advocate Health Care), interview with author, July 9, 2018.

4. Kate Kovich (vice president of high reliability innovation at Advocate Health Care), interview with author, July 9, 2018.

5. Alan J. Stolzer, Carl D. Halford, John J. Goglia, eds. *Implementing Safety Management Systems in Aviation* (Burlington, VT: Ashgate Publishing Company, 2011).

6. "To Care, Comfort, and Heal . . . Without Harm: Creating and Living a Culture of Safety at Holy Redeemer Health System," Holy Redeemer Purpose Paper, revised October 20, 2010.

7. The 73 percent is based on the latest data from HPI*Compare*, an aggregated dataset of harm data in the HPI client community, from calendar years 2014–2016, comprising 4,868 acts leading to serious preventable harm.

8. Marci Vanderbosch (high reliability transformation lead for Sacred Heart Medical Center and Children's Hospital and Providence Holy Family Hospital in Spokane, Washington), interview with author, July 9, 2018.

9. Jones currently serves as chief executive officer of Cancer Treatment Centers of America (CTCA), Chicago (a specialty hospital for cancer care). He conveyed these figures to me in a discussion on July 9, 2018. For Vidant's safety event reduction figures, please see Beth Anne Atkins, "Vidant Health Receives National Award for Quality and Patient Safety Initiatives," *Vidant Health*, January 24, 2014, https://www.vidanthealth .com/latest-news/vidant-health-receives-national-award-for-quality#.

10. Mary Ann Hilliard et al., "Our Journey to Zero: Reducing Serious Safety Events by over 70% Through High-Reliability Techniques and Workforce Engagement," *Journal of Healthcare Risk Management* 22, no. 2 (September 20, 2012): 4, doi: 10.1002/jhrm.21090.
11. Hilliard, "Our Journey to Zero," 14.

Chapter 3

1. Terje Aven, "What Is Safety Science?," *Safety Science* 67 (2013): 15.
2. James T. Reason, *Managing the Risks of Organizational Accidents* (Brookfield, VT: Ashgate Publishing Company, 1997).
3. Richard I. Cook and David D. Woods, "Operating at the Sharp End: The Complexity of Human Error," in M. S. Bogner, ed., *Human Error in Medicine* (Hillsdale, NJ: Lawrence Erlbaum Associates, Inc.), 258–259.
4. Jens Rasmussen's "Risk Management in a Dynamic Society: A Modeling Problem," *Safety Science* 27, no. 2/3 (1997): 190, features an illustration of the dynamic safety model. Rasmussen's model recognizes that forces such as a sudden increase in patient volume act on systems to reduce safety margins, cause time pressure and workload effects, and result in overuse of resources. But this model only points safety leaders to systemic solutions that provide for early warning of conditions leading to harm so that adjustments can be made to prevent actual harm. The dynamic safety model has little to say about how to prevent those conditions. Bonini's paradox tells us that by the time a model is accurate enough to predict system behavior, the model is too complex for users to understand. Another construct, the bow tie model, bridges the gap between the Swiss cheese model and the dynamic safety model by acknowledging both the systemic causes of the event and the possibility that systems can limit the severity of the resulting harm by intervening in a timely way.
5. Christine Sammer et al., "What Is Patient Safety Culture? A Review of the Literature," *Journal of Nursing Scholarship* 42, no. 2 (2010): 157.
6. Press Ganey-Healthcare Performance Improvement (HPI) compiled this list over the decade spanning 1992–2002.
7. Institute of Nuclear Power Operations (INPO), *Traits of a Healthy Nuclear Safety Culture*, Addendum II, April 2013: A-II-4.
8. As Christina Dempsey relayed in *The Antidote to Suffering: How Compassionate Connected Care Can Improve Safety, Quality and Experience* (New York: McGraw Hill, 2018) (200), significant events per reactor site decreased from a high of 0.90 events per reactor site in 1989—that is, nearly one event at every one of those 100 reactor sites every year—to 0.01 events per reactor site in 2014. That is only one event for all 100 of the reactor sites in one year, a reduction of 98.9% over 25 years. And better still, those significant events were precursor events. No actual core damage events occurred during those years.

9. James Reason, "Human Error: Models and Management," *British Medical Journal* 320 (2000): 768–770.

10. Other thought leaders include Rene Amalberti, a physician and aviation expert; Sidney Dekker, an aviation safety expert; Ronald Westrum, a sociologist; Patrick Hudson, a psychologist; Vernon Bradley, a DuPont production manager; Chong Chiu, an MIT engineer and innovator in nuclear safety and reliability; and Charles Perrow, a sociologist and founder of Normal Accident Theory (NAT).

11. Karl E. Weick and Kathleen M. Sutcliffe, *Managing the Unexpected: Assuring High Performance in an Age of Complexity* (Jossey-Bass, 2001), 10.

12. Rene Amalberti and Paul Barach, "Five System Barriers to Achieving Ultrasafe Healthcare," *Annals of Internal Medicine* 142, no. 9 (2005): 756–764

13. Carole Stockmeier and Craig Clapper, "Daily Check-in for Safety: From Best Practice to Common Practice," *Patient Safety & Quality Healthcare* (September/October 2011): 30–36.

Chapter 4

1. Scott Snair, *West Point Leadership Lessons: Duty, Honor, and Other Management Principles* (Naperville: Sourcebooks, 2004), 269.

2. Courtesy of Carole Stockmeier, conversation with author, 2007.

3. These figures, all approximations, furnished by the company's website. Please see Norfolk Southern, "Corporate Profile," accessed July 16, 2018, http://www.nscorp.com/content/nscorp/en/about-ns/corporate-profile .html.

4. Please see Norfolk Southern, "Vision & Values," accessed July 16, 2018, http://www.nscorp.com/content/nscorp/en/the-norfolk-southern-story /vision-and-values.html.

5. Edgar H. Schein, *Organizational Culture and Leadership* (San Francisco: Jossey-Bass, 1985).

6. Ellen Crowe (director of clinical excellence and care redesign), correspondence with author, May 30, 2018.

7. J.M. Gottman and R.W. Levenson, "Marital Processes Predictive of Later Dissolution: Behavior, Physiology, and Health," *Journal of Personality and Social Psychology* 63(2) (1992): 221-233.

8. Dr. Steven Linn (chief medical officer of Inspira Medical Center Vineland), interview with author, July 16, 2018.

9. Mary Walton, *The Deming Management Method* (London: Penguin, 1986), 138–139.

10. Ronald A. Heifetz, *Leadership Without Easy Answers* (Cambridge, MA: Harvard University Press, 2009), 113.

11. The first five elements from this table are taken, with permission, from "Leadership Method Module," *Healthcare Performance Improvement*, April 2011 (revision 2).

12. "30 of Muhammad Ali's Best Quotes," *USA Today*, June 3, 2016, https://www.usatoday.com/story/sports/boxing/2016/06/03/muhammad-ali-best-quotes-boxing/85370850/.

Chapter 5

1. The 73 percent is based on the latest data from HPI*Compare*, an aggregated dataset of harm in the HPI client community, from calendar years 2014–2016, comprising 4,868 acts leading to serious preventable harm.

2. James Reason, J., "Beyond the Organisational Accident: The Need for 'Error Wisdom' on the Frontline," *Quality & Safety in Health Care* 13(2004): ii28–ii33.

3. James Reason, *Managing the Risks of Organizational Accidents* (Vermont: Ashgate, 1997), 68–70. The skill/rule/knowledge (SRK) classification was developed by Jens Rasmussen, a cognitive systems engineer from Denmark. This classification was further developed by James Reason as the Generic Error Modeling System (GEMS).

4. Sylvain Charron and Etienne Koechlin, "Divided Representation of Concurrent Goals in the Human Frontal Lobes," *Science* 328 (April 2010): 360–363.

5. "Making a Difference: One Organization's Approach: Educate to Build Character," *Los Angeles Times*, March 14, 1994, http://articles.latimes.com/1994-03-14/local/me-33766_1_character-education.

6. Michael Leonard, Suzanne Graham, Doug Bonacum, "The Human Factor: The Critical Importance of Effective Teamwork and Communication in Providing SAFE care," *Quality and Safety in Health Care* 13, Suppl. 1 (2004): 85.

7. Walter J. Boyne, "The Checklist," *Air Force Magazine*, August 2013: 52–56.

8. "Procedure Use & Adherence," *Institute of Nuclear Power Operations*, 2009: 9 *et passim*, www.smartprocedures.com/pdfs/inpo-09-004-use-and-adherence-guidelines.pdf.

9. Marianna Pogosyan, "Geert Hofstede: A Conversation About Culture," *Psychology Today*, February 21, 2017, https://www.psychologytoday.com/us/blog/between-cultures/201702/geert-hofstede-conversation-about-culture.

10. Dr. Glenn Bingle (chief medical officer of the Community Health Network), interview with author, November 8, 2007.

11. Janet Jacobsen, "Community Health Network Reduces Deadly Infections Through Culture of Reliability," *American Society for Quality*, June 2008.

12. Joan Wynn (chief quality and patient safety officer of Vidant Health), interview with author, July 11, 2018.

13. "Culture Shift Sets the Bar Sky-High for Patient Safety," Virginia Commonwealth University, 2013 Annual Report, 2013, https://annualreports.vcu.edu/archive/medical/2013/stories/safetyfirst.html.

Chapter 6

1. For this story, I rely on Diane Suchetka, "Burn Victim Hopes Her Story Calls Attention to Dangers of Surgical Fires," *Plain Dealer*, May 23, 2010, http://blog.cleveland.com/metro/2010/05/burn_victim_hopes_her_story _wi.html.

2. Myles Edwin Lee, *Near Misses in Cardiac Surgery* (Boston: Butterworth-Heinemann, 1992), xix–xx.

3. Rhona H. Flin, Paul O'Connor, and Margaret Crichton, *Safety at the Sharp End: a Guide to Non-Technical Skills* (Farnham: Ashgate, 2013), 177.

4. "Safer Air Travel Through Crew Resource Management," *American Psychological Association*, February 2014, http://www.apa.org/action /resources/research-in-action/crew.aspx.

5. For the data about CRM, I am indebted to Jan U. Hagen, *Confronting Mistakes: Lessons from the Aviation Industry when Dealing with Error* (Basingstoke: Palgrave Macmillan, 2013).

6. Jeff Archie et al., "Leadership and Team Effectiveness Attributes," *Institute of Nuclear Power Operations*, May 2015: 2.

7. Amy C. Edmondson, *Teaming: How Organizations Learn, Innovate, and Compete in the Knowledge Economy* (San Francisco: Jossey Bass, 2012), 59.

8. Edmondson, *Teaming*, 60.

9. "Behaviors That Undermine a Culture of Safety," *Joint Commission* 40 (July 9, 2008), https://www.jointcommission.org/assets/1/18/SEA_40.PDF.

10. "Intimidation: Practitioners Speak up About This Unresolved Problem (Part I)," *Institute for Safe Medication Practices*, March 11, 2004, https:// www.ismp.org/resources/intimidation-practitioners-speak-about -unresolved-problem-part-i.

11. "Intimidation: Practitioners Speak Up."

12. In the aviation industry, this concept of decision-making power or the steepness of command hierarchy is referred to as authority gradient.

13. Gert Hofstede, "Power Distance in 10 minutes," PowerPoint Presentation, August 2014.

14. Calvin L. Chou, Laura Cooley, *Communication Rx: Transforming Healthcare Through Relationship-Centered Communication* (New York, NY: McGraw Hill, 2017). Visit www.CommunicationRx.org for free access to Chapter One, "Building the Case for Communication and Relationships."

15. The term *Relationship-Centered Communication* is an extension of scholarship on *Relationship-Centered Care*, which links to Carol Tresolini and the Pew–Fetzer Task Force, *Health Professions Education and Relationship–Centered Care*, Pew Health Professions Commission, 1994.

16. Calvin Chou, "Time to Start Using Evidence-Based Approaches to Patient Engagement," *New England Journal of Medicine Catalyst*, March 28, 2018, https://catalyst.nejm.org/evidence-based-patient-provider -communication/.

17. Edmondson, *Teaming*, 52.
18. Edmondson, *Teaming*, 75.
19. Marvin S. Cohen et al., "Critical Thinking Skills in Tactical Decision Making: A Model and a Training Strategy," in *Making Decisions Under Stress: Implications for Individual and Team Training*, ed. Janis A. Cannon-Bowers and Eduardo Salas (Washington, DC: American Psychological Association, 2006), 166.
20. David R. Urbach et al., "Introduction of Surgical Safety Checklists in Ontario, Canada," *New England Journal of Medicine* 370, no. 11 (2014): 1029–1038.
21. Lucian L. Leape, "The Checklist Conundrum," *New England Journal of Medicine* 370, no. 11 (2014): 1063–1064.
22. "Loss of Thrust in Both Engines After Encountering a Flock of Birds and Subsequent Ditching on the Hudson River, US Airways Flight 1549, Airbus A320-214, N106US, Weehawken, New Jersey, January 15, 2009," National Transportation Safety Board Accident Report, adopted May 4, 2010, 168.
23. "Loss of Thrust in Both Engines," 179.

Chapter 7

1. Barbara A. Brunt, "Developing a Just Culture," *Health Leaders*, May 18, 2010, https://www.healthleadersmedia.com/nursing/developing-just-culture.
2. Philip G. Boysen, "Just Culture: A Foundation for Balanced Accountability and Patient Safety," *The Ochsner Journal* 13, no 3: 400–406, https://www.ncbi.nlm.nih.gov/pmc/articles/PMC3776518/.
3. Kerm Henriksen et al. (eds.), *Advances in Patient Safety: From Research to Implementation, Vol. 4: Programs, Tools, and Products* (Rockville: Agency for Healthcare Research and Quality, 2005), 389.
4. Henriksen, *Advances in Patient Safety*, 389.
5. "Hospital Survey on Patient Safety Culture: 2016 User Comparative Database Report," Agency for Healthcare Research and Quality, March 2016: 25.
6. "Hospital Survey on Patient Safety Culture."
7. Robert Pear, "Report Finds Most Errors at Hospitals Go Unreported," *New York Times*, January 6, 2012, https://www.nytimes.com/2012/01/06/health/study-of-medicare-patients-finds-most-hospital-errors-unreported.html.
8. James Reason, *Managing the Risks of Organizational Accidents* (Vermont: Ashgate, 1997).
9. "A Roadmap to a Just Culture: Enhancing the Safety Environment," Gain Working Group E, September 2004: vi.
10. For the tree, please see Reason, *Managing the Risks*, 209. 7

11. James Stewart, *Blind Eye: The Terrifying Story of a Doctor Who Got Away with Murder* (New York: Simon & Schuster, 1999).
12. L. D. Harvey and S. A. van Riet, *Fair Response to Mistakes*, National Association for Healthcare Quality presentation, 2010.
13. W. D. Reynard, *The Development of the NASA Aviation Safety Reporting System* (National Aeronautics and Space Administration, 1986).
14. "Fair and Just Culture," *CS Energy*, August 2010.
15. David Marx, "Patient Safety and the 'Just Culture': A Primer for Health Care Executives," Agency for Healthcare Research and Quality, April 2001: 4, https://nursing2015.files.wordpress.com/2010/02/mers.pdf.
16. Erika Anderson, "21 Quotes from Henry Ford on Business, Leadership, and Life," *Forbes*, May 31 2013, https://www.forbes.com/sites/erikaandersen/2013/05/31/21-quotes-from-henry-ford-on-business-leadership-and-life/#4863d1f8293c.

Chapter 8

1. Robert S. Kaplan and David P. Norton, "Using the Balanced Scorecard as a Strategic Management System," *Harvard Business Review*, January–February 1996.
2. Robert S. Kaplan and David P. Norton, "Putting the Balanced Scorecard to Work," *Harvard Business Review*, September–October 1993.
3. Catherine Corbett et al., *Maximize Patient Safety with Advanced Root Cause Analysis* (Marblehead: HCPro, Inc, 2004), 7–9.
4. David M. DeJoy et al., "Creating Safer Workplaces: Assessing the Determinants and Role of Safety Climate," *Journal of Safety Research* 35 (2004): 81–90, http://citeseerx.ist.psu.edu/viewdoc/download?doi=10.1.1.476.1620&rep=rep1&type=pdf.
5. "Building a High-Performing Workforce," *Press Ganey* (white paper), January 2016, http://www.pressganey.com/resources/white-papers/building-a-high-performing-workforce.
6. "Pediatric Early Warning (PEW) Score System," Agency for Healthcare Research and Quality, updated March 14, 2012, https://innovations.ahrq.gov/qualitytools/pediatric-early-warning-pew-score-system.
7. "Modified Early Warning System (MEWS), Agency for Healthcare Research and Quality, updated March 12, 2014, https://innovations.ahrq.gov/qualitytools/modified-early-warning-system-mews.
8. J. Gardner-Thorpe et al., "The Value of Modified Early Warning Score (MEWS) in Surgical In-Patients: A Prospective Observational Study," *Annals of The Royal College of Surgeons of England* 88, no. 6 (October 2006): 571–575, doi: 10.1308/003588406X130615.
9. Cheri Throop and Carole Stockmeier, "SEC & SSER Patient Safety Measurement System for Healthcare," *Healthcare Performance Improvement* (HPI White Paper series), updated May 2011, http://www.pressganey.com

/docs/default-source/default-document-library/hpi-white-paper---sec-amp
-sser-measurement-system-rev-2-may-2011.pdf?sfvrsn=0.

10. For an overview of the US government's "Adjusted Patient Days Calculation," please see https://www.hud.gov/sites/documents/46151X1HSGH.PDF.

11. "Serious Safety Event Rate (SSER)," Nationwide Children's Hospital, accessed July 12, 2018, https://www.nationwidechildrens.org/impact -quality/patient-safety/serious-safety-event-rate-sser.

12. Richard J. Brilli, "A Comprehensive Patient Safety Program Can Significantly Reduce Preventable Harm, Associated Costs, and Hospital Mortality," *Journal of Pediatrics* 163, no. 6 (2013): 1638–45, doi: 10.1016/j. jpeds.2013.06.031; "Serious Safety Event Rate," Nationwide Children's, accessed July 13, 2018, https://www.nationwidechildrens.org/impact -quality/patient-safety/serious-safety-event-rate-sser.

13. Deirdre E. Mylod, "One Way to Prevent Clinician Burnout," *Harvard Business Review*, October 12, 2017, https://hbr.org/2017/10/one-way-to -prevent-clinician-burnout.

14. "Safety Culture Indicators: Performance Monitoring & Trending for Safety Culture in Healthcare," *Healthcare Performance Improvement*, revised August 2009: 3.

15. "Rules of Engagement: Assessing and Addressing Employee Engagement and Readiness for Change," Press Ganey, November 2016.

16. "Building a High-Performing Workforce," Press Ganey white paper, 2016.

17. Paul F. Wilson, Gaylord F. Anderson, and Larry D. Dell, *Root Cause Analysis: A Tool for Total Quality Management* (Wisconsin: ASQC Quality Press, 1993), 19–34.

18. Jim Merlino and Gary Yates, "Reducing Serious Safety Events: A Critical Dimension of the Patient Experience," Press Ganey white paper, 2015: 3.

19. Wilson, Anderson, and Dell, *Root Cause Analysis*, 78–80.

20. Corbett et al., *Maximize Patient Safety with Advanced Root Cause Analysis*, 108.

Chapter 9

1. Catherine Corbett et al., *Maximize Patient Safety with Advanced Root Cause Analysis* (Marblehead: HCPro, Inc, 2004).

2. Catherine Corbett et al., *Maximize Patient Safety*, 5–6.

3. For the information in this paragraph, I rely on Catherine Corbett et al., *Maximize Patient Safety*, xi; "SEC & SSER Patient Safety Measurement System for Healthcare," *Healthcare Performance Improvement* (white paper), updated May 2011; Craig Clapper, personal correspondence, July 10, 2018.

4. Data taken from "Common Cause Analysis Data: 2014–2016," *Healthcare Performance Improvement*, 2017.

5. Taken from Appendix C-1 and C-2 of "SEC & SSER Patient Safety Measurement System for Healthcare," *Healthcare Performance Improvement* (white paper), updated May 2011.

6. Material from this paragraph taken from "How a Systems Approach Can Change Safety Culture," MedStar Health video, 5.34, published March 19, 2014, https://www.youtube.com/watch?v=zeldVu-3DpM.

7. "How a Systems Approach Can Change Safety Culture," *MedStar Health* video, 5.34, published March 19, 2014, https://www.youtube.com/watch?v=zeldVu-3DpM.

8. Ibid.

9. All data provided to the author by Glenda Battey (program director, high reliability at Providence St. Joseph Health), e-mail correspondence, July 7, 2018.

10. Data furnished by an assessment undertaken by a team of consultants in 2015.

11. Douglas Cropper et al., "Implementation of a Patient Safety Program at a Tertiary Health System: A Longitudinal Analysis of Interventions and Serious Safety Events," *Journal of Healthcare Risk Management* 37, no 4 (2018): 4, doi: 10.1002/jhrm.21319.

12. Kim Hollon (president and CEO of Signature Healthcare), personal correspondence with author, May 6, 2018.

13. Marc Harrison, "Tiered Escalation Huddles Yield Rapid Results," *NEJM Catalyst*, March 7, 2018, https://catalyst.nejm.org/tiered-escalation -huddles-yield-rapid-results/. For this discussion, I am also indebted to supplemental materials and guidance provided by Intermountain's internal safety consultants.

Chapter 10

1. Catherine E. Shoichet, "Nurse Dies Protecting Patients in Texas Surgical Center Stabbing," CNN, November 26, 2013, https://www.cnn.com/2013 /11/26/world/texas-surgical-center-stabbing/index.html.

2. Daniel Zwerdling, "Hospitals Fail to Protect Nursing Staff from Becoming Patients," National Public Radio (*All Things Considered*), February 4, 2015, https://www.npr.org/2015/02/04/382639199/hospitals-fail-to-protect -nursing-staff-from-becoming-patients.

3. The total case incident rate (TCIR) for US hospitals has declined from 9.1 per 100 FTEs (full-time equivalents) in 2000 to 5.9 in 2016.

4. See "Injuries, Illnesses, and Fatalities," Bureau of Labor Statistics ("Table 1—Incidence rates—detailed industry level—2016 (XLSX)" accessed July 17, 2019, https://www.bls.gov/iif/oshsum.htm.

5. "Injuries, Illnesses, and Fatalities."

6. Scott Harris "Safety Culture in Healthcare: The $13 Billion Case," *Professional Safety*, October 2013: 49.

7. "The Role of Workplace Safety and Surveillance Capacity in Driving Nurse and Patient Outcomes," Press Ganey nursing special report, 2016: 1.

8. Ibid.

9. John Baldoni "Employee Engagement Does More than Boost Productivity," *Harvard Business Review*, July 3, 2013, https://hbr.org/2013/07/employee-engagement-does-more.

10. "Burnout and Resilience: A Framework for Data Analysis and a Positive Path Forward," Press Ganey white paper, 2018.

11. "Guidelines for Preventing Workplace Violence for Healthcare and Social Service Workers," Occupational Safety and Health Administration (OSHA), https://www.osha.gov/Publications/osha3148.pdf.

12. Susan D. Scott, "The Second Victim Phenomenon: A Harsh Reality of Health Care Professions," Agency for Healthcare Research and Quality, Perspectives on Safety, May 2011, https://psnet.ahrq.gov/perspectives/perspective/102/the-second-victim-phenomenon-a-harsh-reality-of-health-care-professions.

13. "Burnout and Resilience: A Framework for Data Analysis and a Positive Path Forward," Press Ganey white paper, 2018.

14. Chief nursing officer (San Diego–based healthcare system), conversation with author, May 7, 2018.

15. Emily Halu, "Preventing Workplace Violence in Healthcare: A Nurse's Perspective," Press Ganey blog, May 22, 2018, http://www.pressganey.com/resources/blog/preventing-workplace-violence-in-health-care-a-nurse-s-perspective.

16. Quotation taken from Audrey L. Nelson, *Safe Patient Handling and Movement: A Practical Guide for Health Care Professionals* (New York: Springer Publishing, 2006), 4.

17. "Facts About Hospital Worker Safety," Occupational Safety and Health Administration, 2013, 5, https://www.osha.gov/dsg/hospitals/documents/1.2_Factbook_508.pdf.

18. "Safe Patient Handling and Mobility," Centers for Disease Control and Prevention, updated April 6, 2018, https://www.cdc.gov/niosh/topics/safepatient/default.html.

19. Don Goble (Press Ganey consultant), conversation with author, May 2018.

20. Tejal K. Gandhi and Gary R. Yates, "Boards Can Be Safety Champions," *Trustee*, May 8, 2017, https://www.trusteemag.com/articles/1244-hospital-boards-can-be-safety-champions.

21. "Improving Patient and Worker Safety: Opportunities for Synergy, Collaboration and Innovation," The Joint Commission, 2012: 16.

22. As an example of similar thinking, Harris's elements of creating a safety culture are: "organization-wide commitment to safety; visibility and transparency; ongoing learning as a key prevention tool; a focus on leading indicators and early reporting of safety and health risks; continuous communication; recognition and rewards; eliminating fear of reprisal for reporting; [and] commitment to continuous improvement" (Scott Harris "Safety Culture in Healthcare: The $13 Billion Case," *Professional Safety*, October 2013: 54).

23. Harris, "Safety Culture in Healthcare," 53.

24. Drake Baer, "How Changing One Habit Helped Quintuple Alcoa's Income," *Business Insider*, April 9, 2014, http://www.businessinsider.com /how-changing-one-habit-quintupled-alcoas-income-2014-4.

25. "Mission, Vision and Values," Sisters of Charity of Leavenworth Health System, accessed July 14, 2018, https://www.sclhealth.org/about/mission/.

26. David Marx, "Patient Safety and the 'Just Culture': A Primer for Health Care Executives," Trustees of Columbia University, 2001: 22.

27. "Safety and Health Management Systems: A Road Map for Hospitals," Occupational Health and Safety Administration (OSHA), 2013: 31, https://www.ors.od.nih.gov/sr/dohs/Documents/DLib_2.4_SHMS _roadmap_508.pdf.

28. "Guidelines for Preventing Workplace Violence for Healthcare and Social Service Workers," Occupational Health and Safety Administration (OSHA), 2015: 17.

29. Ibid., 13–23.

30. Paige Minemyer, "Beth Israel Deaconess Medical Center Battles Workplace Violence," *Fierce Healthcare*, August 11, 2017, https://www .fiercehealthcare.com/healthcare/beth-israel-deaconess-takes-aim-at -workplace-violence.

31. "We Are Northwell Health," Northwell, accessed July 14, 2018, https:// www.northwell.edu/sites/northwell/files/Fact-Sheet-June-2018.pdf.

32. Diane O'Donnell, "Northwell Staffers Compete in Safe Patient Handling Olympics," Northwell Health, December 11, 2017, https://www.northwell .edu/about/news/press-releases/northwell-staffers-compete-safe-patient -handling-olympics.

33. Audrey Doyle, "Focused Efforts Advance Workforce Safety at Sharp HealthCare," Press Ganey, April 2018, http://www.pressganey.com /docs/default-source/default-document-library/focused-efforts-advance -workforce-safety-at-sharp-healthcarebb5fd35d82706b31bd87ff0000a8a bfc.pdf?sfvrsn=0.

34. "HPI Press Ganey Case Studies: Safety and Reliability Consulting," Press Ganey, 2017: 3.

35. Judy Geiger (executive director, Intermountain Health), personal correspondence with author, May 2018.

Chapter 11

1. Christy Dempsey and Deirdre Mylod, "Addressing Patient and Caregiver Suffering," *American Nurse Today*, November 2016: 17, https://www .americannursetoday.com/wp-content/uploads/2016/11/ant11-CE -Suffering-1020-copy.pdf.

2. David Ross Garr and Frank J. Marsh, "Medical Malpractice and the Primary Care Physician: Lowering the Risks," *Southern Medical Journal* 79, no. 10 (1986): 1280–284, doi:10.1097/00007611-198610000-00020.

3. Linda T. Kohn, Janet Corrigan, and Molla S. Donaldson, *To Err Is Human: Building a Safer Health System* (Washington, DC: National Academy Press, 2000).

4. Institute of Medicine, *Crossing the Quality Chasm* (Washington, DC: National Academy Press, 2001).

5. "Majority of Nations Acute Care Hospitals Meet Quality Reporting Goals, Will Receive Full Rate Increase Next Year," Centers for Medicare and Medicaid Services, October 11, 2007, https://www.cms.gov/newsroom/press-releases/majority-nations-acute-care-hospitals-meet-quality-reporting-goals-will-receive-full-rate-increase.

6. Deirdre E. Mylod and Thomas H. Lee, "A Framework for Reducing Suffering in Health Care," *Harvard Business Review Insights Center*, November 14, 2013, https://hbr.org/2013/11/a-framework-for-reducing-suffering-in-health-care.

7. David E. Wang et al., "Association Between the Centers for Medicare and Medicaid Services Hospital Star Rating and Patient Outcomes," *Journal of the American Medical Association Internal Medicine* 176, no. 6 (2016): 849–50, doi:10.1001/jamainternmed.2016.0784.

8. Greg D. Sacks et al., "Relationship Between Hospital Performance on a Patient Satisfaction Survey and Surgical Quality," *Journal of the American Medical Association Surgery* 150, no. 9 (2015): 858, doi:10.1001/jamasurg.2015.1108.

9. "Performance Insights: Health Care Improvement Trends," Press Ganey white paper, 2017.

10. Dennis O. Kaldenberg, Deirdre. E. Mylod, and Maxwell Drain, "Patient-Derived Information: Satisfaction with Care in Acute and Post-Acute Care Environments," in Norbert Goldfield, Michael Pine, and Joan Pine, *Measuring and Managing Health Care Quality: Procedures, Techniques, and Protocols* (New York: Aspen Publishers, 2002), 4:69–4:89.

11. Christina Dempsey et al., "Reducing Patient Suffering Through Compassionate Connected Care," *Journal of Nursing Administration* 44, no. 10 (2014): 517–24, doi:10.1097/nna.0000000000000110.

12. For similar results from other scholars, please see Huey-Ming Tzeng and Chang-Yi Yin, "Are Call Light Use and Response Time Correlated with Inpatient Falls and Inpatient Dissatisfaction?," *Journal of Nursing Care Quality* 24, no. 3 (2009): 232–42, doi:10.1097/ncq.0b013e3181955f30.

13. Megan Trucano and Dennis O. Kaldenberg, "The Relationship Between Patient Perceptions of Hospital Practices and Facility Infection Rates: Evidence from Pennsylvania Hospitals," *Patient Safety and Quality Healthcare*, August 22, 2007.

14. "Impact of Care Attributes," Institute for Innovation PowerPoint, accessed July 15, 2018, http://theinstituteforinnovation.org/findingslibrary/instituteFindings.php?p=2&c=0&m=0&f=8.

15. Christine M. Meade, Amy L. Bursell, Lyn Ketelsen, "Effects of Nursing Rounds on Patients' Call Light Use, Satisfaction, and Safety," *American Journal of Nursing* 106, no. 9 (2006): 58–70, doi:10.1097/00000446 -200609000-00029.

16. "Inspiring Innovation: Patient Report of Hourly Rounding," Institute for Innovation, 2014, http://www.theinstituteforinnovation.org/docs/default -source/innovation-stories/inspiring-innovation-stories_patient-report-of -hourly-rounding_final.pdf?sfvrsn=2.

17. Pamela H. Guler, "Patient Experience: A Critical Indicator of Healthcare Performance," *Frontiers of Health Services Management* 33, no. 3 (2017): 17–29, doi:10.1097/hap.0000000000000003.

18. Erin Graham, "Pennsylvania Hospital's Bedside Bundle Improves Relationship-Based Care," *Industry Edge*, January 19, 2017, http://www .pressganey.com/blog/pennsylvania-hospital-s-bedside-bundle-improves -relationship-based-care.

Epilogue

1. *Oxford Dictionaries*, s.v. "transformation," accessed July 18, 2018, https://en .oxforddictionaries.com/definition/transformation.

2. Gerald Lupacchino (chief experience officer at Hartford Healthcare), interview with author, July 5, 2018.

3. Christine M. Meade, Amy L. Bursell, Lyn Ketelsen, "Effects of Nursing Rounds on Patients' Call Light Use, Satisfaction, and Safety" *American Journal of Nursing* 106, no. 9 (2006): 58–70, doi:10.1097/00000446 -200609000-00029.

4. Paul Sternberg (medical director of patient experience at Vanderbilt University Medical Center), phone conversation with author, June 26, 2018.

5. "Increasing Value in the Emergency Department: Using Data to Drive Improvement," Press Ganey white paper, 2015.

6. Sue M. Evans et al., "Consumer Perceptions of Safety in Hospitals," *BMC Public Health* 6, no. 41 (2006), https://doi.org/10.1186/1471-2458-6-41.

7. "2017 Patient Access Journey Report," Kyruus, 2017, 2, https://www .kyruus.com/hubfs/Whitepapers/Kyruus_2017_Patient_Access_Journey _Report.pdf.

8. Charles Hagood (partner and practice leader, Press Ganey Strategic Consulting), phone conversation with author, July 20, 2018.

9. Patty Adkins, MS, RN (Vice President, Quality and Patient Safety at Sharp Healthcare), email with author, July 18, 2018.

10. Skip Steward (chief improvement officer at Baptist Memorial Healthcare), e-mail with author, July 20, 2018.

Index

About the Authors

Joseph Cabral is the chief human resources officer and president of workforce solutions at Press Ganey, a position to which he brings significant experience driving cultural transformation and caregiver engagement to support Press Ganey's broad client base.

Most recently, Joe was chief human resources officer at Partners HealthCare, one of the largest diversified healthcare service organizations in the United States. With more than 20 years of experience developing and executing strategies that enhance cultural and organizational change, Joe has spent more than a decade driving business objectives, vision, and values forward in all aspects of talent management and human resources in order to achieve the organization's goals. Prior to Partners HealthCare, Joe served as chief human resources officer at Cleveland Clinic and at Northwell Health, and he has held key HR leadership roles at NewYork–Presbyterian Hospital and Boston Children's Hospital.

Joe holds an MS degree in quality systems management, has taught as an adjunct professor at the University of Massachusetts, and has served as a Baldrige Examiner as well as on New York's Regional Economic Development Council. He has been cited by *Time, BusinessWeek,* the *Wall Street Journal,* the *New York Times, Forbes,* and other industry publications for his expertise in human resources best practices, and in 2014 he received the CHRO of the Year Award from *HRO Today.*

Judith Ewald is a senior manager with Healthcare Performance Improvement (HPI) – Press Ganey, performing consulting to improve human performance in complex systems. In this capacity, she manages and participates in comprehensive reliability and safety culture improvement projects for individual hospitals, regional, and mega healthcare systems.

Judith has over 30 years of experience in healthcare operations, leadership, and consulting and, prior to joining HPI, served as the Assistant Vice-President for Quality, Safety, and Outcomes for the Inova Health System in Northern Virginia. Judy holds a Master's in Public Administration and is a Certified Professional in Healthcare Quality.

Emily Halu, RN, MSN, CPPS, is a staff consultant with Healthcare Performance Improvement (HPI) – Press Ganey. Emily is a Registered Nurse with a background in Acute Care Medical/Surgical Nursing. She realized her passion for improving the quality of patient care and took her clinical experience to performance improvement, starting the American College of Surgeon's National Surgical Quality Improvement Program (ACS NSQIP) at Riverside Regional Medical Center (RRMC), Newport News, Virginia. Following that, Emily became RRMC's Patient Safety Manager. She developed expertise in managing safety event reporting and investigation, impacting safety culture, leading safety coaches, teaching safety behaviors, and leading Root Cause Analysis and process improvement.

As an HPI consultant, Emily guides healthcare organizations throughout the United States in transforming their patient and workforce safety through the application of high reliability organizing principles. In addition to her RN, Emily holds a bachelor's degree in Animal Behavior from Bucknell University and a Master's of Science in Nursing from Austin Peay University.

Steve Kreiser, CDR (USN Ret.), MBA, is a partner with Press Ganey Strategic Consulting. Steve has more than 30 years of experience improving safety and reliability in naval operations, military and commercial aviation, and healthcare. During his tenure with Press Ganey and Healthcare Performance Improvement (HPI), he has worked with over a hundred hospitals to improve patient safety, safety culture, leadership, cause analysis, and peer review.

Prior to joining HPI, Steve was an officer and F/A-18 pilot, retiring as a naval Commander in 2008. During his naval career he accumulated 3,500 flight hours and 720 carrier landings, including combat missions in Iraq, Bosnia, and Afghanistan. He also held positions designed to improve reliability and safety in naval aviation, serving on aircraft mishap investigation boards and human factors councils tasked with discovering root causes for aviation accidents and associated human errors.

Additionally, Steve has a unique background and perspective on team training from his commercial airline experience as a first officer with United Airlines where he worked extensively in the area of crew resource management. Steve holds a Master of Business Administration degree from the University of Maryland University College and a Bachelor of Science degree in aerospace engineering from the University of Virginia.

Thomas H. Lee, MD, MSc, joined Press Ganey as Chief Medical Officer in 2013, bringing more than three decades of experience in healthcare performance improvement as a practicing physician, a leader in provider organizations, researcher, and health policy expert. As CMO, Tom is responsible for developing clinical and operational strategies to help providers across the nation measure and improve the patient experience, with an overarching goal of reducing the suffering of patients as they undergo care, and improving the value of that care. In addition to his role with Press

Ganey, Tom, an internist and cardiologist, continues to practice primary care at Brigham and Women's Hospital in Boston. Tom frequently lectures on the patient experience and strategies for improving the value of healthcare and was selected as a stage speaker on the subject at the acclaimed TEDMED meeting in 2015. He has authored more than 260 academic articles and the books *Chaos and Organization in Health Care* and *Eugene Braunwald and the Rise of Modern Medicine*. In November 2015, Tom released his third book, *An Epidemic of Empathy in Healthcare: How to Deliver Compassionate, Connected Patient Care That Creates a Competitive Advantage*, published by McGraw-Hill.

Deirdre Mylod, PhD, is the executive director of the organization's Institute for Innovation and senior vice president of Research and Analytics. In this joint role, she is responsible for advancing the understanding of the entire patient experience, including patient satisfaction, clinical process, and outcomes. Through the Institute, Dierdre partners with leading healthcare providers to study and implement transformative concepts for improving the patient experience.

Throughout her time at Press Ganey, Dierdre has served in a variety of key leadership roles. Most recently, she served as the vice president of Improvement Services, during which she oversaw the organization's Client Improvement Management teams. These teams offer clients quality-improvement strategy and solutions to enhance their performance in patient evaluations of care. Previously, she was responsible for developing Press Ganey's HCAHPS initiative and managing clients' participation in state-reporting projects. Dierdre currently serves as Press Ganey's liaison to the National Quality Forum (NQF) and has served on committees on public reporting through the NQF. Dierdre holds a master's degree and a PhD in psychology from the University of Notre Dame.

Stacie Pallotta, MPH, is a Partner in Advisory Services and Strategic Consulting for Press Ganey. Stacie has gathered extensive experience consulting with organizations across multiple industries to assess and improve consumer and patient experience. Her most recent work has included patient experience improvement strategy, organizational cultural alignment for patient centeredness, and interim executive leadership (CXO).

Prior to joining Press Ganey, Stacie launched and led an independent consulting business. Her most recent healthcare organizational experience includes her role as a senior leader at the Cleveland Clinic. Specifically, she was Senior Director for the Office of Patient Experience and responsibilities included leading strategy and daily operations for several key service lines: Best Practices, External Partnerships, Service Excellence and Culture, Volunteer Services, and International Patient Experience. Stacie was a founding member of the Patient Experience Advisory Group at Cleveland Clinic and is a member of the Board for the Association for Patient Experience.

Stacie earned a Master's degree in Public Health from Case Western Reserve University, and a Bachelor of Science (biology) and a Bachelor of Arts (psychology) from Marietta College in Ohio.

Shannon M. Sayles, MS, MA, is a senior manager with Healthcare Performance Improvement (HPI) – Press Ganey. Prior to joining HPI in 2009 she led the implementation of the safety and reliability initiative at Sentara Healthcare, an integrated healthcare system in southeastern Virginia. In this role she collaborated with and provided guidance to system and operational leaders in implementing behavior-based approaches for error prevention and high reliability, state-of-the-art cause analysis, and other reliability strategies. These efforts received national recognition for Sentara with the 2004 American Hospital Association

Quest for Quality Prize and the 2005 JCAHO John M. Eisenberg Patient Safety and Quality Award.

As an HPI consultant she has worked with over 25 healthcare systems in the United States and Canada. She has over 30 years of nursing and healthcare leadership experience, including over 15 years in performance improvement in hospitals, ambulatory settings, long-term care, and health plans. In addition to a clinical nursing master's degree from Boston University, she completed a master's degree in organizational development from Fielding University.

Tami Strong BA, BSN, RN, MSN-HCQ, is a director at Healthcare Performance Improvement (HPI) – Press Ganey. Tami has over 28 years' experience leading quality and safety initiatives in the manufacturing and healthcare industries. She began her operations management career working in the automotive industry where she used her expertise in materials management and supply chain logistics to achieve highly reliable lean production systems. She is an experienced change agent with formal and practical training in the utilization of the Toyota Production System (lean) philosophy and tools, heuristic manufacturing process design, and ISO9001. Tami is a registered nurse with experience in intensive care nursing and as an executive leader responsible for quality management, process improvement, patient relations, regulatory compliance, risk management, clinical education, and infection control. She has combined her passion for patient safety, high reliability, and operational excellence to lead several performance improvement projects in both manufacturing and healthcare systems to achieve improvements in safety, satisfaction, quality, and efficiency. Tami holds a bachelor's degree in Business Administration–Materials Logistics Operations Management from Michigan State University, a Bachelor's of Science in Nursing from Grand Valley State University, and a Master's of Nursing in Healthcare Quality and Safety from The George Washington University.

Cheri Throop RN, MHSA, BS, RHIT, CPHQ, is a senior manager with Healthcare Performance Improvement (HPI) – Press Ganey. Cheri started her clinical career in neonatal nursing and has more than 40 years of diverse healthcare experience that encompasses administrative and operational leadership for safety, quality, performance improvement, medical management, and integrated data management.

She has worked with HPI clients for over a decade, previously served as chief quality and safety advisor for a pediatric business alliance, and facilitated federally funded initiatives tasked with developing nationally endorsed data standards and measures. Cheri is also actively engaged as a guest lecturer in leadership development programs at several academic organizations and is on the senior evaluation faculty, Health Professions, Western Governor's University.

David Varnes, CDR (USN Ret.), MSAE, is a senior manager with Healthcare Performance Improvement (HPI) – Press Ganey, leading over 16 client systems or single hospitals through comprehensive safety and reliability culture transformation. Dave works with board members and executives as well as staff and medical staff in achieving significant reductions in serious preventable harm.

Dave is a former H-46 and H-3 helicopter pilot with over 21 years of leadership experience in the US Navy. He has over 1,500 flight hours in Search and Rescue, MEDEVAC, ammunition, and personnel transport missions. While attached to USS *Dwight D. Eisenhower* (CVN 69), Dave served as Weapons Officer where his leadership and emphasis on quality and safety—as well as strict commitment to protocol—led to zero mishap incidents. Dave has also served on aircraft mishap investigation and Field Naval Aviator Evaluation Boards as well as human factors councils tasked with uncovering root causes of aviation mishaps and associated human errors.

Dave holds a Bachelor of Science in Electrical Engineering from Purdue University and a Master of Science in Aeronautical Engineering from the Naval Post Graduate School.

Martin Wright is a director in Press Ganey Strategic Consulting for workforce solutions. He has gathered valuable experience through 15 years of working in healthcare market research, process improvement, and patient safety. He is responsible for supporting Press Ganey's advisory services and consulting practices focused on the caregiver experience and delivering workforce solutions to enhance the culture of an organization, including safety culture and employee and physician engagement.

Throughout his career, Marty has served as both a consultant, with the goal of helping client organizations improve patient, employee, and provider experiences, and a leader, with a strong desire to develop his teams. His clients have ranged from small critical access hospitals to large integrated health systems, and he presently leads a team of 20 advisors and consultants.

Marty has been a featured speaker at many national healthcare conferences and has authored several articles in prominent healthcare publications. He earned a Bachelor of Arts degree in English Literature from Purdue University in West Lafayette, Indiana.

Gary Yates, MD, is a partner in the strategic consulting division of Press Ganey. He is the former Senior Vice President and Chief Medical Officer of Sentara Healthcare in Norfolk, Virginia, and served as President of Healthcare Performance Improvement (HPI), which joined the Press Ganey family in 2015.

Gary provided leadership for the quality and patient safety initiatives leading to Sentara Norfolk General Hospital being recognized as the 2004 recipient of the AHA Quest for Quality Prize and Sentara Healthcare being recognized as the 2005 recipient of the John M. Eisenberg Award for Patient Safety and Quality from the Joint Commission and the National Quality Forum.

Gary served as co-chair of IHI's ninth annual National Forum on Quality Improvement in Health Care. He also served two years as President of Virginians Improving Patient Care and Safety (VIPCS), the statewide patient safety consortium for Virginia.

In 2005, Gary was awarded the Physician Executive Award of Excellence from Modern Physician and the American College of Physician Executives (ACPE). He currently serves on the Board of Stewardship Trustees for Catholic Health Initiatives (CHI) and as a member of the AHA Quest for Quality Prize Selection Committee.

About the Editors

Craig Clapper, PE, CMQ/OE, is a founding partner of Healthcare Performance Improvement (HPI) and a partner in Press Ganey Strategic Consulting. HPI is a consulting group that specializes in improving human performance in complex systems using evidence-based methods from high reliability organizations. Craig has 30 years of experience improving reliability in nuclear power, transportation, manufacturing, and healthcare. He specializes in cause analysis, reliability improvement, and safety culture improvements. Craig has led safety culture transformation engagements for Duke Energy, US Department of Energy, ABB, Westinghouse, Framatome ANP, and several healthcare systems.

Prior to being a partner in Press Ganey consulting, Craig was the Chief Knowledge Officer of HPI, the Chief Operating Officer of HPI, the Chief Operating Officer of Performance Improvement International, Systems Engineering Manager for Hope Creek Nuclear Generating Station, and Systems Engineering Manager for Palo Verde Nuclear Generation Station. Craig has a Bachelor of Science in Nuclear Engineering from Iowa State University and a Professional Engineer (PE) license. He is a Certified Manager of Quality and Organizational Excellence (CMQ/OE), American Society for Quality (ASQ).

James Merlino, MD, joined Press Ganey in 2015 as president and chief medical officer of the Strategic Consulting Division. In 2018, he assumed the expanded role of chief transformation officer to ensure that Press Ganey's solutions align with current and future industry needs. In this capacity, he oversees the creation and delivery of individualized plans to help clients achieve transformational and sustainable improvement. An accomplished surgeon and industry leader in improving the patient experience, Jim has played a critical role in shaping Press Ganey's strategic direction. Under his leadership, the Press Ganey Strategic Consulting Division was named one of the fastest-growing consulting groups in the United States in 2017 by *Consulting* magazine and one of "America's Best Management Consulting Firms" by *Forbes*.

Prior to joining Press Ganey, Jim served as chief experience officer and associate chief of staff at Cleveland Clinic health system. He was also a practicing staff colorectal surgeon at the organization's Digestive Disease Institute. At Cleveland Clinic, Jim was responsible for leading strategic programs to improve the patient experience across the system. He spearheaded numerous groundbreaking initiatives to ensure the highest standards for patient care as well as to improve patient access and referring physician relations. He also championed organizational cultural alignment around the patient as a key component of patient-centered care.

Recognized as an expert in improving the patient experience, Jim is frequently invited to speak on strategies to redefine care around the needs of the patient, and has developed and led patient experience programming around the world. Jim has been recognized as one of Becker's Healthcare's "50 Experts Leading the Field of Patient Safety" in 2015, 2016, 2017, and 2018. He has been widely published in academic journals. In 2014 he released his first book, *Service Fanatics: How to Build Superior Patient Experience the Cleveland Clinic Way*. Jim holds a bachelor's degree in business administration from Baldwin-Wallace College and a medical degree from Case Western Reserve University School of Medicine. He completed his general surgery training at University Hospitals of Cleveland and his colorectal surgery fellowship at Cleveland Clinic.

 **Carole Stockmeier, MHA,** is a partner in Press Ganey Strategic Consulting. She has over 20 years of experience in hospital operations leadership. Carole has supported comprehensive safety culture engagements at hospitals and integrated health systems and has helped organizations achieve significant improvement in safety reliability.

Prior to joining HPI, Carole served as the Director of Safety & Performance Excellence at Sentara Healthcare where she guided leaders in the implementation of strategies for human error prevention and reliability performance. She provided operational leadership for Sentara's patient safety initiatives, with outcomes recognized by award of the American Hospital Association 2004 Quest for Quality Prize and the 2005 John M Eisenberg Award for Patient Safety and Quality.

Carole holds a Master in Health Administration from Virginia Commonwealth University, where she is a Fellow of the Williamson Institute of the Department of Health Administration, and a Bachelor of Science in public health from the University of North Carolina at Chapel Hill.

About Press Ganey

PRESS GANEY WAS founded more than 30 years ago, based on a passion to help improve the way in which healthcare is delivered. Today, that principle remains a core element of Press Ganey's mission to help healthcare organizations across the continuum reduce suffering and enhance caregiver resilience to improve the safety, quality, and experience of care.

Press Ganey partners with providers to capture the voices of patients, physicians, nurses, and employees to gain insights to address unmet needs. Through the use of integrated data, advanced analytics, and strategic advisory services, Press Ganey helps clients transform their organizations to deliver safer, high-quality, patient- and family-focused care.

Press Ganey is recognized as a pioneer and thought leader in patient experience measurement and performance improvement solutions. As a strategic business partner to more than 26,000 healthcare organizations, Press Ganey leads the industry in helping clients transform the patient experience and create continuous sustainable improvement to healthcare delivery.

For more information, please visit pressganey.com.

Also from Press Ganey

"This work is a gift of learning and awakening to all health professionals. It offers an effective practice model which aligns compassionate care with safety, quality, and deep personal experiences."
—JEAN WATSON, PhD, RN, AHN-BC, FAAN, Founder and Director, Watson Caring Science Institute, and Distinguished Professor and Dean Emerita, University of Colorado Denver

THE
ANTIDOTE
TO SUFFERING

HOW COMPASSIONATE CONNECTED CARE
CAN IMPROVE SAFETY, QUALITY, AND EXPERIENCE

CHRISTINA DEMPSEY
CHIEF NURSING OFFICER,
PRESS GANEY

THE **ANTIDOTE** TO SUFFERING

DEMPSEY

Mc Graw Hill Education

AN
EPIDEMIC
OF
EMPATHY
IN
HEALTHCARE

How to Deliver Compassionate, Connected Patient Care That Creates a Competitive Advantage

Thomas H. Lee, MD
Chief Medical Officer of Press Ganey

AN EPIDEMIC OF EMPATHY IN HEALTHCARE

LEE

Mc Graw Hill Education

Mc Graw Hill Education